W9-CSO-250

THE RANCH

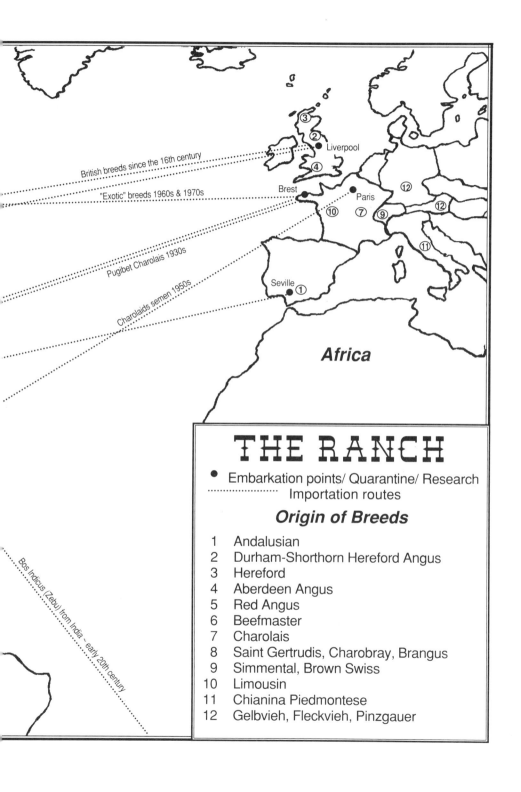

British breeds since the 16th century

"Exotic" breeds 1960s & 1970s

Pugibet Charolais 1930s

Charolais semen 1950s

Bos Indicus (Zebu) from India ~ early 20th century

Liverpool

Brest

Paris

Seville

Africa

THE RANCH

● Embarkation points/ Quarantine/ Research
⋯⋯⋯⋯⋯ Importation routes

Origin of Breeds

1 Andalusian
2 Durham-Shorthorn Hereford Angus
3 Hereford
4 Aberdeen Angus
5 Red Angus
6 Beefmaster
7 Charolais
8 Saint Gertrudis, Charobray, Brangus
9 Simmental, Brown Swiss
10 Limousin
11 Chianina Piedmontese
12 Gelbvieh, Fleckvieh, Pinzgauer

THE RANCH

A Modern History of the
North American Cattle Industry

Sherm Ewing

Mountain Press Publishing Company
Missoula, 1995

Copyright © 1995
Sherm Ewing

Cover painting and drawings by
Wanina Travis

Library of Congress Cataloging-in-Publication Data

Ewing, Sherm, 1926–
    The ranch : a modern history of the North American cattle industry
/ Sherm Ewing.
        p.   cm.
    Includes bibliographical references (p.   ) and index.
    ISBN 0-87842-309-5 : $25.00 — ISBN 0-87842-310-9 (pbk.) : $14.00
    1. Beef cattle—North America—History. 2. Ranch life—North America
—History. 3. Ranchers—North America—Biography. 4. Cattle trade—
North America—History.   I. Title.
SF196.N7E95   1995   95-39631
636.2' 13' 097—dc20   CIP

PRINTED IN THE U.S.A.

Mountain Press Publishing Company
P.O. Box 2399
Missoula, Montana 59806

To those who make a living on the land

Contents

Preface

I don't think of myself as a "real" writer. Don't real writers use pencils? I use a computer. I've heard that Steinbeck routinely sharpened thirty yellow pencils every morning while the "word processor" between his ears booted up for the day's production. With my handwriting, this would be a disaster!

And I'm no longer a "real" rancher, either, not since I've moved to town; and besides, shouldn't a real rancher be ranch born and raised? I wasn't. But then, not all doctors were born in hospitals, and few lawyers were actually raised at the bar. But I have *lived* on the land full time, thinking of important things like cows and grass and the weather and not much else for forty years. I made a good living, too, and have labored long in range and ranch organizations and been tried by epidemic, fire, blizzard, and flood. So I guess I can say I *was* a real rancher, once.

Ranching is a solitary, single-minded business, and success depends on *when*, not *where*, you were born. I was lucky. I was born in 1926, which put me in line for work right after the Second World War and the Great Depression—at the beginning of a period of unparalleled growth. And I was born at the edge of the great North American steppe, where my roots run deep. My mother's grandparents settled in Minnesota before the Civil War and, with peace, stayed on in business: One, a journeyman tanner, started the North Star Boot Company (now defunct); another, a Bay of Fundy fisherman's son, went to Iowa and followed the railroads west across the prairie states and provinces. He built some of the first grain elevators, and the business he founded still prospers.

My father's family floated down the Ohio River in 1792. At first they farmed the edge of the prairies; later they took to the law. I'm proud to claim descent from a number of tough old circuit-riding lawyers and judges, nevermind those who moved to fatter pickings in Foggy Bottom—the modern beltway. "That's where the jobs are . . ." They still say that today.

With my father, a retiring lawyer and aspiring playwright, I spent a few years on the eastern seaboard until something happened that changed my life forever. When I was eight, my parents divorced. My mother took her family to California to recoup, and I've never forgotten the wonders we saw from the Union Pacific cars: big skies, distant mountains, the covered wagons of Depression-era gypsies and/or emigrants in ruts of the Oregon Trail.

I remember Devil's Slide, the Great Salt Lake, a roper on a black horse at a California rodeo. I felt the West in my bones and decided before I was nine that the West was where I would live—where, like my forefathers, I would build a business and be my own boss someday. Ranching came naturally; I have had no regrets.

Half a century later, my wife and I—having raised our family—left our home in Alberta's Porcupine Hills, sold the business that had served us well (to our son, now with a family of his own), and "retired" to Montana. Two ranch-raised daughters, with goals of their own, remained on the land not far away.

I decided to write about our land, our friends, and the life we knew and loved. For three years we traveled—visiting old friends, meeting new ones, recollecting stories and taping discussions; later, at home, we transcribed our tapes onto 2,000 single-spaced pages that filled four large red notebooks with "research." Then came four or five years of sorting, blending, and assembling it all into . . . what? I was curious myself. I've watched in fascination as the words of a hundred characters from many different ranges in the accents of six nationalities gradually interacted in print. I like the results.

In *The Ranch,* part one sets the stage with a discussion of ranching in the first half of the twentieth century. Part two reports (sometimes whimsically) on areas of growth in the 1950s. Part three reveals an invasion that spread fitfully out of Mexico and changed the look of North American beef cattle in the 1960s and 1970s. Part four discusses an importation of "new" and "exotic" breeds and assesses their utility through the 1990s. Like in my earlier book, *The Range,* the characters speak for themselves; my comments appear in italic type.

A defensive word on style: I have chosen capitals without periods for agencies, titles, and departments—A&M, CDA, DVM, USDA; I have used "AI," "AI'd," and "AI'ing" in references to artificial insemination; I have used the phonic "comprest" for the so-called compressed or compact cattle types of the 1950s; and I have taken other unspecified liberties that will, I hope, make for easier reading. (For a guide to most abbreviations and special terms, see the glossary.)

For a short introduction to those who have contributed so much to this oral history, see the "Register of Characters." Most of my Characters checked their pieces for accuracy; in addition, my wife, our children, lawyer Bill Scott and his wife, Shirley, Dr. Dick Lauritzen and his wife, Lorena, and other literati searched for gaffes and inconsistencies. Dr. George Carlson, a medical geneticist at McLaughlin Research Institute, checked references to his new, fast-changing field. Carmen "Chiquis" Gonzalez, of Juárez, Chihuahua, corrected Spanish, while our Norman neighbor, Jacqueline Heffern, advised us on French.

Photographers Ted Pritchett and Roman Hrytsak, of Calgary, and Professor Harlan Ritchie, of Michigan State, generously contributed classic images. M. Pierre Gautier faxed snapshots and shipping data from his St. Pierre-Miquelon office. Gadfly to a generation of ranchers, Dr. Roy Berg, of Edmonton, has guided me for years; and my earnest, erudite editor, Dan Greer, of Missoula, has labored hard to make my work look professional.

My goal has been to produce an interesting account of twentieth-century ranching, focusing on some of the people, animal breeds, and events that have been important to me and to the cattle industry. I haven't meant to dump on any breed; I like 'em all! And I like the people who raise 'em. Above all, I've tried to be true to my Characters while providing a real good read.

And I've tried to remember the advice of Samuel Langhorne Clemens—a very real writer and very tough critic, who said: "A book should be judged by *words left out*."

Having culled two-thirds of my "gather," may the remainder suit my readers, if not "Mark Twain."

PROLOGUE

In my first book, *The Range*, my characters spoke of grass—their basic resource. Range scientists explained that grass, equipped with billions of tiny roots, provides a reservoir for water and material for organic soil; the deepest soils on earth, they said, developed under grass—and grazing animals. Then, ranchers and other land managers told how domestic livestock help maintain and improve the range by seeding, fertilizing, and pruning for the benefit of all—at little or no expense to the taxpaying public.

I live today on the old grass range near "the falls" of the Missouri—in recent years a fertile, grain-growing area. What makes this land so fertile is a rich, organic soil that developed over thousands of years under millions of trampling, defecating, belching, farting, expiring wild "cattle."

When Meriwether Lewis and William Clark arrived here in 1805, they noted incredible numbers of bison; they also noted much riparian damage—and that was in a time pristine, before the longhorn. When the sodbusters came, they found soils rich in organic matter ready to supply the world with wheat. They turned under much wild grass, but modern calves and lambs still drop and play and grow on unplowed acres of native rangeland.

In *The Range*, one lifetime student declared the land in better shape today than when the buffalo roamed free.[1]

Range is a renewable resource! Where grass goes about its business of building topsoil. Which produces more grass. Which is converted by grazing animals into:

- protein and mineral-rich foods;
- bone charcoal for high-grade steel;
- coverings for baseballs and footballs;
- hair for yarn and felt;
- gelatin for film;
- fat for soaps and lubricants;
- hoof material for glues;
- blood for cancer research;
- glands for insulin, ACTH, and adrenalin;
- and so on, and so on, and so on.

Even vegetarians should thank ranchers and food animals for contributing to cool-running tires, razor-sharp blades, foaming beer, pharmaceuticals, and hundreds of other by-products of digestion. But more on all that, someday, in a future book I'll call *The Roast*.

Now, on to *The Ranch*, where ranchers and animals are the characters.

"We can almost say that everything that was then is not now, and everything that was not then now is."

—William Manchester, historian

PART ONE

The Way Things Were

Part One: The Way Things Were

The SN Brand

The SN Brand

*T*HERE'S A STORY UNDER EVERY BUTTE *and in every coulee on the range, a human interest story of one who passed this way—most likely in pursuit of a four-footed animal.*

Most of the events have gone unnoticed and unrecorded, but occasional place-names survive. In Alberta, for those in the know, "Head-Smashed-In" brings to mind a nameless Peigan boy trampled to death in a buffalo jump or "pishkun." But how about Hungry Horse, Moose Jaw, Spotted Bear, Lame Deer, or any one of dozens of Dead Horse Hills?

As a pilot, my imagination stirs as I home in on the navigation aid near Buffalo, Wyoming: "Crazy Woman VOR . .. Crazy Woman VOR . . .," a recorded voice goes dismally, incessantly through the wind. Who was she? What? When? Why? I wonder. No doubt, at least one interesting yarn resides at every crossing, pass, and water hole on earth.

On Cripple Creek in southern Alberta the SN brand is all that's left of Noah Sitton. And, since I use the SN ranch as the backbone for my tales, I'll begin with what I know of the human characters behind that brand.

Noah Sitton was born in eastern Oregon in 1862 and, as a teenager, set out to make his fortune in a time-honored way—by stealing horses. Everywhere in range-land history we find equine entrepreneurs filling demand in one place with supply on the hoof from another: Nez Perce horses to Blackfeet country in prehistoric times; Oregon horses to California with the gold rush; Wyoming horses to Montana when the range was free; and so on.

So, in the 1880s—under the guidance of hard-riding Noah Sitton and his partner Jimmy Gunn—horses wearing North Dakota brands arrived in British Columbia to be swapped for gold with very few questions asked. The boys and their horses would have come a long way, dodging vigilantes in Montana, mounted policemen in the territories, and fellow "horse lovers" everywhere. They could have crossed the Porcupine Hills, where, according to Gunn family lore, they stopped to rest their "cavy" in a sheltered, well-grassed coulee—perhaps the very coulee where squatter "Mormon Bill" Schaeffer had a horse camp. (I've always called the place Stove Coulee; recently I learned the exact location of Bill's campsite when a bulldozer unearthed a rusted tent stove.) Was "Mormon Bill" in cahoots with Jim and Noah? Could have been, but no matter: Bill moved on.

But Noah never forgot that good grass country below the butte called Skimmerhorn. In 1911 he returned and bought the coulee for cold hard cash from Riel Rebellion dispatch rider Billy Stewart, whom the Cree called "He Rides Wild Horses." (I conjure some of the rides that old homesteader must have made as we gather cows in our so-called Stewart Field.)

Then, in 1911—with his pick of marks and brands—Noah H. Sitton applied for a cumbersome NHS. The Alberta Brand Office turned him down and suggested his initials backward, adding a "half diamond, underneath, points up." And with that, Sitton branded his cows and a few years later sold land, brand, cows, and all to Hoosier T. C. Milnes, who gave the place to his English son-in-law, remittance man Tom Riddle.

In 1946 Albert Alm (whose story is in The Range) bought the ranch and nine years later sold it to my wife, Claire, and me. In the 1990s it's home to Charlie, Sherry, Calvin, and Lonni Jo Ewing and their long-time assistants Don, Debbie, Justin, and Morgan Snider. The cows, after much crossbreeding, now produce "Beefbooster" bulls, but they still wear the SN brand. And the Porcupine Hills still produce many characters and stories.

But Noah Sitton and his tough old ways are now almost forgotten. According to one crop-eared, old-time SN hand, Regis Morkin, Noah wouldn't allow his men to wear a cap—even in the coldest weather: If they wanted to work for him, he said, they would "play out their string like cowboys," and Noah himself set them an example.

Noah and Mrs. Sitton (he called her "Duzzie"; she called him "Doozie") had no heirs; an only child was eaten by a vicious sow, they say. And those who rode the grub line in the years between the wars remember SN hospitality as frugal. I have it from neighbor William Oliver that the best the Sittons ever offered was billy goat sandwich (Bill said it "smelled" like billy goat, anyway). Furthermore, just before dinner the hosts would call the coyote hounds to lick the breakfast dishes clean—which saved on grub as visitors remembered appointments elsewhere.

In the end, both Sittons died intestate and insane, leaving the remains of their ill-gotten gains to the province of Alberta.

Which is the sad, but (mostly) true, story of the SN brand.

1   A Place to Start

WHITEMUD CREEK, *a two-day ride to the east of the Porcupine Hills: There the Gilchrist family of Prince Edward Island filed Dominion Land Act homestead claims in the spring of 1904.*

Capt. William Gilchrist must have been a resourceful man, having survived the seven seas in the days of sail. Yet, when he moved his family west to become in middle age a landlocked greenhorn, his sons (soon grown to hardened plainsmen) had trouble finding jobs for the old man; they would mount him on gentle horses and set him to herding bulls or fetching milk cows, as one might treat a city cousin today.

But, green as they were to its ways, pioneers like Captain and Mary Gilchrist were the seed stock of the West, and their descendants populate the range today. Their youngest son, Joe, was four when he arrived in Assiniboia, and before he died in Medicine Hat at age ninety-two he told me about old-time ranching ways.

JOE GILCHRIST

I was born on the second day of the century and grew up running cows and ranches before the days of rural telephones and electrification, improved roads and "possum-bellies" [cattle semitrailers], and two-way radios.

When I was fourteen, my four older brothers made a deal for a ranch called the Whitemud place south of Maple Creek, Saskatchewan, and took me in as a partner. The deal included 700 head of cattle branded Q7 on the hip, 20 head of horses, and a haying outfit. It makes me tired to think of all the hay we pitched by hand in those old days, but we built a big feed reserve and, over the next ten years, took on several other places and saw our herd increase to 2,500 head.

Looking back . . . what a lot of time and planning just to get the routine chores done! For instance, weaning in 1922: It was late October when Bert Ingram, Johnny Chourrout, and I left the Whitemud with four hundred head of yearlings bound for winter pasture at Manyberries, sixty miles west in Alberta. We packed our camp outfit on horses and trailed a dozen extra; the grass had

"Brocklefaces" and roans in this mid-century herd indicate earlier dominance of the Short-horn (Durham) breed. —City of Lethbridge Archives

been good, the steers moved well, and a couple days later we turned 'em loose on winter range and made ready to gather the she-stuff at the dipping-vat corrals.

That night it started to snow and got mighty cold; with the temperature twenty below, we worked the drys and pushed them out of the way. Then, corralling the pairs, we split the cows away at dark and hit for a shack on the Black Tail, four or five miles away. The night was short; we were back at dawn to corral the cows while their hungry, bawling calves went out to graze.

On the fourth day, we packed and got ready to move the calves home to the Whitemud. The first day we figured to make it to the Q [ranch], where a fellow named Speedy Jim would let us have some hay. Well, the sun came up bright that morning; you could have roped a coyote easy—if your horse didn't step in a badger hole under the snow. A few cows were hanging around, so we pushed them over a hill; then 700 fresh-weaned, hungry calves rushed out of the gate—a pretty fair bunch for three cowboys to handle.

Everything went fine until a couple of cows returned; then, of course, the calves broke back; more bellering cows appeared, which meant corralling them all again, which took all day.

Next morning we struck out for the Q again and this time had no trouble, arriving in time to get everything fed and settled well before dark. By next sunup, Mrs. Speedy Jim had packed us a lunch, and the three of us headed the calves for the railroad pens at Altawan, twenty miles away. It was a nice clear day—but twenty below, with a foot and a half of snow—and we picked up thirty head of a neighbor's steers that wanted to go home . . . let 'em break trail. Even so, it was dark when we dropped the calves in a field with plenty of grass and shelter at Altawan.

At daylight, I rode into town and ordered fifteen cars for the forty-mile move to Vidora [Saskatchewan]. The train was to come at four; it came at eight, and the trainmen helped us load. We pulled into Vidora at five o'clock next morning—five days after leaving the dipping-vat corrals.

Now, the stockyard at Vidora had just one loading chute, so it took several hours to unload fifteen cars, turn the calves out to graze, feed our horses, and get breakfast. That afternoon we gathered the bunch and started for the Whitemud, ten miles away, but the going was tough and it was midnight before we got home. Then, gulping our supper like coyotes, we turned in for a very short time before brother Sandy woke us, loaded our saddles in a sleigh, and drove us to catch the morning freight back to Altawan, where, in a howling blizzard, we caught our horses and struck for the Cross Z ranch where we batched till spring.

Looking back, I think how many days it took to get a few things done, things that would take just hours now, with modern trucks and trailers. But I also remember, after all those days of weaning, trailing, and shipping, that not a single calf got sick! Not a one! Try that today with your preconditioned calves and high-speed travel![2]

A ND TWO HUNDRED MILES NORTHWEST, *in the beautiful Bow Valley west of Calgary, the steep banks of Jumping Pound Creek had been a killing place for buffalo for centuries when John and Richard Copithorne arrived from County Cork and set to ranching.*

First they worked as bullwhackers and mule skinners; then they squatted, illegally, on the rich, organic rangeland already under lease to eastern interests. Soon the Lands Act was applied within those leases and the Copithornes filed on homesteads. Today their descendants populate the valley.

I count many of them as friends—the kind you make in the ranching business: You meet once or twice a year and may never know them well, but you know how they think as ranchers and would bet your life on their word. Here one of them tells of earlier days on the CL ranch.

MARSHALL COPITHORNE

When I was a kid, my dad, Percy, was raising "commercial" [meaning unregistered] Herefords. They were about as close to purebred as you could get;

By the 1950s many ranchers were ashamed to own anything but well-marked, whitefaced Herefords. —City of Lethbridge Archives

we were ashamed to put our brand on an off-color cow. But that was a recent development.

The CL cow of Grandad Richard's day was another matter—a multicolored, dual-purpose Durham. But, soon after the Calgary Bull Sale started in 1910, he began buying Hereford bulls and slowly our herd became "whitefaced and feather necked"—typically Hereford. But, whatever the breed or cross, we were always *meat producers* as opposed to *breeders*.

When I was a kid, we roughed calves through the winter, and I mean *rough*. If they weighed 380 pounds at weaning, they went out next spring at 400 and disappeared in the bush till November, when they'd weigh 450. A year later they might go 800; eventually, as grass-fat three- and four-year-olds, they'd go to market at 1,100 or 1,200 pounds.

Dad was of the old school, where the main criteria for a cow was easy wintering and dropping a calf each spring. It didn't matter what some judge might pick; Dad wasn't the least bit interested in showing. I was never in 4-H. Dad saw no sense in *leading* cattle; he was more for chasin' 'em—within reason—consistent with the business of selling *pounds*.

A high point of the CL year was shipping the steers. Dad and his brothers liked to trail to Calgary, where, as their string of big old three-year-olds headed through a residential area, the "drag" would see the leaders up in front and take a shortcut through the roses and petunias.

12

This went on through the thirties until one day when they had their steers lined out along a thoroughfare, a lady stepped out on her porch and shook a tablecloth or bedspread. Pop! Snap! Crash! Those steers went in all directions, taking clotheslines and fences with 'em.

A cop was there with a warrant when we finally reached the stockyards, and we never trailed through Calgary again.

LET'S CONSIDER THE CATTLE used on northern ranches in earlier years. Some of the very first came to our range from the goldfields to the west, from the mountain valleys of Oregon and British Columbia. Following the Civil War came the famous Texas longhorns, pushed north by cowboys. By the early 1900s, however, there had been a heavy infusion of British genes—direct from England or via the eastern states and provinces.

A decade before Nelson Story drove the first range herd into Montana over the Bozeman Trail, thirty years before the first herds trailed across Milk River into Canada, a range-cattle industry flourished in Colorado. My friend Dick Goff is a lifelong student of that range.[3]

DICK GOFF

In 1859, 150 Durhams, known as Shorthorns, were trailed west from Missouri and crossed with Texas longhorns. Once that cross got going, more Shorthorns were brought in—the first so-called blooded cattle on the range.

Herefords came soon after the Civil War, when hundreds of limited companies were organized to cash in on free grass; capital was subscribed by eastern and British interests, and many English families sent second sons with tons of money and bunches of "blooded" bulls. In a fascinating out-of-print book [written in 1885 by Baron Walter Von Richthofen] called *Cattle Raising on the Plains of North America*, we learn that Shorthorn and Hereford bulls were used to "breed up" nondescript Texas cattle in the early 1870s and, while both breeds did well in the upgrading process, the Hereford (with distinctive marking and markedly better promotion) soon prevailed.

I always like to point out that what *really* made those old-time Herefords great was crossing them on longhorn-Shorthorn cows. *Hybrid vigor!* With all the hype, it's easy to forget about hybrid vigor.

IT'S ALSO EASY TO FORGET that those old-time, "mongrel" cows were self-propelled. They had to have good underpinnings, as did the bulls that bred them. In this, the aboriginal British breeds excelled, as John Cross of the A7 Ranche reminded me.

The old English Durhams were growthy beasts: This 1835 Smithfield champion heifer weighed 2,200 pounds when just three years old. The 1937 Oklahoma A&M champion (front) weighed 1,100 pounds at twenty-one months. —Harlan Ritchie/Don Good montage

JOHN CROSS

In the 1880s my father came west from Montreal and put our ranch in the Porcupine Hills together. First he imported Shorthorns to upgrade the Montana cattle on our range. He bought his first Hereford in Chicago in 1910; next it was Galloway, but all the British breeds were tough enough to survive on the range in the early days. They liked to live! I like 'em still.

I visited England in the 1930s and saw the British breeds on their native ground. Each district had its own: Lincoln, Devon, Hereford, Durham, Aberdeen—you name it. And they all went to market on the *hoof*, starting in Scotland and walking to London. That required good feet of man and beast!

I remember one old gent who pointed to a Hereford bull that nobody would buy. The reason? A very long head.

"Of course," he explained, "that bull's ancestors were never picked for *heads*; nor were they picked for *color*. They were picked for the way they *walked* before a plow."

"That bull is full of meat," the old man said, "and look how he strides along."

Full of *meat* and *strides* along—that's what gave the British breeds their reputation.

A S RELATED IN THE RANGE, *Fred Burton came out of Ontario and squatted on a lease in the Porcupine Hills. By 1900 he had married Oregon-born Minnie Furman and was building a ranch. Twenty years later their four sons were making names for themselves on the rodeo circuit from Calgary to Cheyenne. The wild, free life of the cowboy suited the Burton boys; they were tough and smart without spending much time in school, and they didn't have time for hay or fences, either.*

When Gordon, the youngest, arrived in 1916, Mrs. Burton decreed he should go to school! She would move to town herself and make it happen! And when neighbor Warren Cooper heard of those plans, he exclaimed, "We got trouble enough without educated Burtons!"[4]

But Gordon finished high school, finished college, and went on to earn a Ph.D. in ag-economics at Iowa, and when he came back to the ranch his education served the entire industry.[5] He remembers the way things were:

GORDON BURTON

When I was a kid, our neighbors were desperate; they'd had heavy losses from blackleg, and my father tried to immunize his calves by running a copper wire through the brisket. Veterinarians were scarce, and people would try anything. Bill Lyndon, in the next coulee, had the idea that you could prevent blackleg by making a slit in the neck and inserting a quarter—presumably there was silver in a quarter in those days, and presumably silver was as powerful as copper.

It might have worked, but the neighbor's kids were rotten! Once they discovered where quarters came from, they were rich—and had the added fun of roping calves.

I went on to university in 1934, and about that time a brother took over the ranch. He wasn't interested in cows. He preferred low-risk investments like racehorses and poker. So, somewhere along the line, he sold our good old cows and replaced them with worn-out crocks out of the stockyards.

My father saw what was going on and was most unhappy; he was getting old and, in 1950, asked Jean and me to take over the ranch. I knew right away that we had to have better cattle, and about that time a local Hereford breeder held a dispersal sale (I don't know how these breeders have "dispersals" every year). Well, the cattle were highly touted and the breeder was smart! He weaned his calves a few weeks early, and gee! I bid on fat, square, 1950s-style purebred cows and brought 'em home delighted. Next spring they calved out easy but didn't have enough milk to keep a cat alive! Their calves were puny! I'd bought good-looking, no-good cows, and I disposed of them right smartly.

Later, I bought more Herefords, but before long I was crossing them with Angus. Then the Gilchrists "discovered" a new breed in Arizona. I tried a couple of the new Charolais, and what a hell of an improvement! I've been crossing ever since.

THIS BOOK IS ABOUT CATTLE AND CATTLE PEOPLE, and I need a few more characters to help me set the stage.

Now, where would a northern rancher meet a character whose family was on the New Mexican range a century before the first herds arrived in Montana? At a cow-college or short course or conference, that's where. And I think it was at the 1959 PRI meeting at Miles City, Montana, that I first met Bob de Baca.

BOB de BACA

Even our family name comes from *vaca*, Spanish for cow. My great-great-great-grandfather had five land grants from the king of Spain, and even my great-grandad owned 100,000 acres near Los Alamos, where he ran cattle, sheep, and horses and freighted on the Santa Fe Trail. The bones of one de Baca are buried beside that trail . . . died of cholera, they say. They poured a barrel of whiskey over his shallow grave.

The cow was not a major food animal in New Mexico in those days; you were limited to what you could corral inside your village—the Apaches and the Navajo saw to that. For meat, my people depended on bison and traveled to the buffalo grounds in Texas, where they killed large numbers Indian-style—a colorful and dangerous way of life. You rode bareback into the herd, which was probably stampeding, found a nice fat cow and drove a lance clear through her pleural cavity—no gun, no bow and arrow, just one good *caballo* and a spear.

Later, the wagon people came and dressed and salted down the kill and dried it and hauled it home to the ranch.

As the buffalo disappeared, rails replaced the trail, and my family settled down to ranching with Texas longhorns. Around 1910 they brought in Herefords, which proved to be right for the country, and when I was a kid everything was whitefaced on our range. Black Angus or roan Shorthorns were virtually unknown, and the Hereford people did everything they could to keep it that way. I remember a college girl who asked us not to mention Angus or Shorthorn in her presence; she considered it a form of harassment, so to speak!

"Spearing a Buffalo" by C. M. Russell. —Minneapolis Institute of Arts

At any rate, cattle are in my blood, and I started learning the business at a very young age. We had a neighbor who would steal an occasional calf, so it made sense to earmark soon after calves were born. When I was thirteen, Dad fell off a windmill and was too stove up to work; later, supervising the branding, he asked who'd notched the calves. "I did," I said with pride.

"Did you do it the day they were born?"

"No, sir."

"Then, you been runnin' and ropin' these calves!"

"Well, I got the job done, Dad."

"You can rope the milk cow's calf and any dog in town," said Dad, "but you leave my calves alone! I sell pounds!"

So, I never became a good roper—you only rope the milk cow's calf about twice before it knows to run for the barn.

But I did learn something else: *Calves are sold by the pound*, which I've never forgotten.

Not always by the pound as JIM GRAY used to say:

We usually didn't sell calves at all; usually, it was three- and four-year-old steers. But in 1935 Dad contracted his calves at $5 a head—I think we had fifty or sixty head—and when Peter Massie, the buyer, came to get 'em, Dad told him he wasn't happy with the price. "Lookit these calves; they're great!" Dad said, "I never shoulda taken a penny less than $6 for any of 'em."

Peter Massie looked them over and said, "Neil, they look so good, I'm gonna *give* ya a whole six bucks a head, straight through." And he did.

And that same fall our fat, dry cows sold for $12 a head, and we were mighty glad to get it!

*T*HE DEPTHS OF THE GREAT DEPRESSION—1935—*every pound and every penny counted. For fifty years resourceful ranchers had been building homesteads into viable family businesses based on guts and determination. Cash had always been scarce; in 1935 it was almost nonexistent, and expectations were exceptionally low. Even by the standards of those times it had become increasingly hard for a range cow to return a satisfactory living to her owner.*

In 1935 Ray Woodward, a kid from a ranch near Bozeman, entered Montana State College. He went on to earn an advanced degree in animal science and a Ph.D. in genetics and, finally, to an illustrious career in consulting.

RAY WOODWARD

Up to the early thirties there had been much interest in livestock breeding but little real improvement; then a few people said, "Hey, cut the horseshit! Let's dig out some *facts*."

I was at Montana State in the 1930s, and a guy named R. T. Clark lectured us on something new called "performance testing." Other than that, the only thing was a smattering of nutrition.

Genetics? Forget it! In those days there was no real application of genetics to livestock breeding, no objective criteria in selection, and in my opinion the professors generally did everything they could to head off that sort of nonsense. Hell, the two most important livestock judges I remember were deans of agriculture! Imagine! Their contribution to science: judging shows!

When I left college in 1939, I was dumb and happy—and lucky as all get-out. I got a key job as assistant animal husbandman at Havre in northern Montana, where I soon met Harry Hargrave, my counterpart at Manyberries, the Canadian range experiment station across the line.[6]

I was in contact, too, with animal scientists at Fort Keogh, at Miles City, where the first *real* beef cattle breeding work was done.

So, Fort Keogh, Miles City, the 1930s . . . Yes! That's the perfect place and time for a book like this to start.

2   Miles City—1935

BY 1935, WILL HUGHES (as related in The Range) had expanded on his homestead in Montana's Judith Basin and was doing a nice business in hogs, milk, beef, and grain. He was freighting for construction crews and digging coal from a coulee on his land, and his two sons, Harley and Gerald, were helping him run several bands of sheep and a thousand cows.

GERALD HUGHES

It was late in the 1930s that Pa happened to meet Art B—, a well-known rancher who was just getting started in purebred Herefords and planning a sale at Butte. So Pa says, "Jerry, you better go pick up some of them good bulls."

"Ah," I said, "I dunno nothin' about 'em."

"You go ahead," Pa says, "and don't come home without 'em."

Well, we didn't have no truck, so brother Harley put me on the bus, and next morning it was cold and snowing when I took a cab to the stockyards at Butte.

Some fancy bulls came through the ring, and I bought five at 500 bucks apiece. I didn't know the other bidders, and I'm sure the auctioneer doubled up on me once or twice, but towards the end of the sale I picked up an off-color red neck a whole lot cheaper, just to make a load. Art bought me dinner that night at the old Finlen Hotel, and next morning I hired a truck and headed home with six "blooded" bulls costing more than a whole damn carload of good ranch cows.

And the bastards didn't know enough to eat grass! They had their heads in a bucket until spring when we turned 'em loose in Gooseberry Coulee where they got to fightin', and we found one in the creek bottom with a broken neck before he ever bred a cow.

Well, I guess I learned somethin', anyway. You could walk right up to those bulls in the pasture—they was that gentle. But they never did grow much—

The old cavalry barns of Fort Keogh became part of the famous Miles City range livestock experiment station. —Montana Historical Society

just little, short-bodied bulls—and Dad was disgusted. "Gotta have size," he says; "I sell *pounds*."

So, early in the spring of 1942 my young brother Curt come home from college talkin' "performance," and Pa says, "Gerald, we better give them Miles City bulls a try," so I called superintendent Quesenberry at Fort Keogh, and he says, "Sure. We got two dandy big, long four-year-olds you can have."

"Ship 'em up on the Milwaukee," I said, "and send us the bill," and by God he did. And that's how we got started with the famous Line One strain. Later, I drove down to see for myself and bought a couple more—got 'em for a song. Nobody wanted them government bulls, ya see, and before long we had more Miles City Line One bulls than any other ranch in Montana.

M ILESTOWN," IT WAS CALLED: A tent city just outside the Tongue River cantonment. Col. Nelson A. Miles established the fort for his 5th Infantry regiment following the fight on the Little Bighorn. Later that year, 1876, Congress decided to build a permanent fort to be named for Captain Keogh, the Irish soldier of fortune who fell with the 7th Cavalry. (Keogh's horse, Comanche, was the only known survivor of the 7th; he lived to a ripe old age at Fort Riley, Kansas.)

By 1879 the Indian Wars were over, and Milestown became the center of Montana's vast range cattle industry. For the next two decades, cowboys shared the rich surrounding grasslands with soldiers; then the fort was decommissioned and became a world-famous remount station where horses were bred and trained for the U.S. Cavalry and other mounted troops around the world.

Finally, as horse soldiers rode into history with the First World War, Fort Keogh became a place for peaceful research, to be shared by federal and state agricultural scientists—which brings us to the Miles City of the 1930s.

RAY WOODWARD

Until the thirties, those who professed to be expert in livestock breeding were actually detrimental to the industry; all they knew was visual appraisal. Then, a few good scientists got together at Miles City and put three things in motion: they began *performance testing*; they began *linebreeding*; and they planned a follow-up with *crossbreeding*.

R. T. Clark was chairman of the animal husbandry department at Bozeman [Montana State], and he worked closely with the USDA in planning the Miles City project. Born in Scotland, "Scotty" Clark had a Ph.D. from Minnesota, where he was the protégé of the prominent geneticist Laurence Winters. Clark himself was a controversial character but responsible for more advances in beef cattle breeding than any other man I ever met.

The initial Miles City work wasn't classic, but, by God, it broke ground. Studies were made of the birth, weaning, and yearling weight characteristics of beef cattle in fourteen inbred lines, and heritability estimates proved that

R. T. "Scotty" Clark, beef cattle performance pioneer.
—Montana State University Archives

you could expect continuous improvement while selecting for performance within those lines. In addition, fertility was found to improve significantly when inbred lines were crossed—an indication of *heterosis* or *hybrid vigor*. When the first heritability estimates were published in 1947, based entirely on Miles City data, there wasn't much left for critics to shoot at. That work was a milestone in the history of livestock breeding.[7]

*R*AY DIRECTED RESEARCH *through the decade of the 1950s, during which fourteen unique "Miles City" beef cattle lines were firmly established.*

*A*NOTHER BOZEMAN GRAD *and veteran of Havre went to Miles City in 1961 and worked with the inbred lines for twenty-five years. Here's what Joe Urick told me about the first and most famous, known as Line One.*

JOE URICK

In 1933 two half-brother Herefords, *Advance Domino 20th* and *Advance Domino 54th*, were obtained by the station from Colorado and put with fifty-eight registered Hereford cows purchased from George Miles, the colonel's nephew, who had become a local banker and part-time rancher. The cows were divided into two groups and, thereafter, the sons of one bull were bred to the daughters of the other. Then the line was closed; no more genes were added while it grew to 200 head. That was Line One, the first, largest, and most famous of the Miles City lines.

Advance Domino 20th, *a progenitor of Line One.* —USDA

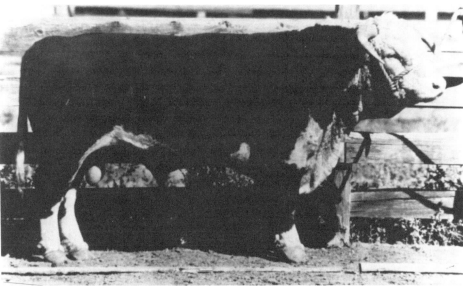

22

Thirteen other inbred lines were established, most of them small in number: twenty or thirty head—small enough to be bred by a single bull. A line might be built from six or eight half sibs and held to thirty head, in which case inbreeding would go up fast with expected loss in fertility, semen quality, and number of calves born alive. One mistake in such a small population, and a line might fizzle out.

The 200-head Line One didn't fizzle out. Half-sib, mother-son, or father-daughter matings were avoided so that inbreeding never rose above 30 percent. Furthermore, Line One was a multi-sired line; if one bull was a lemon, others would cover up. But in my opinion the greatest advantage came from George Miles's cows—born and raised in a rugged environment. And they were big! And the year was 1933—before the "comprest" trend got started. And now we know from experience that both the original Miles cows and the two *Advance Domino* sires must have been free of any recessive genes.

Now, just a word about *type*: Line One cattle are long bodied and longheaded. Our old Montana extension specialist, N. A. Jacobson, used to say that animals grow proportionately: if an animal is longlegged, it'll probably be long bodied and longheaded. Now, an animal suited to rough country will probably have long legs; therefore, a good range animal is apt to be long, overall. So, Line One was never selected for length of head or body. Length came naturally with the foundation animals and with selection, over the years, for growth.

Scotty Clark was only one of many people involved in setting up and studying the Miles City lines. Clark's expertise was in designing the research projects; he wasn't the greatest teacher I ever had, but he had a wonderful sense of humor, and he sure could put you straight on what he considered important. When judging a class of cattle, he'd put his cards on the table: "How good are the records?" he'd ask. He liked to say that studying the records was even more important than seeing the animals.

Dick Quesenberry was superintendent of the station when Line One started. He was a top animal husbandman raised in the Southwest, where cattle had to be good rustlers to survive. I'm sure Dick knew George Miles and liked the way he "roughed" his purebreds through; he was probably instrumental in getting George's cows into the program.

Fred Baker was herd manager and animal husbandman in the thirties and early forties, and the people responsible for publishing the first heritability estimates were Arne Nordskog, animal science professor at Bozeman, and Brad Knapp, who had come to the station after a productive career at Beltsville.[8]

No matter who was in charge, there was political pressure from those who didn't like what was going on—or what they *heard* was going on. I could name quite a few whose jobs at Bozeman were on the line because of their support for the Fort Keogh project. Fortunately, the station had the support of a few influential ranchers like the Hughes brothers whose feedback surely helped keep the program alive.

23

Miles City research
station superintendent
Dick Quesenberry.
—USDA

*R*UTH UNDEM HUGHES *was raised on an eastern Montana sheep ranch. Her dad called her "Tommy" and sent her off to Bozeman where she met and married rancher G. Curtis Hughes.*

After service in World War Two, Curt returned to Bozeman to design, build, and supervise the new Montana Wool Laboratory while his brothers, Gerald and Harley, ran the ranch. Then, in 1950, old Will Hughes summoned him home, and Curt and Tommy became working partners in the ranch.[9]

"TOMMY" HUGHES

Curt had always known that his dad liked big cattle, so it was natural that he would advise him to visit Dick Quesenberry, the tall, slow-speaking New Mexican superintendent at Fort Keogh.

Fort Keogh was not a popular place with most ranchers in those days; few of them knew what was going on, they just disapproved on principle. Not so Father Hughes, who was using Line One bulls by 1942.

Curt Hughes and Tony.

We had been home on the ranch for several years when Curt began saving the best of our home-raised calves and growing and testing them right on the place. He was afraid the Fort Keogh supply might dry up, and a geneticist suggested raising our own.

So that's how it happened that Curt was out in the feed yard sorting bulls when Harry Hargrave and Joe Gilchrist stopped by one day in 1953. They were looking for rams, but when Harry saw our bulls, he said, "These are exactly what my brother Bert is looking for in Alberta. What'd it take to save him a couple?"

Well, $175 a head sounded okay, so next April, Bert and Amy came down from the Hargrave ranch and bought the first bulls we ever sold.

Soon word got around. In November the Watson boys came down from Abbey, Saskatchewan, and, even in the midst of blizzard, liked what they saw so much that they bought a few bulls and, with neighbor G. D. Elkink, have been coming back ever since.

John Minor, another Saskatchewan rancher, had a vibrio problem in his herd of 1,000 cows and was looking for clean, young bulls to follow a pioneer AI program, settling cows he missed. Later, when calves from our "cleanup bulls" outweighed those from AI, he was naturally very impressed and kept coming back for more for the rest of his life.[10]

The size of the "reverse 2 standing N" brand on this "Newford" bull's hip indicates that he was branded as a calf on the Hughes ranch—the brand has grown with the animal. The smaller "flat H triangle" rib brand indicates the bull was purchased by the Frank Kelly ranch of Fort Benton as a full-grown, performance-tested Newford (the Hughes ranch trade name). —Roy Berg, 1956

And there were other Canadian customers. I'll never forget the Grays and the Cotters.

THE GRAY AND COTTER FAMILIES *were connected to Claire and me, and fourteen other families in the Porcupine Hills, by miles and miles of Number 9 telephone wire.*

Hold the button: one long crank would get you Central.

Release the button; crank in a code for a neighbor: Two "shorts" and one "long" was our ring on the SN ranch.

The 700 line ran from Meadow Creek through Schaefer Coulee, over Sixteen Hill, across Cripple Creek, up Skimmerhorn, through Windy Pass, and down to the Box X ranch, and most of the subscribers—good neighbors that they were—spent much time "rubbering" on the phone.

Now, rubbering wasn't any invasion of privacy. Since we owned the phone company, we shared responsibility for the line; how else could we know when the elk had torn it down? Rubbering wasn't entertainment, it was duty! So everybody agreed.

Of course, when a dozen phones came off the hook at once, the line got noisy and voices faded. Wheezing old Bill Oliver kept a loudly ticking alarm clock on his phonebox, which was annoying, but it didn't pay to holler, "Hey, Bill! Get off the line!" I did that once, and it made old Billy mad. He didn't speak to me for a month; others thought the Ewings had something to hide. Besides, Bill did more than his share of work on the Meadow Creek phone line.

Instead, we developed the habit of shouting; Wes Alm always claimed that if neighbor Butch McLeod would step outside he wouldn't need a phone at all. At any rate, while rubbering one day in 1954, Jim Gray heard me hollering at Curt Hughes in the Judith Basin, hundreds of miles away.

Only recently there had been a meeting at the one-room Meadow Creek school-house. Harry Hargrave had explained the new "performance testing." Jim Gray and Lawrence Cotter had been interested. Now here was a fellow selling bulls on their party line. Jim learned about the Hughes bulls while rubbering on me—or so he always claimed. It made a good story.

JIM GRAY

That's right! I was rubbering on you, and those bulls sounded like something we could use at $300 a head. So Lawrence and Phyllis Cotter jumped in their truck straightaway and went and bought four bulls—two for them and two for me—and, whenever the Hugheses think of us, I bet they see silver dollars.

In 1956 Alberta banks were discounting "Montana cartwheels," which they hated because it cost so much to ship 'em back. But that's all Montanans used, and tourists spent 'em here, and we could buy 'em at our banks for eighty cents on the dollar.

So, when Lawrence went buying bulls, he bought up 1,200 cartwheels and packed 'em in cookie tins (they weighed about seventy-five pounds!) and hawked 'em in for safekeeping whenever they stopped for coffee. Curt and Tommy never said a word when Cotters paid for the bulls. Later, they went to the bank and made the deposit in cookie tins . . . never said a word.

Old Curt and his brothers were no-nonsense, forward-looking cowmen who put a lot of effort into culling genetic trash. They were the first to use Line One, and their bulls worked well for us! Almost worth their weight in silver, you might say.

RAY WOODWARD

When Miles City Line One bulls went out to ranchers like the Hugheses, they triggered lots of antagonism. At one point, the Hereford people tried to shut us down; now they love Line One. Slowly, a few farsighted breeders woke up. By the time we celebrated the line's fiftieth anniversary in 1984, it could be found in 60 percent of modern Hereford pedigrees.

Sixty percent is a pretty big share for a line built up from sixty head just fifty years ago, but success didn't just happen—*boom*! There had to be a sound, scientific basis, and that basis was the development of *performance* and its acceptance by ranchers. A few good breeders spearheaded the state performance groups, but commercial ranchers were very much involved. They were the guys who said, "Look! We're tired of this horseshit where calves get lighter every year. We don't want dwarfs! We're looking for something better. We sell pounds!"

3   Going for Small

M EN LIKE PERCY COPITHORNE, Will Hughes, and Bob de Baca's father may have liked big cattle, but it was tempting in the 1920s and 1930s to
upgrade with "modern" bloodlines supplied by the growing purebred industry.

By the 1940s, however, it was also apparent that, as breeding stock became
"pure," size and performance dropped. There were scales on the Gilchrist ranches,
and records show shipping weights decreasing, while pictures show the cattle getting
purer. What was going on?

Joe Urick was raised on a Montana stock farm where, as a teenager in the
thirties, he became an enthusiastic judge and showman. He remembers what went
on.

JOE URICK

In 1936 us kids showed a couple of 4-H steers that weighed about 1,100
pounds. But one of our neighbors, a registered Hereford breeder, brought in a
well-bred steer that was 200 pounds lighter, and the judge—an Iowa man—
gave him the nod.

Then my dad challenged him, saying, "Here I am, raising good, big cattle,
and you're telling my kids we oughta be raisin' *small*. What's the idea?"

"Well," the judge said, "there's been a change. I'm putting this steer up
because we're going for *baby beef*. We're looking for 500-pound carcasses," and
he slapped that little steer on the rump and made him grand champion of the
show.

You see, the old judging system was based on subjective, visual criteria like
color and smoothness and shape. And I learned, as I went on to college, that
those criteria didn't turn feed into beef. In fact, I learned, in working with
some of the very first bulls ever tested, that productive types could be very
different from the popular style of the day. Productive animals might have big
long heads and weren't what you'd call "smooth," and they certainly didn't
win ribbons. They were simply more efficient meat producers.

BY THE MID-TWENTIETH CENTURY, there was a very large gap, it seems, between producers of beef and producers of seed stock, as Bob de Baca remembers:

BOB de BACA

When I was in high school, Dad was renting pasture to one of the largest Hereford breeders in the state. His cattle were in our backyard, so to speak, where we could see what was going on, and we noticed at least two bulls in every breeding pasture.

I hit him up one day: "How in the world d'ya know, for registration, which calf is from which bull?"

"Why, any good cowman knows by eye which calves are sired by which bull!" the breeder said.

Yeah, sure! I thanked him for his instruction. And we also couldn't help noticing that his calves were getting smaller every year. Finally Dad asked him, "What the hell happened to those good, big ol' cattle you used to raise?"

"Well," the breeder says, "the trend's toward *small*. Selling my bulls at Denver, I get an extra hundred dollars for every inch I take off. Small is what's winning shows."

"Well, I want volume and scale in my bulls," said my father. "I don't sell cattle by the *inch*; I sell *pounds*."

IN SEPTEMBER 1949 I visited a ranch with a reputation for well-bred seed stock. For many years the owners had imported high-priced bulls from Cheyenne and Denver, had topped the big Canadian shows, and were selling "better breeding stock" to breeders and commercial ranchers on both sides of the border.

On this occasion, visitors were invited to inspect a curiosity—misshapen, stunted, wheezing "Little Minnie." No one in our party, including several old, experienced cowmen, knew what we were looking at that day. Certainly, the owners didn't recognize a large genetic problem in "Little Minnie," or they would not have shown her off.

What we saw was an interesting freak, that was all. But a few weeks later a headline in Life *magazine caught my eye:*

DWARFS OF "LOST CANYON"
Miniature cattle find proves to be hoax of the year

L IFE HAD ASSIGNED PHOTOGRAPHER *Wallace Kirkland to do a story on a "race of midget cattle" discovered in a mysterious "lost canyon" in North Dakota. Wrote Kirkland:*

"Sure enough, there were the midgets—one bull and four heifers. Though full-grown they were small enough to walk under a card table and weighed between 160 and 210 pounds."

But good reporter Kirkland smelled a rat. The cattle were very fat, and for having come out of the "breaks" they were certainly tame. Further investigation showed the owner to be a burgeoning sideshow promoter who failed to locate his mysterious canyon—it was really lost. And three days later, a Montana rancher turned up who claimed to have raised the tiny cattle and sold them to the promoter for $100.

And so, with a hoax exposed, reporter Kirkland returned to Chicago, said Life, "leaving the promoter with five midget Herefords and a face as flushed as a North Dakota sunset."[11]

A bogus "midget" of Lost Canyon. —Wallace Kirkland; Life Magazine © Time Warner Inc.

*N*OBODY KNOWS WHAT'S GOING ON *in ranch country better than a good ranch veterinarian. Dr. Jim Bailey of Great Falls remembers what happened next.*

DR. JIM BAILEY

Cattle breeders have never been content with a good product; they're always swinging to extremes, and the first extremes I recall were little compact, compressed-looking things off the TO ranch in New Mexico. Cute little devils, they were—the hottest things going; you could almost put one in your pocket. Somehow, someone had gotten the idea that we needed petite carcasses for smaller cuts of meat, and the purebred fraternity began a trend toward smallness that came to a tragic end.

One day a Hereford breeder looked around his calving barn and cried, "My God! I see a *dwarf!*" Suddenly, the "comprest" type had a brand new name—and some very undesirable characteristics.

*I*N 1990—*boxed beef having largely replaced wholesale carcasses swinging on the rail—the meat packers tell us we must raise cattle that "fit the box."*

It was a different box they spoke of in 1950. The ice box was being replaced by the refrigerator, designed for the compressed kitchens and compact families of the post-war era. Howard Fredeen—geneticist and meat industry consultant—questions how the trend to "small" got started.

HOWARD FREDEEN

As I remember, it was the packer not the breeder who started the "comprest-compact" fad that ended in dwarfism in 1950. Meat processors theorized that modern families were smaller, therefore meat cuts must be smaller. Perhaps we can excuse the judges and professors for jumping to the conclusion that smaller animals were needed to supply the trade.

*B*UT BOB de BACA, *by 1950 on staff at Iowa State College, recalls how best intentions went awry.*

BOB de BACA

One of the great old livestock specialists in this country was a man by the name of Beresford who was on the faculty at Iowa State for forty-five years. He used to say he was sorry he ever heard of "baby beef." Then he'd shake his head and add, ". . . and I'm sorrier to say I coined the expression."

A TO ranch steer weighing just 965 pounds became grand champion at Denver in 1945. —Harlan Ritchie/Don Good

He had tried to help producers of the 1930s cut their costs. He had preached that they could save two years' production by better feeding and earlier finishing. Instead, producers had gone to smaller breeding and were calling their smaller animals "baby beef."

Rex Beresford was pushing a hundred when he died, still shaking his head and muttering, "Breeding small was never my intention."

WHATEVER A WELL-MEANING EDUCATOR *like Rex Beresford may have meant, hundreds of young ranchers graduated from ag colleges fifty years ago with confidence in their well-educated eyeballs and little understanding of genetics.*

Well-known judge and showman JACK PHILLIPS *remembers:*

I was raised in the "compact-comprest" era when a square, blocky, short-legged, early-maturing, fat-type critter was ideal. As a Hereford kid, I was raised to believe that a beef animal should be "yeller and meller" and have "a top like a table."

I hitchhiked once to the American Royal at Kansas City and watched Francis Miller show his string of three-foot-wide, navel-high *Double Dandy Dominos*, the prettiest things I'd ever seen in my life. Their type was my ideal, as I watched the old professors place the shortest-legged, fattest steers on top. Then—all of a sudden—*dwarfism*! The TO in New Mexico called itself the "Compress Hereford Ranch"—even showed a few dwarfs, were proud of 'em, but didn't know what they were.

A "comprest" Hereford bull like *Larry Domino 50th* became so popular that everybody had to have a son, and they doubled up on him and the *Baca Dukes* and the *Royal Dominos*; some of the Wyoming Hereford Ranch bulls were such powerful show winners that all good Hereford breeders had to have

It wasn't just the Hereford breed that foundered. Here's a 1950s triple-compounded Eileenmere Angus, affectionately nicknamed "Short Snorter." The nickname was unfortunate since the "snorter" gene was soon to devastate the purebred beef cattle industry. — Harlan Ritchie/Don Good

their names in their pedigrees. So, all of a sudden, all Hereford cattle were bred almost the same and, when they started doublin' up, these little dudes [dwarfs] started fallin' out. Many dwarfs were snorters—you could hear them breathing clear across the barn. Most were knocked in the head before they died from natural causes; the genes weren't lethal, but they sure killed a lot of business. "Hey, we've made a mistake! We've been picking the wrong kind of cattle," the professors said. Hell, they wouldn't grow; they would put on fat; they didn't have much muscle. . . But, of course, few of us ever saw a carcass in those days. We were flying blind! Our thinking had to change.

A year or two later, we were placing the sorriest cattle—what we'd been *taught* were the sorriest cattle—at the top. We didn't have to choose; they were *all* we had. They weren't much bigger, but their pedigrees were clean. And that's when things began to work again. That's when Dr. Watson's Here-

Typical "snorter" dwarf of the 1950s. —Harlan Ritchie/Don Good

ford ranch in Oklahoma imported English bulls that were clean pedigreed and *big*. Everybody talked about how big those Herefords were, and they reversed the trend for the entire purebred industry.

*C*LAIRE AND I GOT MARRIED IN 1950 and headed for California where the hills were paved with gold, as everyone knew. Along the way we saw the sights—including WHR, the Wyoming Hereford Ranch, one of the wonders of the world for purebred breeders—or so we thought. Idealistically, we supposed that purebred cattle were the ultimate food animals. Disillusionment came with experience, and we finally found our niche in commercial (unregistered) cattle.

With promotion and dollars and hype, purebreds are often seen as the ultimate food animals; in reality, as many ranchers realized even then, purebred selection was based on subjective appraisal. It was common in the fifties for a breeder to substitute a "nurse cow" for a mother deficient in milk; it was common to use creep feeders and other gimmicks to beef up the farm environment. No wonder cattle performance was in a downward spiral.

One who explained this well at short courses from Banff to San Antonio was a professor at the University of Alberta. Here's his story:

ROY BERG

Just before World War Two, the Canadian Pacific Railroad and the Alberta irrigation districts were promoting *better breeding stock*, by which they meant the British breeds. The promoters maintained registered herds from which they distributed seed stock to the settlers. My family got Holsteins delivered at Brooks; I went with my brothers and "walked" them home, seventeen miles across the prairie.

And I was exposed to *better breeding stock* in 4-H, where we learned that beef cattle had to be a certain type and size, and everybody believed that production was determined by shape. Beef animals had to be very square and blocky; if you had the right shape, you had "quality," by which was meant the right kind of beef and the right size of roast. But nobody looked at carcasses or talked about inheritance or performance. We were deeply influenced by a show-ring mentality.

University professors (like me, a few years later) were often proud to be asked to judge—so we were partly responsible for that show-ring mentality. 4-H kids were told that the "comprest" or "pony" type was exactly what the industry wanted. How could that be, when beef was sold by the pound!

Anyway, the idea developed that *big* meant *bad*, and all through World War Two cattle got smaller and more compact, and it just so happened that, in

Crowning the champ at the 1955 All Angus Futurity show. —Harlan Ritchie/Don Good

selecting for small, a gene for dwarfism popped up and helped us get there quicker.

That dwarf gene got the attention—to put it mildly—of the seed stock breeders and brought us around to trend reversal quicker than anything else imaginable. Soon, the "pony, comprest, compact" type was just a blip in history—prominent for awhile, but not long lasting. And, right at that point, "performance" appeared in curricula across North America.

RAY WOODWARD

The well-remembered dwarf gene was in cattle right along; I remember a dwarf at Havre in the thirties. There was a strong correlation between the heterozygote dwarf carrier, and the new, small "comprest" type that the professors—in their wisdom—were promoting.

But it was really the show jockeys—bless 'em—that spread dwarfism across the country. The age of technology was at hand, but it would be a while before the industry came to realize that the eyeball wasn't the ultimate tool of selection.

Meanwhile . . . still plenty of room for showbiz on the ranch.

4   Niceties and Necessities

I HAVEN'T MANY FRIENDS *in the purebred business, fewer yet who are professional judges and fitters, so I treat the few I have with respect. Here, two discuss a business in which I have never been involved; it's important to many people, nonetheless.*

The late Paul J. "Jack" Phillips was a well-known judge and breeder of registered beef and dairy cattle and, in later years, the president of the American Chianina Association. Chianina—an interesting Italian breed of which you'll read more later.

JACK PHILLIPS

People say, "Chianinas are not efficient beef animals."

I say, "Whoa! You're tellin' me that because a cow weighs a ton, she can't be efficient?"

"That's correct."

"Then, what if her first calf sells for $5,000?"

"Oh, well, that's not what I mean."

"Well, it's what *I* mean," I say. "I'd rather sell a $5,000 purebred than a 600-pound grade calf at a dollar a pound. Talk about efficiency—you're talkin' dollars, too."

*J*ONATHAN FOX III *is a third-generation breeder. His grandfather bred horses (sometimes artificially) before the turn of the twentieth century near Rochester, Minnesota. His father raised Percheron horses, dual-purpose Shorthorns, mutton-type sheep, and lard-type hogs for homesteaders settling the plains before World War One.*

Jonathan grew up on Justamere Farm in Saskatchewan, where, from his earliest years, he was fascinated by genetics; he bred cats and ducks and mink, experimenting to see what colors he would get. Later, he became famous judging all kinds of stock including poultry and llamas at the largest shows on earth—often presiding in

Justamere Hal, with Jonathan up, presiding at Regina. —Ted Pritchett

the ring on horseback. Meanwhile, he became known as a breeder of fine Holsteins and Polled Herefords.

Horse lovers always, Jonathan and his wife, Molly, "retired" to British Columbia in the seventies; they still raise Morgan horses in the nineties, while their son Lyle carries on at Justamere Farm *in Saskatchewan.*

JONATHAN FOX

Us Foxes always had a limited land base, so we always kept purebred livestock—fewer numbers, higher prices, eh? Of course the cattle business is, always has been, and always should be an international business, but in the 1940s my neighbors kept bringing home these dumpy, little cattle from the States, and I was about fed up.

One fall day in 1955 Molly and I were returning home from Denver when we saw a poster advertising a bull sale in Great Falls. "Gosh," I said, "let's see what's goin' on."

Well, the sale was over when we got there; the barn was dark, and there was nobody around but we found the light switch and a tattered old sale program, and I started lookin' the cattle over. Pretty soon I come across three bulls in one stall; they were very much alike, and I fell in love with them on sight.

"I'm gonna stick around," I said to Molly, "and see if I can't buy one of these bulls tomorrow." And that's when I bought *Beau Trumode*, one of the best Polled Hereford bulls I ever owned.

In looking over *Trumode's* pedigree, I found that it was completely clean of dwarfism. His sire had come from British Columbia (exactly one-half mile from where I live today), and his background was a bigger type than was common. I was surprised to find a bull like that in the States in the 1950s.

Funny thing, too: when I got home to Saskatchewan with this Canadian-American bull, my neighbors said, "Whaddaya want with a big ol' horse like that?" He would have been a seven or eight on the so-called Missouri frame-score at a time when they were lookin' for threes and fours. They'd all like a bull like *Beau Trumode* today.[12]

A FEW YEARS LATER, Jack Phillips (Ph.D. in animal science) started what he called the American Herdsman Institute at Kansas City—a company whose business was the "custom fitting" of show cattle for a percentage of the sales. Jack had a great eye for cattle and a great memory for detail, and before he died he told me this story:

JACK PHILLIPS

I overheard two guys talkin', and one of 'em said, "You see that long, tall doctor a-holdin' that bull? Well, he's done more damage to our breed than anyone in the country."

We were at a major Polled Hereford show, and the speaker—one of the most prestigious breeders in the country—was talkin' about *me*! The "long, tall doctor" (the kind that don't do nobody no good, as somebody said) was *me*.

That was over twenty years ago, and the bigger-type Polled Hereford that I was accused of "putting up" at the shows has been "doing damage" ever since. If I started the trend, I'm proud.

Time was when hornless [polled] Herefords were a laughingstock compared to the horned variety. The saying was: "Breed the horns off; breed the ass off," and they sure *were* assless cattle—plain as snakes, and ugly, but at least they didn't have horns.

Back in the early days, some of our smarter guys stuck some *Larry Domino* [bloodline] into the Polled Hereford breed and were proud of what they'd done until they found they'd introduced dwarfism. Fortunately, there wasn't much, and we got rid of it pretty quick, and our ugly, old assless cattle stayed "clean." The polled Hereford breed actually gained on the horned through dwarfism; horned Herefords went backwards, by the standards of the day.

Anyway, in 1967 I went to Denver looking for bigger bulls for our American Herdsman Institute in Kansas City. I got there late for the National Western show but in time for the sale, and I quickly went to the Polled Hereford barn for a look.

As I walked down the rows of bulls, one stood four or five inches taller and six or eight inches longer than the rest. I thought, "What have we here?"

Just then somebody punched my arm, and here's this short little guy with a great big belly, a big ol' hat, and a big cigar a-standin' there grinnin'. "You're Jack Phillips," he said.

"Yes, sir, I am."

"I'm Jonathan Fox."

We shook hands, and he said, "You're lookin' at my bull. Would ya tell me what ya see?"

Well, we were spooked on dwarfism in those days, so I said, "Mr. Fox, do you have an extended pedigree on this bull?"

He reached in his coat. "Just happen to have one here that goes back eight generations."

I studied the pedigree, and it looked pretty solid to me; the bull was sired by *Predominant 25U* out of a daughter of *Beau Trumode*. I started away; "Hey, where ya goin'?" said Jonathan.

"Why, to try to buy your bull."

"You are?"

"Yep. And, I'll tell you somethin' else, Mr. Fox. Just as soon as the snow melts, I'm coming to Saskatchewan to see the sire of this bull."

"Anytime," said Jonathan. And he was grinning.

Well, the Herdsman Institute was just getting started, and I didn't have much money, but I'd rode old Jonathan's bull to $2,000 when two new guys walked into the ring and started bidding against me.

Well, they didn't know who they were bidding against; I was duckin' the competition, but at $3,000 I was just about out of money. So I decided to bluff; I jumped the bid $500 thinking, "If this don't buy ya, Mr. Bull, I'm in trouble." But it worked. They quit. I bought the bull, and now I'll tell ya something funny, coming from a judge of Hereford cattle: That bull had red pigment around his eyes! He looked like a spook. He was ugly. His head was about *that* long; he was tall; and when we came back later that evening the other breeders were leading him in the alley and pokin' fun at my ugly ol' assless, red-eyed bull.

I told a customer, Mr. Buford of Caledonia, Missouri, about ol' "Red Eye," and he come up to Kansas City and took one look and said, "Jack, that's the ugliest bull I ever saw."

And two months later he gave $10,000 for a quarter interest.

Next April I visited *Justamere Farm*—"It's just a mere farm," says Jonathan, "not a ranch or anything"—and in a clearing in the bush we came upon Red Eye's father: the biggest, longest, highest-topped, meatiest bull I'd ever seen. That was *Predominant 25U*, and I had to have him.

I made a deal to bring *Predominant* to Kansas City; I'd manage him; Jonathan and I would go partners on his semen. That was the year they first certified artificial insemination in the breed, and they allowed a hundred certificates per bull.

I sold all hundred of *Predominant's* certificates at $1,000 a crack. What I call a very efficient bull!

Ol' *Red Eye: Justamere* Roundup Ian 176X (*notice the red pigment around the eye*).
—from an old sale catalog

JONATHAN FOX

I have a saying: "In cattle breeding it's the *niceties* and the *necessities* you're concerned with." You can't afford the niceties till the necessities are looked after.

Historically, red pigment around the eyes of a whitefaced Hereford have been grounds for disqualification from the herdbook. But I didn't cull old Red Eye; in a breed that's plagued by cancer eye, I consider pigment a *necessity*.

When I judge, I start from the inside out, not from the outside in. You gotta know where the bones are; then, in your mind, you add layers: the meat, the fat, the hair. When I judge, I'm like an X ray, lookin' in.

What they teach in 4-H clubs is "presentation." *Good* presentation is worth teaching; what I don't like is the phony stuff like fillin' the flanks with air or silicone—the sort of thing you hear of now and then. When they pump up the flanks, they're not changing a bull's genetics, eh? And I was amazed when I first saw purebred calves on nurse cows, and all this fancy, phony hairdoin'. It's trying to pass something off as genetic that isn't! That's what I call a nicety we don't need.

JACK PHILLIPS

I don't know about nurse cows. Gettin' $10,000 for a bull that's spent his first year on a Holstein? Makes the nurse cow very efficient in my book. [Jack laughs at the thought.]

Of course, eventually they quit paying. The practice of using nurse cows is no longer acceptable, but people did get what they paid for: 1,300 pounds in thirteen months . . . at only a year of age. That's genetics!

But, getting serious about *Predominant 25U*: The rest of the story will show, I hope, that not all breeders are con men, and that not all purebreds are raised in a hothouse environment.

Jonathan's great old *Predominant* was sired by *Roundup 3L*—a tremendous bull from the Spidell ranch near Roundup, Montana, at a time when most cattle breeders were going to small.[13]

Bill Spidell was one of the most interesting stockmen I ever met, and he had a philosophy of cattle breeding that still makes sense today—for those with the money and guts to follow through. For instance, he never believed in weaning; he'd wait till the cows kicked 'em off. And he crowded his bulls together and let 'em fight; he thought the survivors made the best herd-sires.

His cattle sort of migrated from summer to winter pasture without fencing, and he never fed his cows a supplement. A neighbor told me he had gone to old Bill once, cryin' that there was too much snow for grazing: "Bill, you gotta feed your cows," he'd said—and remember, those were purebred cows.

"No," said Bill, "my cows can live off the fat on their backs for weeks, and I ain't gonna spoil 'em."

44

And, again, he paid $5,000 for a class-winning bull at the National Polled Hereford Show at Atlanta back when $5,000 was a hell of a lot of money. And he turned that pampered, southern farm-raised bull out with his heifers on a section of Montana rangeland where there was only one watering place a half mile off; the bull stayed right by the gate—I'm talking about a two-year-old bull standing at the gate while heifers came and went.

One day Spidell spied a cowboy saddlin' his horse. "Where ya goin', Jim?" he asked.

"That new bull's never found water; I'm gonna show him where to drink."

"Put your horse away," Bill says. "Just leave him be." And a couple days later the boys were lookin' down at a $5,000 stone-cold national stock-show winner.

Spidell put his foot on the carcass. "It's a blessing," he said. "This dumb son-of-a-bitch lay down and died before he did any harm by reproducing his kind."

That was back in dwarfism days, and people said Spidell was some kind of a nut: he didn't cull his red-eyes; he didn't cull his linebacks; he toughed his valuable purebreds through the winter. What a nut!

Bill Spidell was really a breeder who understood the laws of God and Nature. He knew what man could do and what he couldn't. He kept things simple. He might have saved the whole Polled Hereford breed just by keeping the *niceties* and *necessities* separate.

The Beef Steer of Tomorrow
by James V. Rawe

The beef steer of tomorrow
will change a lot we know;
He may be extra long and wide
and maybe not so low.

Professors tell us what he'll be,
his weight and grade and yield;
They tell us how he'll fatten
on roughage in the field.

The Hereford people know for sure
that they will set the pace;
That this steer of tomorrow
will be a red whiteface.

The Durham men declare and say
there surely is no doubt:
The beef steer of the future
will take the Shorthorn route.

The Angus folks will never agree
(their breed, it nothing lacks);
And who in heaven's name could think
of anything but blacks.

Charolais breeders firmly stand;
they know their kind's supreme;
In weight, in gain, in everything
of course he will be Cream.

Now no one knows for sure who's right,
though we each hope we are;
But we could find some dismal day
that we have gone too far.

For safety's sake, let's not condemn,
as great may be our sorrow,
If we wind up rejecting
the Beef Steer of Tomorrow.

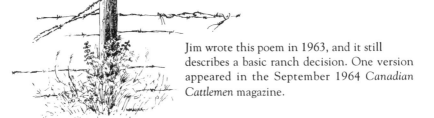

Jim wrote this poem in 1963, and it still describes a basic ranch decision. One version appeared in the September 1964 *Canadian Cattlemen* magazine.

5   The Fat of the Matter

SEED-STOCK PRODUCERS and their "commercial" bull customers were divided at midcentury: At the heart of their controversy was fat—an excess of
which is laid on last, as animals develop.

Now to oversimplify a complicated subject: A young animal grows rapidly, making
lots of bone and muscle. Then, as growth slows, food not needed for maintenance
turns to fat. Selection for slow growth or early maturity results in animals that are
overfat at an early age—as in the "comprest" type.

This wasn't well understood in the 1950s.

ROY BERG

In the early fifties, the University of Alberta took a championship at
Toronto with a Shorthorn steer of the standard type that put on fat in patches.
The judge called that steer "the best *fleshed* animal I ever put my hands on in
my life"— his actual statement.

And somebody took a picture of the rib eye of that steer (an unusual thing
to do in the 1950s), which has allowed us to see that it had six square inches
of lean and was covered by a three-inch rind of fat. The point is that the
experts in those days never saw a carcass; yet they talked a lot about "flesh-
ing," meaning what they *thought* they felt through the hide—actually, gobs of
fat.

We at U of A were as quick as anybody to be suspicious. Certainly I was
when I came home from Minnesota in 1955 thinking, "Let's find out what's
really under the hide. That should be simple."

Of course, it wasn't simple. You can't really tell what's hidden under the
rind of fat without cutting through to the rib eye, as in quartering. And in
those days sides weren't quartered before grading. That would require a major
change in the system.[14]

47

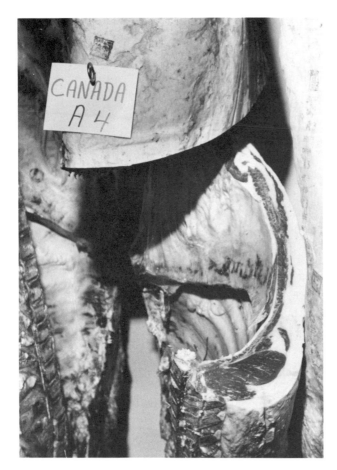

The eye of loin, or rib eye, from a Canada A4 (overfat) carcass. The nutritious red meat is covered with about 2" of expensive, undesirable fat that will have to be trimmed before retailing.
—Ted Pritchett

*I*N THE *1950s the nutritional value of animal fat had not been rendered suspect, but the economic message was clear. As the production of meat and fat and bone was scientifically studied, cattle feeders found that it cost twice as much to produce a pound of fat as a pound of muscle—that is, red meat.*

That meant that, in response to supposed market signals, millions of dollars were being wasted every year in producing expensive fat. It's appropriate here to consider briefly the forces behind those signals.

The late, great JIM BALDRIDGE, *cattle auctioneer, put it this way:*

I used to fatten cattle back in Iowa in the fifties when you bought a set of steers and fed 'em until the corn was gone. That was the state of the art.

When they had so much brisket that their front legs couldn't carry 'em, they were *almost* ready to sell.

When your corn was gone, you sold 'em. There was nothing more scientific about it than that.

And W. D. "BILL" FARR,
the grand old man of western cattle feeding, told me this:

Before World War Two and pretty well through the fifties, most so-called fed beef was produced in relatively small farm lots in the Corn Belt, and the amount of beef in the country depended entirely on the corn crop. If Nature was kind, why, farmers bought lots of cattle and fed 'em for a longer time and produced lots of meat—and lots of fat.

I judged Chicago once, in the early fifties, and the judging committee was made up of three packers, two Corn Belt feeders and myself; we were on horseback around the stockyards for three days, judging the 350 loads of "fats" in the competition. The lightest load averaged 1,400 pounds—they were *really* fat!

Now, the thing most people don't understand is that there were once some valid reasons for laying on fat. Meat animals were supposed to be fat in the early days.

Let's go back to the early 1900s. In those days there wasn't much population in the middle of the country where we raised and finished most of the beef, so our meat went east or west to the population centers without much refrigeration to preserve it. Sides of beef swung from rails on the ceilings of railroad cars whose floors were covered with sawdust, and now and then, with all the swaying, a side would fall to the floor. At the destination a gang of big, strong guys would pick up the sides and carry them off on their backs; if the carcasses were dirty, why, just trim 'em down to nice clean fat; it was insulation and wrapping paper both. Fat served a double purpose in those days.

When the meat came off the cars in an eastern city, they'd hang it some more while it aged and got tender—and moldy. Restaurants in those days didn't think a carcass was ready to cut till there was plenty of mold on the outside cover; then they'd simply trim off some fat, and the beef was ready to eat.

Even then, they didn't trim too close, because cities like Boston, Philadelphia, and New York had very large foreign populations which liked large amounts of tallow, while old-timers, here long enough to accumulate wealth, demanded the very best—by which they meant the fattest.

In the old days, you couldn't sell a carcass to any butcher in Boston at less than 800 pounds, better yet 1,000, and the fatter the better. Those were the days when the packers developed *house grades*, names that described their product for any given market: "Swift's Premium" meant something entirely different in Denver than it did in Boston, where they liked those great fat cattle.

Government grading, on the other hand, was something new and different. It was an attempt at standardization, and it started in Portland, Oregon, just before World War Two. Nobody paid any attention to it at first; then, because of wartime price controls, it became mandatory as a measure of quality in pricing the product.

*I*N 1850 THE REPUBLIC OF CALIFORNIA *became a state. Before the gold rush, the big industry had been cattle, and—forget about meat and fat—the primary trade had been* hides, *to be shipped round the horn and tanned for industrial belting.*

When I went to California a century later, one big product was citrus, *and the company I worked for grew oranges, lemons, and grapefruit as well as walnuts, barley, and beans—and cattle. Irrigated orchards and crop fields were surrounded by steep, hilly rangeland where Dewey Culbert, a fine old Californian, coached me in traditional cowboy skills as we roped and doctored yearlings for foot rot and screwworm.*

We sometimes helped at the company's large feedlot where walnut and citrus byproducts were converted into manure for the orchards. In fact, in 1950 the main product of that feedlot was natural compost—manure. So, were Dewey and I really "organic cowboys"? I would not have said so.

*O*NE DAY *when Dewey and I arrived for work at the feedlot, we got the impression that our boss, Herb Lyttle, was mad!*

HERB LYTTLE

That was the day that beef grading became compulsory; I remember it well. We had shipped to both Armour & Company and E. B. Manning & Sons in Los Angeles—so many steers for Armour, so many for Manning—gate cut [at random] from the very same pen.

I shipped lots of cattle to Manning, a man who had built a successful business catering to high-class outlets in southern California back when grading was optional. In those days the packer had a choice whether he did, or did not, wish to grade the cattle he bought, and Mr. Manning did *not* grade. He did everything with flourish; his trucks were spit and polish, all black with a

*California cowboy
Dewey Culbert.*

red stripe around, and everything was spotless at his plant. If meat grades had been useful, Mr. Manning would have used them; instead, he relied on his personal reputation for integrity. It's indicative that his firm is still in business forty years later!

The federal meat-grading system was designed to establish prices during World War Two. Both price controls and grading were discontinued in 1946 but brought back for the Korean War—that was the excuse. Then, after 1950, every animal going through a federally inspected plant had to be graded.

Now, grading has nothing to do, of course, with health. Sanitary inspection is carried out by government veterinarians. Grading is done by federally appointed graders whose work is, by nature, very subjective.

Well, that day in 1950 we shipped our steers to Armour and Manning, and a day or two later the guy from Armour calls: "My God, Herb! Those cattle didn't grade! Only five of that carload of eighty head made USDA Choice; the balance went Good."

"Oh, no!" I said. I'd sold them at a price based on "U.S. Choice," and there was lots of money at stake between Choice and Good. Maybe I'd goofed; I called the Manning buyer:

"Lou, how'd those cattle grade for *you?*"

"Just fine! Wait a minute. . ." And when he came back with the numbers, he verified that pretty near all had gone Choice, just the opposite of the cattle that went to Armour. And, remember! They'd been sorted at random from the same pen at our feedlot.

Of course, I immediately called Armour, and they had a great confrontation. It turned out that the same man had graded both loads at the two plants on the same day; it was simply an error in judgment—an error repeated many times, up to the present day.

I always thought that, in California at least, one big force behind compulsory grading was Safeway Stores. They liked the USDA grades. No longer

In this 1989 photo, professors Jeff Savell, of Texas A&M, and Harlan Ritchie, of Michigan State, demonstrate a classic variation in red meat production. The plastic bag on the left holds the thirty pounds of fat trimmed from a U.S. "Yield-Grade 1" (lean) carcass in readying it for retail. The bags on the right hold the hundred pounds of trim from a U.S. "Yield-Grade 4." Live and carcass weights were almost identical, and both were trimmed to a uniform quarter-inch rind.

were they saying that their own product was good—not like Swift and Armour with their Premium or Blue Ribbon house grades. Now, the U.S. Government was saying Safeway's product was good! Better yet: Uncle Sam was calling their product "Choice."

Safeway always advertised nothing but U.S. Choice—a paradox, really. Choice was wastefully fat, not what the housewife wanted. But, with that stamp of approval, Choice was what she would buy. It was important. She felt safe that way.

BILL FARR

Following the Korean War, the Corn Belt feeders became the "U.S. Prime" beef producers in the country: they were kings of the mountain; they got the premiums.

Here in Colorado, we were outlaws—didn't belong to the same church, couldn't afford to meet the highest grade. We were regarded as producers of underfinished butcher cattle, not quite ready to eat. And the federal grading system, with the premium it placed on fat, reinforced that notion for the next thirty years.

ONCE AGAIN *we have a practice (in this case, the production of fat) that began at the grass roots with very good reason.*

Then Uncle Sam, in his wisdom, locked everything in with a rolling stamp that passed for the Great Seal of Approval of the United States of America. Ranchers who toured the carcass-breaking plants of the 1960s saw meat being readied for retail. They remember sides of beef stamped US Choice—*and nearby mountains of very expensive "trim" to be shipped abroad. Even in the 1960s we didn't need—and couldn't afford—all that tallow here.*[15]

6   Two Ranches

I STARTED WITH HEREFORD CATTLE and stuck with them through the 1950s. Shorthorns were out of style; Angus were especially small; Herefords had been the breed of choice for fifty years. I believed that with good management and without much capital outlay, a whitefaced herd could pay for a ranch. Some dream!

But Hereford cows had problems: They didn't have much milk. Worse, when a bright, hot sun came out on a late spring snow, unpigmented Hereford udders would sunburn, teats would chap, and newborn calves would be brutally kicked away. That's when a north-country rancher puts in long days roping and hobbling cows, and salving their teats with goose grease or store-bought ointments. It may sound funny to city folks, but sunburnt teats are no joke for a cowboy (or a cow!).

The commercial herd that wore the SN brand in the 1950s was standard for the times. Purebred Hereford bulls had been used for years; yet as Butch McLeod, my neighbor, said, "You can't expect 400-pound calves in the hills; we don't get the rain. And, as for fertility, be happy with 80 percent."

Well, I wasn't happy with 80 percent crops of 350-pound calves, but I kept on greasing banana-shaped teats that gave more trouble than milk for a few more years.

MEANWHILE, a thousand miles to the south, some big white cattle were quietly making the scene. So, let's go south. I want you to meet Mack Braly—oilman, lawyer, rancher, entrepreneur—who had much to do with providing alternative breeds.

I first met Mack at a cattle meeting in Denver in 1970, and many years later, when Claire and I visited his Oklahoma home, he and his wife, Claudia, and their son, George, entertained us long into the night with stories of red tape and golden cattle.

Now, when Mack told a story, he always liked to start at the beginning. So, let him start at the beginning—before he owned any cattle, before he owned a ranch.

Well, Mack didn't want a ranch, but he had no choice. . .
His old friend Charlie Bates would see to that.

MACK BRALY

I'm a lawyer by profession. Been in the oil patch on my own since '32. Practiced law from '35 to '40. Drilled my first well as a law-school freshman. Saw the bottom drop out of oil in '29 and '55 and '82, and it's always the same: Short of oil, and the price goes up; all the smart guys drill new prospects; they hunt, they find more oil; then, 'stead of cutting prices and competing for the market, they conspire together and promote production quotas.

What's more, Congress approves; Congress helps confound its own anti-trust laws. And so it was in 1955: The price got soft; the oilmen cut production to fifty barrels a day; at $25, the price stayed soft; at $8, folks with any sense quit drilling.

So, one day in 1955, I was sitting around with nothing much to do when here come my old Sunday school teacher, Charlie Bates. Now Charlie had been a successful oil broker in his day, and he'd been an absolute heretic till he joined the Baptist Church. An exceptionally fine man was Charlie Bates, and many things got started with what he did to me that day.

He walked into my office, says, "Mack, go get your hat on. Come with me."

"Where we goin', Brother Charlie?"

"I wanta show you some Bermuda grass."

"I got a yard full of Bermuda grass; I don't need any more."

"But this is special," said Charlie. "A brand-new hybrid, Midland; full of hybrid vigor."

Now, him bein' an old friend, and me not havin' much to do, I put my hat on and got in the car, and we drove all the way to Tulsa where he showed me several thousand acres of sandy bottom, cleared of willow and blackjack, and knee-high in Bermuda grass. As we walked through the field, he says, "Look at this, Brother Mack! Now, I want you to go home and buy a demonstration plot and plant it to this Midland. We'll show the people of poor old Pontotoc County what to do with their worn-out land."

"Charlie, you must be nuts," I said. "I don't know anything about farming, I'm not interested in grass, and I sure ain't interested in showin' a bunch of damn ol' jug-headed farmers how to make their land produce; let 'em figure it out themselves."

But, as I say, I didn't have much else to do, so I was willin' to look when a real estate man came in one day and, "Get your hat on, Mack," he says. Now, when those guys tell me that, I generally strap my pistol on, too, but this one took me to a bottom thick with "bo-darc," flat as a table with an inexhaustible supply of water running through it, and I was glad.

Bois d'arc, or Osage orange, is the finest wood in the world. The Indians made bows of it; it's strong and resilient and *very* tough to clear, but I couldn't resist. Right then and there I bought 1,100 acres of the finest bottomland in the nation—"bo-darc," creek, and all—and I spent the next five years clearing it of brush. Then I bought more; I needed this forty, that eighty, everything adjoining, till I had 4,000 acres cleared and could call the place a "ranch."

So I called on Bates: "Well now, Brother Charlie, you got me into this. You gonna hafta supervise the spriggin'."

You see, you can't plant Bermuda grass from seed; you got to *sprig* it, and you can imagine findin' sprigs for 4,000 acres! They cost me plenty at $5 a tow sack, and there wasn't such a thing as a spriggin' machine so it was a big, big job, but Charlie was intrigued; he supervised until the place was knee-high in Midland, and at that point I was ready to go ranching.

I didn't know anything about cattle, so I hired me an old-time cowboy, Norton, who had worked the range from Chickasha, Oklahoma, to Tucumcari, New Mexico. "Nort," I said, "What kind of cows you think we oughta have?"

"Well," he says (and he was always spittin'), "we sure don't want no dwarfs."

"Whaddaya mean? Tell me about dwarfs. And what about the cattle we see at shows?"

"I don't know," he says. "I don't think I like 'em much at all. I kinda like them big ol' rangy cattle."

"Well, d'you know where we can find some of the big kind, like you're talkin' about?"

"Yeah," he said, "I think I know a place out in New Mexico."

So I sent Nort out, and he bought five carloads of big, long, rangy Herefords and those ol' cows hit the Bermuda grass a-runnin' . . . hit a fence and followed it for miles. It was five days before they stopped exploring and settled down to become real efficient meat-producin' critters, and, if all my cows had been like them, I'd still be raising Herefords.

Well, perhaps it was beginner's luck. On his next trip Nort wasn't so successful; the best he could find was some little short-bodied, dumpy kinds, and I commenced to get uneasy. Once again, I was talkin' to Charlie Bates as we was leaning on the fender of my pickup watching the cattle graze.

I said, "Charlie, what I'd really like is some of them big ol' white cows like I saw in France. I remember 'em layin' out where an artillery shell had killed 'em with their legs stickin' up in the air, and they was the biggest doggone things I ever seen. Later I saw some alive. Can't remember what they called 'em but, Boy! they looked like what a cattleman ought to have."

"It just so happens," Charlie says, "that I was visiting last night, and a guy was talkin' about a bull that a trucker dumped off in his yard—the biggest, whitest bull that fella ever saw. The way he said it was somethin' like 'Shar-lay.'"

Big growthy Herefords of the type bred by George and Verna Peterson of Highwood, Montana, might have kept Mack Braly happy with the breed in the 1950s.

"Get your hat on," I says, and we went to see the man with the big white bull. He gave us a little ol' magazine with these big white cattle in it, and I saw an ad for a breeder named Gilmer A. Morriss. Later, I called my manager: "Nort," I said, "be here at dawn. We're goin' to Texas."

We set out early next morning and by late afternoon had come to a place called Rocksprings. "We'll stop here overnight," I said, "and walk in on Gilmer Morriss right at daybreak; we don't want him settin' up for us." But, when we drove into Morriss's yard just after sunup, here was this great big guy with a chest sticks out to here, already workin' some big white cattle through a chute with a crew of Mexican cowboys. He wore a little bitty brimmed hat, turned up all the way around; he wasn't one of these big-hat kind of Texans.

"How de do, Sir," I says; "I'm lookin' for Gilmer Morriss."

"I'm Morriss," and he just kept workin'.

Nort and I just stood watchin' and—boy!—there was nothing tame about those cattle. Finally, I got a chance: "Mr. Morriss," I said, "I heard you had different cattle; we were just drivin' through and hopin' to see what they look like."

Well, Gilmer was a cagey old trader, and he smelled a mouse. He knew he had a greenhorn: he could smell it, he could feel it, and he started whettin' my appetite. "Yeah, I might have somethin' interestin'," he says.

So we drove around his ranch, which was pretty rough and ready, and we looked at his neighbor Jim Chittum's herd, and then old Gilmer says, "I'll tell ya what. I've got some cattle at Kerrville. . ." So we drove a hundred miles or so to find eight or ten yearling bulls and heifers, all clean and white, with a Mexican groomin' them and everything.

"Why, Mr. Morriss," I says, "these don't look like your other cattle or Chittum's."

"Well, those were range cattle; these are show cattle. I'm gettin' these ready for the San Antonio show."

Well, I didn't know much about cattle, but there was one I really liked, a little old bull about ten months old. "What about him?" I asked.

"I call him 'Seguter'; he's gonna win grand champ in the yearlin' class," he said. (The bull's real name was *Saguaro*, like the very old, long-armed cactus, but Gilmer was talkin' Texan, and it sounded more like "Seguter" to me.) "He's gonna live a long time and make my reputation."

So we talked around from one thing to another, and I got the bug on for that bull. "Mr. Morriss," I says, "do you want to sell Seguter?

"Well, I dunno. . ." And he starts playin' hard to get. "I sure got to have him for that show."

"What kinda price you got on him?"

"Ten thousand dollars, but I wasn't aimin' to sell him!"

Well, Nort and I stopped at a hotel in Kerrville, and we kept talkin' and gettin' back to Seguter and, as the night wore on, I knew I had to have that bull. Next mornin' I was knockin' on Gilmer's door as the rooster crowed, and he came to the door in his bath robe, looked through the screen: "Who's that?"

"It's Mack."

"Mack who?"

"Mack Braly. I was with you yesterday afternoon."

"Oh . . . Oh . . . What you want this time of day?"

"I came to get my bull!"

"What bull?"

"Why, the Seguter bull—*Saguaro*." I just about die laughin' when I think how Gilmer never let on, never showed his surprise. He just said, "I get to put him in the show!"

So, in the fall, Claudia and I drove all the way to San Antonio and were disappointed when *Saguaro* only placed fourth, but we hauled him home and turned him out with the Herefords. "You're a damn fool, Braly," I thought, "puttin' a $10,000 bull on a bunch of $165 cows."

But, if a fella does something dumb, he should do it with enthusiasm! So I bought more Charolais bulls, some of 'em halves and some three-quarters;

Saguaro had a five-generation pedigree, but they all traced back to the Mexican importation by a French guy named Pugibet in the 1930s, and they all had a shot of Brahma in them. Their first crop of calves were the prettiest golden colored critters I ever saw; we called them our "golden nuggets," and they grew and were big for their age and were meaty-lookin' calves, and we were very, very pleased with what we were doing.

It was Carlton Corbin, a performance-minded neighbor on the Stony Broke Angus Ranch and later president of PRI, who said, "Mack, if you think your calves are so good, why not send 'em to Tishomingo and let them prove it?"[16]

One of the very first performance test stations ever was at Murray State College at Tishomingo, Oklahoma, and it was only thirty miles away, so that's what we did. We put our golden nuggets up against all the fancy Angus and Hereford bulls that had been winning shows from Texas to Alberta, and—whaddaya know! We won! Our nuggets outgained everything else on test.

They became the foundation of OCR, our Oklahoma Charolais Ranch, which produced well-known seed stock for thirty years.

THAT WAS 1957 or 1958. The large, well-muscled white or cream-colored cattle that had been showing up in Texas for two decades were thousands of miles and several generations removed from their center of origin in France. They had come to the United States from Mexico.

Foot-and-mouth disease (FMD) had long been a problem in North America; wherever it had been found, it had been eradicated, only to break out elsewhere at a later date. Following outbreaks in 1923 and 1929, the United States, Canada, and Mexico had signed an agreement banning it from our continent forever. No cattle would be allowed to land from any country where foot-and-mouth was tolerated—which took in most of the world.

Interestingly, even before the ink dried on that agreement, the first of several small importations appeared in Mexico from France, to turn up north of the border a few years later.

NOW, ANOTHER three-generation pedigree: that of the Michaelis family of Coahuila and Texas.

Max G. Michaelis, the first, was born to German parents near Round Top, Texas, in 1864. During Reconstruction he was sent to school in Germany, where the family still had ties. On his return, post–Civil War Texas was still unsettled, so he went to Mexico, which, under President Díaz, was a very advanced country with many European settlers and more foreign embassies than the United States.

But land was cheap in Texas, so in 1890 Michaelis sold high in Mexico and bought a place at Kyle near San Antonio, where I found his grandson Max G. III, known to his friends as "Maximo."

M. G. "MAXIMO" MICHAELIS III

Grampa Max *won* this ranch from Captain Kyle, a local hero, in a horse race; the 1890 deed record shows a consideration of one dollar for 260 acres. He added to that, substantially, only to lose much of it again in the Great Depression.

Mules were worth a lot when Grampa arrived, and mammoth jacks helped put Kyle, Texas, on the map. In 1911 Grampa sold a three-year-old jack that was seventeen hands high—supposedly the biggest in the world—for $5,000 in gold. Then, along came World War One and internal combustion engines; by 1920 the day of the jack was gone.

But, along with jacks, Grampa raised Durham and Hereford cattle; I still use the scales he weighed 'em on. Performance records, of course, were around for a long, long time before heritabilities were known, and I have pictures of Grampa weighing and measuring jacks in 1908. I even have the weights he kept on Shorthorns.

By 1925 Daddy [M. G. Michaelis, Jr.] was ready to take over, but central Texas was experiencing one of the worst droughts in its history, so Daddy went to Mexico as his father had done before him; that's when he got *Rancho El Fortín* at Músquiz, Coahuila. The revolution was over; Mexico was restocking and American ranchers were allowed to summer their cows in Mexico and bring them back in the fall, duty-free, with unweaned calves at side. Naturally, they all weaned 100 percent calf crops. [Maximo chuckles at that improbable thought.]

Now, as everybody knows, cattle came to the New World five hundred years ago with the first conquistadores, and each Spanish ship thereafter brought more animals—with, no doubt, a full complement of disease. Spanish cattle then spread throughout the Americas: "Criollo," we call the survivors of slash-and-burn agriculture in the tropics and uncontrolled grazing in the north; an example is the famous Texas longhorn.

Cattle breeding goes in cycles. I'd say Texas cattle went downhill during the 1870s and 1880s (the classic "cowboy" period) when all good bulls were castrated and driven north as steers. Those not good enough for market stayed home and bred the cows; sounds like negative breeding to me, though modern longhorn breeders wouldn't agree.[17]

From 1890 through the 1920s, many criollo herds were "improved" with the British breeds and the East Indian zebu. Nobody gives it credit, but I think criollo should be added to our modern herds to improve hardiness and vigor.

Grampa, though, believed in the Shorthorn breed, which was famous for size; one of his bulls tipped the scales at 2,700 pounds. The downside was that the breed was becoming "wasty," with lots of fat, big briskets, and poor fertility; by the time I came along in the 1930s, the trend was toward small, slow-gaining cattle. Again: *negative* selection for performance.[18]

But, back to Charolais. A Frenchman born in Mexico—Juan, or Jean, Pugibet—became interested in Charolais cattle during World War One. After the war he worked with a French export syndicate to bring three importations to Mexico; they arrived in 1930, 1931, and 1937, and Pugibet kept the shorter-bodied, easier-fleshing animals for himself; they became known as the Pugibet herd.

The Mexican secretary of agriculture and livestock, Gen. Manuel Peréz Treviño, took a longer-bodied bull called *Iroquois* and some heifers, and they became the Peréz Treviño herd.

Now, in 1934 at El Fortín, Daddy was given two Peréz Treviño calves, *Blanco* and *Plato*—the gift of a neighboring rancher, Gen. Miguel Acosta. My grandfather, who happened to be visiting, saw these two white animals and said, "My goodness! Those are the growthiest Shorthorn bulls I've seen in years."

"Not Shorthorns." Daddy said, and added, "I don't know what to do. I got no use for two Charolais." He had a good business producing Hereford calves for the U.S. market, and he wasn't eager to change, yet he almost had to accept these exotic gifts from a very good friend who was also influential in government.

Then Grampa, remembering the herds of good white cattle he'd seen in France on his way to school, said he'd take the bulls to Texas and see what they would do on his pure white Shorthorns. So Daddy, who was ready to trail north, threw *Blanco* and *Plato* in with his steers and strung them out for the border.

That was 1934, and the port veterinarian at Eagle Pass was a good friend of my father's. He knew what he was doing, and a couple of young white bulls didn't seem to matter; he said something about "other off-colored steers—Shorthorns, roans, or whatever," and he was used to seeing one or two bulls in the bunch. "They look healthy enough to me," he said, "and you're payin' the duty. Run 'em across."

Grampa Max was seventy years old when *Blanco* and *Plato* came to Kyle and went to work in his purebred Shorthorn herd. He was almost eighty when *Isaak* and *Nero*, two more *Iroquois* sons, joined them. Before he died in 1950, at age 86, he saw his herd reach "full-blood" status. I consider Grampa, Max G. Michaelis Sr., the first real Charolais breeder in the United States.

And Daddy always swore that *Blanco* and *Plato* were not really smuggled in. He paid the duty in full when they crossed the Rio Grande with the rest of his steers.

A T THIS POINT, *you may have learned more about sprigging Bermuda and crossing criollos than you ever wanted to know. But you've also met Mack Braly of Oklahoma and the Michaelis family of Texas and Coahuila and have had an introduction to the Charolais breed.*

Maximo's grandfather may well have been the first true Charolais breeder in the United States; because of him and a few other farsighted Texans, the breed spread like wildfire across the range into Canada in just a few years.

Charolais-cross calves were appearing on northern ranches by the early 1960s.

Mack Braly was not, and never claimed to be, a pioneer Charolais breeder; when he talked to me, he referred to himself as a "greenhorn." Maybe so, but his work had tremendous influence on ranching, and he was one of the most interesting characters I have met. More of both Michaelis and Braly later.

Ideas have consequences, and the Charolais idea had tremendous impact on modern North American ranching. The traditional British breeds were prodded to change by competition. One who knew the Angus breed of the 1950s would hardly recognize it today, except for color. Competition is a wonderful thing.

I used Charolais sparingly on my SN ranch in the 1960s, and the bull I remember best was El Fortín, bred on a ranch by that name near Músquiz, Mexico, and available in the U.S. and Canada through American Breeders Service, the AI giant. Much more of such things, later.

Now, I want to introduce two innovative breeders, and two interesting and important homegrown breeds.

7 Two Breeders

*R*ANCHERS WERE CHALLENGED *in the 1950s by postwar rising costs and the declining productivity in our increasingly inefficient established breeds. Little was known of the French Charolais that were finding their way north from Mexico. Few ranchers had even heard of the many other breeds that supply the world with beef. But, even then, new and productive domestic strains were appearing on the range.*

ROY BERG

The organized breed registries go back to the industrial revolution, and histories like to tell us that the various breeds evolved from *linebreeding* or *inbreeding*; that is, some very wise person settled on one great animal and started a breed.

In reality, I believe that breeds evolve from ongoing selection—from picking the best on a continuing basis—and there's a difference. My theory is that breeds are the result of selection, rather than of conscious inbreeding to concentrate genes. Selection comes first: *Selection fixes type.*

Let's say a stockman decides to develop a breed. It would be natural to select the best that has worked for him (very few famous breeders, so far, have been *her*). So, before long, he'd be linebreeding without thinking, and where would he look for a continuing supply of seed stock?

Why, to his own production, of course, and that is, in fact, what all breed founders have done.

*A*ND, IN FACT, *that's what Berg himself did in selecting the "Kinsella" lines at the University of Alberta research ranch.*

Well, there are a number of important domestic breeds, but most important to me have been the Red Angus and Beefmaster. Both breeds were established by the 1950s, and I used them in building my SN herd in the 1960s. I learned about Red Angus from my friend Neil McKinnon, who was using the new breed heavily on the LK ranch, east of Calgary, by 1960. With Neil, I visited Beckton, the "calving ground" of the breed, and there, on the slopes of the Bighorns near Sheridan, Wyoming, we met the redoubtable Sally Forbes, who, with her husband, Waldo, began selecting "Reds" in the 1940s.

With Neil McKinnon, too, I visited the Lasater ranch on the high plains of Colorado, where I have returned many times with my family to pay homage to Tom Lasater—ranch philosopher and founder of the Beefmaster breed. I profited from Tom's brain as well as his bulls, since ideas as well as genes are important in my business.

N OW, HERE'S A SLICE *of Red Angus history, carved by one who made it happen:*

SALLY FORBES

It was my late husband, Waldo, not I, who started the Red Angus breed; we met in Georgia, when I was in college, and were married in 1939. A New Englander, I had been west twice as a kid, but Waldo didn't want me "falling in love with the ranch" before we married; his theory was that too many girls fall in love with the country and the life. Next, they want to run the life, and there wasn't room for that on a ranch like Beckton.

Well—that was Waldo. And I was probably obnoxious with all my "bright ideas," but ranching really is a wonderful life.

Beckton Stock Farm has been in the Forbes family since 1898, but, to my knowledge, none of the family lived here until 1934, when Waldo moved out after college and brought in some registered Herefords and, later, registered Shorthorn and Angus cattle. As he learned what was going on, he decided that purebred cattle should be selected on efficiency, not on show-ring standards, which he considered fads. So Waldo decided to start afresh, with a brand new selection program and a brand new set of cattle; and, sometime in the 1940s, he started gathering Reds, which were very unpopular in the predominantly black Angus breed.

Actually, it's estimated that 60 percent of all the world's cattle are red, and it says somewhere in the Bible that "a red animal without white spot is a special beast." But breeders of the 1940s were ashamed to admit they ever had reds; they would blame them on a "neighbor's bull," which was probably "less than pure," and they'd get 'em out of sight as soon as possible. I sometimes make a rather poor joke that the Angus enjoys its great reputation for meat because the blacks were held back for breeding while the reds were culled for sale in the butcher shops.

The breed originated in Scotland—a combination of Buchan "humlies" and polled "doddies"—descended, perhaps, from the old Norwegian Reds, since invaders like the Norsemen often brought their cattle along. At any rate, red individuals have always been accepted in the Scottish Angus breed; in fact, a dozen or so are listed in the first American herd book. They were only first excluded in 1916, and I'm very glad they were.

I believe few American breeders had any idea that a gene for red occurs naturally in their breed. Of course, the red gene is recessive, which means that "pure" black parents may be carriers. If both parents carry the gene, then one calf in four (by Mendelian theory) will be homozygous for red and therefore red colored, which is very convenient for us. A red cow and a red bull (having no black genes) must *always* produce red: the basic genetic principle behind the Red Angus breed.

This extreme "belt-buckle" type was popular in 1950. —Harlan Ritchie/Don Good

For Waldo this was made to order. I used to say the Reds were handed to us on a silver platter. Some would call it gold!

By 1945, we at Beckton had acquired, without advertising, ten Red bulls and eighteen heifers. No one knew what we were up to; Waldo had a nice relationship with Mr. Tomhabe, the Aberdeen Angus secretary, and several of our foundation animals came from association presidents and other influential breeders—all very quietly and on a very friendly basis. It was only as we became effective that love was lost between us and the Angus officials.

Meanwhile, we built the herd on three foundation bulls acquired from well-known breeders around the country. The first and, in my opinion, greatest was *Larkspur 1F* bred by Norm Smith of Larkspur, Colorado.

Churasco 16F came from the Angustora Ranch at Steamboat Springs, and I always thought his name was Waldo's play on Tobasco Sauce—which I relate, somehow, to Angustora bitters. And, Mr. F. B. Davis wrote from his South Carolina plantation offering us a "Red too good to be discarded"; I still have his letter and the crate that *Serenade 23F* arrived in—an interesting bull, though I didn't like his type.

Beckton Larkabeau 13601, *son of* Larkspur, *became a prolific AI sire for American Breeders Service of DeForest, Wisconsin.*

Anyway, *Larkspur, Churasco,* and *Serenade* were our three foundation sires, and we never used their names in full again. But you can see how *Larkabeau* and *Larkabelang,* our famous AI bulls, trace back to good old *Larkspur 1F.*

We started collecting weaning weights in 1954, birth weights shortly thereafter, and from the start we emphasized performance records, not appearance. As I often say: "Looks are the last thing to look at"—except for structural soundness.

Forrest Bassford, the great livestock journalist, knew exactly what we were doing. We invited him out early on and explained that we were building basic values—using color as a mark of excellence only. Forrest never wrote a word about us till we were ready five years later, which was very decent of him; we didn't want to start a fad for color.[19]

And, frankly, we never tried very hard to be accepted by our peers. In fact, when a few other breeders began propagating (instead of eating) their Reds, we became an embarrassment to them. At Phoenix they did us the favor of disqualifying our feeder calves half an hour before the show. Then they changed the rules so our purebreds couldn't compete at Denver, which made us eligible to win with crossbred steers—as we did for years.

However, in March of 1954, a small group of pioneers agreed to meet at Fort Worth to start a breed. As we drove to that first meeting, we called on Dr. Paul Stratton at the University of Wyoming and Dr. H. H. Stonaker of Colorado. "Above all," Stony told us, "you must get it in your rules to outlaw nurse cows!" He agreed with Waldo that the widespread practice of substituting a milk cow for a calf's genetic dam was fraudulent. And he thought the greatest single problem in all the purebred breeds was poor fertility. I remember those statements well! If we accomplished only half of what we hoped, he thought we'd accomplish miracles. So, a few days later, the Red Angus Association of America was established at Fort Worth, based solidly on performance. That was 1954—well before the formation of PRI!

Waldo was elected president just before his untimely death from cancer. I served as secretary for a couple of years, just for convenience' sake.

I VISITED H. H. STONAKER at his farm outside Fort Collins, Colorado. Known to generations of friends and students as "Stony," he had come to CSU (when it was A&M) in 1947 and founded its famous beef cattle research program.

Stony spoke to me of the history and art and science of breeding cattle, and of cattle people.

H. H. "STONY" STONAKER

I'll never forget my evening with Waldo and Sally Forbes over thirty years ago. They were on their way to the Red Angus organizational meeting, and

Sally Forbes with sons Spike and Cam on their ranch in the Big Horn.

they outlined very clearly what they were trying to do. We talked of what they had done so far; we discussed their decision to quit the established Angus breed; we talked about their fears of starting a "fad."

Sally is a very strong woman who kept the family intact after Waldo's death; several children now run the ranch. Many others have been successful in the business, but the Forbes family has kept the Red Angus breed firmly based on performance.

Another rancher, Tom Lasater, has more to show for a lifetime of cattle breeding than anyone I know. His cattle are famous for performance, but he's not a "numbers man"; a scientist analyzing his work would have a difficult time. In other words, if a cow needs culling, she's gone! Tom lets Mother Nature keep score. He doesn't need a computer to figure it out.

Tom Lasater is one of the really true "greats" as a breeder and as a producer. I regret that his cattle haven't been entered in more crossbreed production tests where, no doubt, they would do very well. With one of his sons, Dale, now taking the reins, I expect that will soon happen.

SAID TOM ABOUT HIMSELF, *when my son Charlie and I visited the Lasater ranch at Matheson, Colorado, in 1987:*

TOM LASATER

The Monfort feed yard at Greeley is, or used to be, the largest in the world, and they always have lots of problems with wild cattle—anything startles 'em, they run to the back of the pen, away from the feed trough.

They also get lots of visitors at Monfort's, and people walking up and down the alleys disturb the cattle constantly. So Kenny Monfort built a huge tower, a hundred feet high, where visitors can look down and see what kind of cattle are in the various pens; there'll be Herefords, Angus, black baldies, and what-not. And, even as the feed truck drives down the alleys, the wilder cattle move to the back while the others keep guzzlin' feed as fast as they possibly can. Well, I was up in the visitor's tower some years ago with three or four men who were talking back and forth and around, and one of them said, "You can see every breed in America from here—every single breed!"

"Why, no," I said, "you can't."

Tom Lasater, 1991.

They all turned to me: "What do you mean, you can't?"

"I don't see any Beefmasters."

"What the hell is a Beefmaster?" one of them asked. [Tom chuckles.]

So I told them how Beefmaster was the second recognized beef breed developed in the United States. The King Ranch's Santa Gertrudis was first, but of course the King Ranch had a tremendous amount of pull with the federal government, what with the owner, Richard Kleberg, being in Congress. He got his cattle recognized first, but Beefmaster was second. That was in 1954.

*S*PEAKING *in a soft, south Texas drawl, Tom "rides circle" in telling his stories. He doesn't always start at the beginning, and he sometimes visits unexpected places. Ride along as he takes a turn about the ranch.*

My father, Ed Lasater, of Falfurrias, Texas, owned and operated a 350,000-acre ranch "next door" to the King Ranch. There were lots of Herefords and Durhams down in that country; it wasn't all longhorns or criollos back in 1906 or 1907—that was when Father started selecting for red-pigmented eyes.

Beefmaster cow and calf. —Watt M. Casey Jr.

Then, about 1908, he got some of the first Brahman or zebu that came to the country, and they worked well because of the climate. But everything was *wild*—wild Mexican cowboys, and the cattle were *really* wild! I mean, you could hear 'em crashing through the brush while the cowboys practiced ropin'— just a very wild situation, there in the south Texas brush.

But my father had a number of other enterprises in addition to beef cattle. He had a big bunch of pigs—all sorts of 'em—and the only herd of English Dorset sheep in the country; he had the largest registered Jersey herd in the world, and he owned and operated the Falfurrias Cream Company. I'll tell you about that.

My dad sold dairy cows from that huge Jersey herd to a lot of his smaller neighbors, and they would all start milking about three o'clock in the morning; they all had little ol' hand-cranked cream separators, and some of 'em had old Model-T Ford trucks, and every morning they'd come zooming in to the creamery, deliverin' fresh cream.

Now, the man who ran the creamery was a very hard-boiled gentleman named Procter, and the cream had to be there by 8:30 sharp, and he was brutal. About 8:25 he'd go out and stand on the platform with his pocket watch in his hand, and the little old Model-Ts would come roarin' in and unload until his watch read half past eight. Exactly at that point he'd hold up his hand, and there would be no more cream accepted that day; the next farmer would have to turn his Model-T around and go back home and feed the cream to his hogs. But, Falfurrias sweet-cream butter was famous; it was the only butter I ever heard of that would last ten or twelve months without refrigeration of any kind and still be perfectly edible. All the mining companies across the border in Mexico would buy up huge amounts and haul it up to their camps so their people could have fresh butter.

One of my first jobs in any branch of the cattle business was to go around and visit the stores that sold our butter. I was supposed to ask whoever was in charge how the distributor was treating him. Was he delivering on time? Was he doing everything right? They usually had nothin' but good to say about our butter, but they treated young salesmen like mud.

Of course, we were all supposed to be well dressed; I'd wear a white linen suit and necktie and all the rest, and I'd have to go back to the hotel two or three times a day to take a shower and get organized with a nice clean shirt and tie. Then out I'd go to take more beatings.

Well, there was one big, tall man that owned a little family store in Uvalde, west of San Antonio, and the first time I called I walked up dressed to kill and scared to death. "I'm Tom Lasater," I said. "I'm with Falfurrias Cream Company."

This big, tall man had known my brother before me, and he stood there lookin' down for a couple of minutes until finally he said, "Hell, kid, your brother was good lookin'! What the hell happened to you?" So, I learned to be thick-skinned and what it takes to get out and sell—whether you're big and tall and good lookin', or feeling bad, or what.

When my father died in 1930, I was at Princeton. I resigned in the middle of my sophomore year and came back to Falfurrias to help my mother run the ranch—or what was left of it. The very first thing I did when I got home was to order all our cowboys to hang cowbells on their horses; that way they couldn't run our cattle through the brush without me knowin'. Talk about mad! If it hadn't been the depths of the Depression, every cowboy woulda quit. But I knew you couldn't make money with wild cattle.

I started with a Durham-Brahma cross and then a Hereford-Brahma cross. Then, after several years and just as an experiment, I decided to cross the crosses. I took my top Durham-Brahma bulls and bred 'em to Hereford-Brahma heifers, and the minute the three-way crosses hit the ground, I could see they were a whole lot better than their parents. That's when I really started using a three-way cross.

Most cattlemen are conscious of all the various scientific improvements with cattle—changing genetics up, down, and sideways, and so forth, But, no matter about technology, any stockman who decides to develop a breed has, first, to define what he's lookin' for—whether for dairy, beef, or racetrack, or for the plow. He's got to take into account all the scientific evidence and everything else available to obtain his ultimate goal, so when I started out in the thirties I wrote all the leading livestock shows and asked them to send me copies of their scorecards. Then I spread 'em all out across the table and started checkin' on what they wanted.

Well, they were judging on color, shape of horn, length of tail, ad infinitum; and 90 percent of the characteristics had nothing whatsoever to do with beef. So I decided to make a list and found about twenty I considered important.

I got to thinkin': If I start selectin' on twenty characteristics, I'll have to live 500 years to change a thing. So I boiled 'em down to what I called my six essentials: disposition, fertility, weight, conformation, hardiness, and milk— in no particular order; the absence of any one would be unthinkable.

Probably because of my youthful experience with those wild south Texas cattle, I usually start with disposition. Poor disposition increases management problems on the range and cuts efficiency in the feed yard. You just can't make money with wild cattle, and what people don't realize is that disposition is highly heritable. In other words, a mean, wild cow produces mean, wild calves.

Fertility should probably come first. After all, you ain't got nothin' till a bull impregnates a cow, but . . . disposition, then fertility.

But, weight is equally important. If Jim's calves outweigh Jack's by fifty pounds at a given age, why, obviously they're better. If they continue to outweigh other cattle at two and three years of age, they're better again. So, down the line: disposition, fertility, weight.

Then, conformation, and by conformation I mean type on the *hook*, not the *hoof*. In other words, after you strip the hide off, what's hangin' on the rail is what counts.

Then hardiness: the ability to survive under all conditions. We've had cattle survive at seventy below in Canada; we've seen it thirty below on our Colorado ranch, and our cattle still get the job done without any hay. We don't put up any hay. We run our cattle as close to nature as possible; that's why they fit most situations wherever they're used. To me, that defines hardiness.

So, disposition, fertility, weight, conformation, hardiness, and last on our list of "essentials" is milk production. Maybe it should be first; the cheapest gains are produced from birth to weaning, and weaning weight reflects milk so accurately that selection is a very simple matter. We simply pick the bulls with the highest weaning weights and cull the lightest heifers.

Creep feeding, of course, has no place whatsoever in any serious breeding program; even in the bad years we leave the job of raising calves to the cows. We leave as much as possible to Nature, and—over the years—she has provided Lasater cows with remarkable udders; they have tremendous milk capacity but stay compact and trim to fit the ranch environment.

Tom and an easygoing Beefmaster bull.

I've often made the statement that, if anyone can show us how to eliminate any of our six "essentials," we will make them a very handsome Christmas present. I wish someone would take us up on this, because the fewer traits we select for, the more progress we will make. But so far no one has shown me one characteristic that can be dropped. All are absolutely essential in beef production.[20]

*T*HE FIRST REAL GOOD-PERFORMING COWS *I ever owned were half Red Angus, the products of artificial insemination in the 1960s. Some of our Beckton Larkabeau-sired cows weaned above-average calves every fall for sixteen or seventeen years (a very good record), and the Beckton influence is still evident in the SN ranch herd of the 1990s—a tribute, I think, to the Forbes family and the emphasis they placed upon performance.*

Beefmaster bulls are also still at work in our herd; their genes are a valued component of the trademarked "synthetic" strain we produce. From his ranch in Colorado, Lasater's ideas and his cattle's genes have spread across the continent from Florida to California, Mexico to Alberta, and across the wide Pacific to Australia. They work so well in so many places, I think, because they were developed under honest, practical conditions by a thoroughly honest cowman.

*B*UT IT WOULD TAKE A HARDY COW, INDEED *(and a mighty tough cowboy), to produce very much at seventy below. The coldest I've seen in Canada was forty-four below (F or C—little difference); that's the temperature where LP gas quits boiling and furnace flames go out, as we saw in 1953 and 1968.*

At that point, if you want to keep warm while waiting for a chinook, you must keep a straw bale smoldering under the propane tank. And be careful not to look at the thermometer.

"The Obvious is never real; the Real is never obvious."

—Jonathan Fox III

THE AGE OF GROWTH

Part Two: The Age of Growth

The Innovators

The Innovators

SURELY, THE TWENTIETH CENTURY *has seen more technological change than all previous human experience—which is not to say that the greatest modern innovation is as consequential as the first willful lighting of a fire, perhaps 3,000 centuries ago. Power at the fingertips! Heat on demand!*

And how about the ingenious woman who first set seed where she could nurture and protect it. What an idea! Then, to give the lady of the cave more to nurture, her partner thought of hitching a sharpened stick to a captive animal. Quite an idea: Room and board for an ox, in exchange for power! And, with more free time to think, food growers progressed to the John Deere plow and McCormick reaper of the 1830s—by which time dozens of "improved" animals were available for power, food, and fiber.

At mid-twentieth century, following a war that introduced many of my generation to technology, we saw a marked exchange of capital for labor, a substitution of horsepower for horse power, and a steady "investment" of tax money in infrastructure, with enormous impact on rural society. I think there has been, since homestead days, a "cost-price" squeeze on farmers, but rising expectations after World War Two (soon to be focused by television) tightened the vice. No longer would a ranch woman be content with outdoor plumbing and coal oil light; no longer could a ranchman tolerate a cow that weaned a 350-pound calf every other year. "We sell pounds!" the rancher cries. "And we're going broke!" his wife replies—which brings us to what I call The Age of Growth.

8   Of Tools and Men

GORDON BURTON

More improvements in agriculture in the last fifty years than in the past five thousand! Say what you will, advances in veterinary medicine and animal breeding rank far behind the allocation of resources to infrastructure and all the innovations in farm machinery.

Consider the knotter: a big innovation a century ago; still in use today. For thousands of years man harvested with a scythe. Then in 1834 came McCormick's amazing reaping machine, just a horse-drawn scythe until somebody mounted a ball of twine and a knotter which turned the reaper into a binder—an incredible contraption held together by cotter keys that would churn out grain bundles day after day for decades.

We've long since replaced our horse-drawn equipment with remote-controlled machines, and what a hell of a difference between a six-foot horse-drawn mower and a fourteen-foot air-conditioned, self-propelled New Holland "hay-bine." [21]

And how we've increased output! My father used to cut 160 acres of hay around the buildings and pasture a large herd of work stock while my mother fed a crew of a dozen men. Now, we cut 1,000 acres in several scattered coulees, and sons Jay and Rick haul it home at high speed over miles of well-graveled roads. I'm seventy years old, but I went out early this morning and ran the tractor till noon; then, after a nap, I went back and put up hay till dark. If I'd had to round up, feed, and harness a dozen horses—much as I love 'em—I'd never have done it.

So, the *infrastructure*—power, telephones, roads, natural gas, and so forth—has given us a standard of living comparable with town, and that's very important. If a rancher needs one thing, it's a shower that runs hot water! If you're gonna work, you gotta be comfortable, and these things keep us comfortable on the ranch while we invest our time and labor in production.

Binder operation in 1908. The second man is shocking or stooking freshly tied bundles, later to be pitched onto wagons and hauled to the threshing machine. —City of Lethbridge Archives

GORD'S WIFE, JEAN, *my wife, Claire, and most ranch wives of the 1950s and 1960s could write books of their own about the "hired hands"—some wonderful, some strange—who ate at their tables—till the minimum wage and other wonders caused them to stay in town. Here's a sample from the foothills of Montana:*

TOMMY HUGHES
(reminiscing with family and friends in her ranch house kitchen)

Twelve to fourteen men was normal at lambing. Town folks thought they were drunks—saw them at their worst—but many were good help and came back year after year; we couldn't have done without 'em, but they were . . . *different.* Many of them found a refuge, here in the hills.

Take Big Sam: he read the Bible and *National Geographic*—wouldn't read a newspaper; "Full of bad things," he said. He was big—the Paul Bunyan of Judith Basin, they called him. Len: he worked here most of twenty years; drank, but never came in drunk, never used bad language, stayed in the bunk house till he was sober—unlike his brother Joe. Joe would come in slaphappy, want to dance, tell me how much he loved me. And Jack—shot up in the war and mean when drunk—we didn't want him around then, at all. And Jerry—the kids never saw him sober.

LIANE "NONNIE" HUGHES
(one of the "kids," home for a visit, remembers them all with nostalgia)

We thought the sun rose and set in all of them; we just didn't understand when they came home from town with shoes that didn't match or without their hats. Remember "Johnny Beaver"? Old-time Utah cowboy, and how we loved him! When he saddled the horses and hollered, "Come on, sweetheart!" it was heaven; we'd ride with him all day. He was great with kids, though covered with scars from knife fights—pulled knives on people in town, they say—but we never knew any of that.

TOMMY: . . . and "Smoky Joe," who rode in Madison Square Garden and had the blackest, beadiest eyes you ever saw; he looked kinda mean but was thoughtful! I remember a warning sign he left on a tree when we were trailing sheep to the mountains: "Bar Are Bad."

NONNIE: . . . and Len, who was quite a student and helped us with sixth grade history at the table. And "Sir Arthur," who claimed to have nine-teen kids in New Jersey and was a regular intellectual . . . such beautiful handwriting . . . quoted the Bible and Shakespeare with every word cor-rect—you could look it up.

TOMMY: . . . but, obnoxious! Ten men waiting for breakfast: oatmeal, fried eggs, bacon, pancakes . . . The first dozen eggs I put too close to Sir Arthur, and he took six on top of his hotcakes. I've seen big eaters, but—oh my!—none like him. I learned to put the food at the other end of the table from Sir Arthur.

NONNIE: In grade school days, we had enough men to pitch and catch and cover all the bases for a ball team; all we girls had to do was bat. The biggest change today is the big bands of sheep are gone, and so many men have been replaced by machines.

*M*Y FAMILY *had "Mr. Clean" for a while—a very short while. Mr. Clean was a bald-headed giant who believed that Claire was poisoning him; after that, raw eggs were the only food he would eat. When the ranch hens couldn't supply his needs, I had to take him to town, where he told his story to anyone who would listen.*

In Montana, there had been Mel. He played the fiddle. When he felt we didn't appreciate his talents, he'd hike for the mountains thirty miles away. I'd find him there in his shack a few days later and bring him home.

For extra help during haying I might stop at the local jail where, after consulting police chief Dewey Bray, I could make a deal with a prisoner, pay his fine, and have a sober, pleasant, hard-working hand for a few days, at least. Here's a letter I treasure from one who made that bargain several times.

August 26, 1953
Browning, Mont.

Dear Sherman

I am writing a few lines while I am in here at the jail. My sentences $32 fine, if you could come get me out it will be right. I will stay at the ranch for good. I must close it now

yours truly,
— Tom

A T $5 A DAY *and found, the bargain was good for six days; then a well-fed Tom would head for town. The system worked well for rancher, prisoner, and taxpayer in less guilt-ridden days.*

L IKE ALL *Montana ranches, the T Bar at Augusta has seen many changes in infrastructure, as Rol and Carol Mosher remember.*

ROL AND CAROL MOSHER

CAROL: We were ranch kids who met at Bozeman right after World War Two—Rol was in animal science; I in home economics. I spend my time on *ranch* economics today.

ROL: My folks ran 2,000 ewes until herders got scarce with the war; then coyotes got the sheep, and that's when we switched to cattle. And there've been other changes—big ones. We didn't have the power till I was in high school; then a little 32-volt generator kept batteries charged for lights.

CAROL: . . . and that was news, I can tell you. But a lot of big changes came to the ranch in the fifties, and four-wheel drive was one of 'em.

ROL: Before the war, we never owned a truck of any kind; we trailed our stock the fifteen miles to the mountains. Later, we got a recon car with a rack that hauled two horses; then a two-ton truck; then a two-horse trailer; then a four-by-four pickup; now, a gooseneck stock trailer—big leap forward!

CAROL: And the way we put up hay! Remember the International "Farmall A" with the six-foot mower?

Hydraulic rams make moving and feeding three-quarter–ton bales a snap.

ROL: Were we in business! Then the side-delivery rake that went 'round and 'round the field, instead of back and forth—big jump over the dump rake! But, even then, I dreamed of a machine where you could sit right over and watch the cutter bar: the self-propelled swather or "hay-bine." I should have invented it; I sure as hell *thought* about it a long time ago.

And big round bales—they've taken all the labor out of haying; hydraulic lifters make handling them a snap! So many labor-savers run on hydraulics these days. What'd we ever do without 'em?

ONE WINTER DAY *in 1987, son Charlie and I stopped at Farr Feedlots, Greeley, Colorado, where we had some steers on feed. We took time out for a visit with W. D. Farr, a cattle feeder for almost seventy years. He knows where many labor-savers came from.*

BILL FARR

Modern cattle feeding and all the machinery that goes with it began right here around the sugar plant at Greeley. It started with Warren H. Monfort,

Bert Avery, and myself—I was the youngest; Mr. Monfort's farm was two miles south, Mr. Avery's three miles east; I had a couple of farms nearby where I fed lambs. [22]

Now, when feeders arrived in the fall, you see, we'd unload 'em at the shipping pens and drive 'em home down the county road—on foot with the lambs, horseback with cattle. Then, every two or three weeks, we'd sort some off and drive 'em back and load 'em up for market. Mr. Monfort and I would get to the stockyards early, and we'd sit on the fence and settle affairs of the world while we waited for the switch engine to come. Then we'd help each other load.

Lamb feeding was a very successful business in those days; wool was worth something before synthetic fibers were invented, and young lamb was a desirable product that consistently sold above beef. We didn't do as well with steers, with just one shot at the market; what made it work was beet pulp. Beet pulp, a by-product of the sugar industry, was cheap and made up the bulk of our rations.

Sugar beet culture, irrigated farming: just plain, backbreaking work! Wet beet pulp was an awful thing to handle; in those days you picked it up with a many-tined fork and pitched it onto your wagon; then you got on the wagon and pitched it into your cattle bunks or sheep troughs. The corn came in by rail, and you went into the box car and shoveled it up to the door and scooped it onto your wagon; then you pitched it up through a hole in your granary roof and scooped it out with a bucket. You know that was *brutal* work!

Then, in the early forties, we began to see what machinery could do. With portable welding outfits, we could build machinery and fix things in the field. Mr. Monfort and I were not mechanical geniuses, but we both had little shops and hired mechanics and sent them off to welding school and began designing equipment. We'd make a rough little sketch and say, "Why can't we do this?" They'd study it for a minute and say, "Well, maybe . . ." Then, in a week or two, or a month, here'd come some crude design; we'd try it and find weak spots; they'd fix and improve until we had a practical, working machine that our neighbors would copy.

All the equipment around this feedlot today evolved in our two shops. We developed the first front-end loader to haul wet beet pulp: took an old tractor, rigged a bucket that dumped the pulp over-head into a wagon. Everything worked mechanically, with cables, until a man by the name of Harsh introduced hydraulics.

Leo Harsh—they called him "Bud"—was a mechanical genius. A submariner in World War Two, he was badly crippled in an explosion, but not before he had learned all about hydraulics. As a farm boy, he saw many applications for hydraulics on the farm, so he came home to Eaton, Colorado, riding a wheelchair, and started building pumps and rams and mounting them on equipment. Soon we were dumping pulp hydraulically from Harsh feed trucks; then,

Inventor "Bud" Harsh supervised production from his homemade electric wheelchair until his death in 1960. —Harsh Manufacturing Co.

inspired, we were mounting his pumps and rams on our front-end loaders, bulldozers, cattle squeezes and augers—and the rest is history. People came to see. Ideas spread. Today, most of the brutal, backbreaking work on any farm or ranch is done by hydraulics. Thanks largely to a man named Leo Harsh.

I DIDN'T KNOW Bud Harsh, but I'm grateful for the hydraulics that replaced my eighteen-pound post maul and the rams that do the heavy lifting on our ranch. I could describe hydraulic applications on farms from Alberta to California. But this is a book about ranching and ranchers and livestock, not machines.

CATTLE AND SHEEP are self-propelled feed processors, and methane gas (the much-maligned exhaust of their internal combustion) is a perfectly normal product of digestion. All carbon burners from bacteria to bison have been exhausting methane gas since life began—and "windiest" of all is the lowly termite.

Now, because our four-legged "reapers" cover such large areas, those who herd them have, traditionally, accepted a low-tech lifestyle: solitary, independent, removed from the mass of humanity. Freelance cattle writer Chris Mills has observed their freedom-loving ways on all the continents.

CHRIS MILLS

I know of no country in the world where graziers are socialists, and sheepmen are often the most right wing of them all—which isn't to say they were born that way, or because they are American, African, or Australian; it simply goes with the turf. You don't have to tell a ranch kid or a bedouin, "Watch out for government!" He or she has seen what government can do from an early age.

Swine, chicken, and dairy producers are usually at the other end of the spectrum, looking for government help, while graziers are free enterprisers, opposed to the strappings of government. I expect this is due to the very nature of the business, which requires large areas of land and depends heavily on Nature over extended periods. Such businesses wilt under regulation.

I'M GRATEFUL *to the never-to-be-forgotten drifters and part-timers who helped us run our ranch over many years.*

But special thanks to the steady, resourceful people who came and stayed a few years, especially Nick and Marie Peters in the 1950s, Richard and Mary Berringer and Dave Brackley in the 1960s, John and Connie Loree in the 1970s, Don and Debbie Snider in the 1980s and 1990s. They and others whose children learned to ride and drive on the SN ranch are remembered as friends. All were self-starters who contributed good ideas as well as muscle.

I'm grateful, too, to the aforementioned infrastructure—though I suspect we have been partially socialized by it. When our family was young, we depended on wind for power, trees for a phone line, and unpaved ruts to a town for store-bought goods and "refugee" ranch help. Now, our wind charger has been blown away by hydro, propane displaced by natural gas, Number 9 wire unstrung by cable, trails filled in with gravel or asphalt paving—while "Mr. Clean" and "Mel the fiddler" and "Tom the jailbird" are among the homeless and will never again leave town.

We know that most of this a drain on other taxpayers, but we accept it. In fact, we love it!

We are firmly snared in infrastructure's web.

9   Know-How

MANY OBSERVERS *of change on the ranch have zeroed in on high-tech education. I could focus on land-grant colleges in the States, similar institutions in Canada, Dr. Ensminger's well-attended International Stockmen's School, or the Western Stock Growers' short course held for many years at Banff.*[23]

Instead, I present the Graham School, for decades a movable feast of new ideas for stockmen, bringing hands-on training to every corner of the continent.

Here's Jonathan Fox of Kamloops, British Columbia, to introduce (in a round-about way) the Grahams of Garnett, Kansas.

JONATHAN FOX

When I was born, my parents were homesteading in Saskatchewan; my mother was forty-five years old and wanted to be with her folks in Minnesota. So I arrived at Rochester with the help of one of the world's great doctors, Dr. Will or Charlie Mayo (I don't remember which).

You see, the Mayo brothers were good friends of my grandparents, who had farmed in southern Minnesota for decades. Dr. Will and Dr. Charlie both loved agriculture and horses, and one year in the early 1900s they commissioned an employee to buy a top-notch stallion. The horse seemed sound, and they "stood" him with a hundred mares that season, but he only got eleven of them in foal—which was kind of hard on the Mayos' reputation.

They believed the problem was with the mares rather than their horse (as is often the case), so they hired a top veterinarian at the incredible fee of $100 a day, and they organized a breeders' clinic for horsemen. They slaughtered some barren mares and hung 'em up in a standing position, natural-like, with their sides cut out to expose the reproductive parts. (You've seen this done at modern AI schools, I suspect; but remember, this was almost a century ago.)

And then, in front of the crowd, that vet examined the carcasses and discussed reproductive problems: fallopian tubes plugged up; uteruses seamed shut—whatever goes wrong with a mare. And the spectators could watch his hand movements as he palpated the ovaries; and they were able to try it themselves, getting the feel of the reproductive parts in the light of day.

Dad believed this was done to save the Mayos' reputation, and he also believed it was one of the greatest things ever done for farmers in his district—a prototype of a brand new kind of school. It wasn't long till a veterinarian named Graham, who knew and admired the Mayos, founded a regular school which my dad attended; that's where he learned "artificial impregnation," which he sometimes used in his horse breeding business in the early 1900s [as will be described later].

And half a century later his grandson, Lyle, attended the Graham Cattle School.

COW FOLKS *the world over have attended the Graham School. Here, the son of the founder tells its story.*

BILL GRAHAM

I feel my age when a kid says, "Hey, my grampa came to your school," but it happens all the time. So let me tell you about the founder, Frank B. Graham.

My dad was born on a Kansas farm in 1871, and at seven years old his stepmother run him off with only the clothes on his back and a little old horse named Topsy. He stayed alive in cow camps on the unfenced open range until a kindly old banker backed him in the cow business.

Well, there'd been emigrants goin' west, and maybe they'd have a worn-out cow that could be bought for a buck or two. She'd be worth $5 fat in the fall, so Dad's making money in cattle at a very young age. Then—it must have been 1886—he rode to Texas and bought 500 heifers at $5 apiece. While he was gone, a very tough winter wiped out 80 percent of the cattle on the range, so his heifers were worth $35 a head when he got 'em home. Suddenly, Dad was a wealthy man.

Then, missing an education, he decided to go to school and, because of his age and bein' around, he picked things up pretty fast. With the basics behind him, he entered the Kansas City Veterinary College run by Drs. Borren, Brown, and Stewart, and he went into business with Stewart in 1907.

In those days horses were the *absolute* mode of transportation, and there was always a shortage of stallions and plenty of problem mares. The horse business was good, and Dad spent a few months traveling, learning all he could about the business. He went to his friends, the Mayos, to learn what they were doing about sterility. They hadn't yet learned about hormones, but they did understand that treatments effective on human females often worked on mares and vice versa. Later—and this is important—they found that equine hormones resemble human; the chemistry is the same.

While they were at it, the Mayos impressed my dad with the importance of sanitation. Most doctors and all veterinarians still wiped their tools on their pants and went on about their business. The Mayos built their reputation around attention to sanitation, and some of what they knew rubbed off on Dad.[24]

Well, one fine day around 1908, Dr. Graham and Dr. Stewart announced they would hold a horse clinic at a certain time and place. Owners could bring problem animals for examination. Going down the line, they soon came to a mare with a very large ovary, and they knew she was unlikely to conceive, so Dad turned to the owner and said, "Here's a mare that won't settle."

Well, those Missouri farmers had to be shown! They didn't believe you could stick your arm in a mare and know for sure she was infertile.

"Okay," says Dad, "I'll show ya. Trim your fingernails. Now, reach in there. . . . D'ya feel something hard as a baseball?"

"Yeah! I feel it. Yeah." And a number of people felt that ovary and agreed it was big and hard and became believers.

Of course, that made the owner angry—he already knew his mare was barren. Now, *everybody* knew, and he wouldn't be able to trade her off for nothin'.

Then a stallion owner standin' by, watching this procedure, started laughing—makin' fun: "Just bring your mare to my stud," he said. "He'll settle her." And, by golly, so he did. And the mare dropped a foal next spring, and two vets lost their reputations in a hurry!

Dad and Dr. Stewart were buffaloed. As far as they knew, it was the first time such a mare had settled, and they were sure of their diagnosis; they had handled that ovary, themselves, as had a dozen students.

Around that time Dad come under the influence of a famous M.D. with a withered hand who had a good reputation for treating human infertility by massaging the ovaries—which gave Dad a clue to treating mares. He and Dr. Stewart manipulated the ovaries in dozens of barren mares and—sure enough!—many caught.

Slowly, a pattern developed. They didn't yet understand that they were making the mare produce the right hormones in proper balance, but they got conception in more and more mares, and they taught their method to others.

Dad used to tell this story—take it for what it's worth: One day some vet officials came to his place and said, "Dr. Graham, we understand you're teaching pregnancy testing."

"Yeah . . . a valuable management tool."

"We also understand you're teaching sterility treatment."

"Yep, I'm doing that, too."

"Well, Dr. Graham, you must stop teaching farmers to treat their own stock, or we'll lift your license."

Now, Dad, raised the way he was, was a very rough man. He reached up and took his certificate off the wall and made a necktie of it around the spokesman's neck. Then, without opening the door, Dad threw him out! That was just how quick and fast he was, and that's the way he related the story to me. And he continued teaching without that piece of paper and did as much for the farmers as any ten highly trained professors. And he ran his school for horsemen at 225 West 12th in Kansas City until Henry Ford kinda blew him outta the water.

After World War One, the horse business faded, but interest in cattle grew, so Dad took the school on the road and, from 1919 to 1958, held classes along well-advertised routes in all corners of the country. In winter, it was Burlington, Newark, Harrisburg, and Cincinnati. In spring, it was Denver, Fort Worth, and probably Atlanta. Next year it was Cleveland instead of Cincinnati, Philadelphia instead of Harrisburg, Jacksonville instead of Atlanta. They covered the west from Portland to Los Angeles; then Phoenix, Salt Lake City, Billings, Great Falls, Calgary. And they covered Canada from Moncton to Vancouver.

As soon as I was old enough, I joined them on the road, and we went on teaching thousands of cattlemen to manage health, sterility, and calving. We'd drive maybe 700 miles on Saturday night and Sunday, with our equipment in a trailer. First thing Monday morning, Mr. Monsees, who was with us for thirty-seven years, set up the classroom, while I went out and bought cattle. Tuesday would be a skull session; Wednesday to Saturday, classes at the hotel or the stockyards. We took good care of the cattle, of course, and sold 'em when we were through. We kept the school on the road for forty years.

After Dad had a stroke in the 1950s, we decided to quit the road and have since made our permanent home at Garnett, Kansas. My son, Frank B. II, joined the staff in 1964; grandson Bill in 1989. We teach AI, pregnancy testing, herd health, fertility management, and over the years more than 45,000 pupils have come to our school, but we don't profess to give a college degree.

We just say, "Hey, do this. It works!"

Or, "That *might* work, if you can afford to experiment."

Or, "Here's something that *ain't* gonna work, for sure. Better not try that at all!"

It's a great satisfaction to have given so many people the skills to hold a farm together—obviously doing a few things right, or they wouldn't be coming back to the third generation.

I been teaching all my life, and I love teaching. Especially the practical stuff: prevention and nutrition. Go into one of our classrooms, and you'll see a dollar sign on the board. If something fits that dollar sign, we discuss it! If it don't, we don't say nothin' about it, at all.

And you say I don't speak the king's English! But it's like Will Rogers said: "Them that ain't sayin' ain't, ain't eatin'!" I'm with Will; I been eatin' high on the hog for seventy-five years.

S EVERAL CHARACTERS *in this book attended the Graham School. I sent at least four men from the SN ranch, including my son, Charlie, and my half brother, Truck Morrison, who later sent his wife, Adrienne.*

And they all came home loaded with knowledge, exotic equipment, and enthusiasm for the many new things they'd learned. And many of them quit their jobs soon after graduation to put their skills to work at higher wages—a common result of higher education.

This ancient photo, captioned "Calf born in 1907 in the herd of R. L. Hughey, Alva, Oklahoma," is from an issue of A.I. Digest kept in Graham School files. After learning AI at the Graham School for horsemen, Hughey bred 800 mares to a single stallion in 1910. Bill Graham believes the calf in this photo could be the very first one born by artificial insemination in North America. The primitive technique involved removing a sample of semen from a cow bred by natural service and depositing it near the cervix of a recipient cow.

I never attended the Graham School, mistakenly thinking myself too busy. Rather, my own information has usually come from friendly veterinarians such as Dick LaFrance, of Hardin, Montana.

DOC LaFRANCE

Graham School graduates become good clients. They are aware. Typically, they'll have three hundred cows to pregnancy test and come home eager to start. Usually, they'll find sixty or seventy head they aren't real sure of and, not wanting to send good, pregnant cows to town, they'll call me out for a checkup. Now I'm doing sixty or seventy head I never did before, and chances are good I'll be doing the whole herd in a couple of years. It takes patience to build a practice.

Modern ranch clients, in general, are better educated than they used to be. Sometimes they call me for help; sometimes I call them. Not long ago I was called to sew up a horse for a Crow Reservation rancher and was forty miles from home when—my God!—I forgot my suture needles. What in hell will I do?

I was just passing Blaine Small's place; I know he does his own caesareans, so I pulled into his yard: "Blaine, I need some needles." "Sure, Doc. What size?" And that was all there was to it. There are many good native stockmen who can handle most situations.

'Course, there are some who would be ahead to call me sooner. Pius Crooked Arm, for example.

Pius comes to me one day: "Hey, Doc, I got dis horse got a real too-bad on da right forefoot; I know you gonna be pissed off, but I need your help."

"What can I do for ya, Pius?" I says.

"Well, you goddam white-guy doctors don' un'erstand art'ritis; I hadda go to old-time Indian way."

"Yeah?" I said. "Like what?"

"Like . . ." says Pius, "gouge a knife in da fetlock . . . gouge da hell out, make it bleed. Den wrap him up, give him some penicillin, and kick him out for the winter. In da spring he goes sound."

"Is that what you want *me* to do, Pius?"

"Hell, no! I already done it."

"Then what *do* ya want me to do?"

"Well," says Pius, "I broke da f——in' knife blade off. I want ya to fish it out."

That time, preventive medicine would have paid.

10   Good Medicine

VACCINES AND MEDICINES *are vital tools for ranchers, and vets are important members of any ranch management team. In addition to advice on preventive medicine (which we hope not to have to pay for), they provide emergency services (formerly handled, humanely enough, with a rifle) late at night and in bad weather, and they maintain a handy inventory of very expensive drugs.*

And ranch-land veterinarians sometimes have to act as government agents—filling out forms for interstate livestock movements and vaccinating calves for brucellosis. Some prefer to contract their skills to feedlots, dairies, and racetracks.

Jim Scott, a food animal vet, specializes in "theriogenology."

DR. JIM SCOTT

I grew up in Colorado, working with animals and thinking it would be neat to be a vet. Colorado A&M—now CSU—offered a six-year course: two years pre-vet; two years anatomy, physiology, pathology, medicine, pharmacology, and so on; into surgery, radiology, and clinical pathology. We served several weeks in the clinic, at least a week in the beef barn, and another in the dairy barn diagnosing pregnancy. By graduation, I had palpated a couple dozen cows and evaluated a hundred bulls while traveling with a clinician, all of which whetted my appetite for practice.

I was still in school when Montana rancher Buddy Cobb stopped at the college bull stud and told me about Big Sky country. Well, it sounded pretty good to me, so right after graduation off I went to Great Falls.

My boss was Dr. Pat Dorn. In 1956 there were six veterinarians in a five-county area now served by forty-five vets; I remember putting 375 miles on my pickup in making just two ranch calls. In those days, ranchers did the routine work themselves and tried some of the specialties as well: spaying, pregnancy testing, even caesarean sections. They acquired these skills at "four-day-wonder" schools like Graham's in Kansas or Hedrick's in Colorado—study four days and come home wondering. We figured the specialties were better left to professionals.

THE HARD SCHOOL of experience has been well attended.

JOE GILCHRIST

Wintering "calvy" heifers would have taken more feed than we had in the 1920s, so a neighbor, Sam Cooper, taught us to spay. Before we had chutes and squeezes, we'd just raise a heifer up with a block and tackle, make an incision, remove the ovaries, sew her up, and turn her loose—slick as a whistle. My brother Chay was the specialist, and he did all right as long as he kept things clean.

But I remember once we sure got into a jam. That was when Rube [the eldest brother] decided to spay all the culls—some up to ten years old—to keep 'em from comin' in season. So that's what we did, and the very next day we trailed 'em into the hills, several miles from home. Well, the flies got to 'em and made the darndest mess you ever seen; we had to ride up and rope and doctor every cow at least once—often two or three times. I think it was gasoline we squirted into the wounds, which sure brought the maggots out. But what a mess!

We learned everything by experience, in those days.

*T*HAT SORT OF THING *has happened thousands of times. Here's how one old friend, the son of a country doctor, brought veterinary medicine to the ranchers of one Alberta district.*

EION CHISHOLM

In 1950, fresh out of college after three years in the Mounties and four in the Navy, I jumped at the chance to become DA [district agriculturist] at Rocky Mountain House, Alberta, one of the oldest settlements in the West. Rocky was back in the bush—dirt streets, no roads, no town water—but Thelma and I enjoyed it, and the settlers really appreciated whatever we did.

Most of my clients were immigrants, many of them Dutch, who knew how to drain the swamps; they didn't have much, but you never packed a lunch in the Rocky district. Hell! They were offended if you didn't come in and eat. It might just be a fried egg and a piece of bread, but you were welcome to your share.

First chance to pursue my interest in livestock came when a farmer rode in from the Clearwater district: "Calves dyin' . . . Better come look."

I found a pretty good herd of cows and three or four dead calves; one was fresh, and when I ran my hand over his bloated hide it crackled. "Ya got black-leg," I said. This was easy.

"What's blackleg?" the guy asked.

"Oh," I says, "a bacteria; drops 'em like flies. You vaccinate these calves?"

"Hell, no. I don't vaccinate nothin'."

So I went back to town and asked the druggist if he had any blackleg vaccine. "Nope," but he'd order some in on the bus.

Soon as it came, I went back out and helped the settler vaccinate. The calves quit dying. I was a hero. [Eion laughs.] A hero! A few more cases like this, and I'd hang my shingle out as a veterinarian—there was no vet within a hundred miles of Rocky.

But my boss, the deputy minister, O. S. Longman, had other ideas. He sent me a stinkin' letter: "You're a district agriculturist, not a vet! Henceforth, you'll restrict your activities to things you know something about!"

I put away my shingle and became a feeder.

*A*ND A VERY PROMINENT *feeder, too. Eion organized and built Canada's first large commercial feedlot, Western Feedlots at Strathmore, Alberta, which he managed for many years.*

*D*ICK LaFRANCE, DVM, *was in practice in North Dakota and Montana for forty years.*

DOC LaFRANCE

When I told my friends I wanted to be a vet . . . Well, a lot of them are still rolling on the floor. I wasn't thought of as a student in my youth. Anyway, I took the challenge and graduated from Iowa State, where pregnancy testing by rectal palpation was the only thing I excelled at—probably because I have long, skinny arms and a good touch in tight places.

When you first get out of college, it takes a while before you say, "Hey, here's who I am; here's what I do." Most young people need a transition before they settle down, and Dickinson, North Dakota, was that stopping-off point for me. There were plenty of real cow outfits in the badlands; the cowboys were well mounted and knew how to use a rope, and the ranches had good corrals and working facilities. I got a job with Dr. Johnny Bryan.

*A*T THIS POINT, *Dick's wife, Esther, whom he affectionately calls "Ole," says, "We didn't have much to work with in those days. It seems to me that anesthesia has been one of the big developments in your practice." That jogs Dick's memory:*

Yeah. I remember one time back at Dickinson, Ole and I and Johnny Bryan and his wife were at a dance. We had a bottle of Haig & Haig scotch whiskey and were feelin' good when a rancher named Fred came around to get us: He had paid a lot of money for a heifer; she was having trouble calving. If she had a bull calf in her, it was gonna be his herd sire. We *had* to save her calf.

When we got to his ranch, I reached inside that heifer and could feel the calf's eyes about *this* wide apart. "I'd bet my soul," I says, "you got a bull calf!"

"I want that bull alive!" the rancher says.

"So, we'll have to destroy the mother," Doc Bryan tells him.

Now, there have been several times in my life when I hear a voice—I know it's mine—and I shudder when I hear it. This time the voice says, "Wait! Let's do a caesarean."

"What the hell is that?" the rancher wants to know. I explain what I've learned in college; I say I think I can save both cow and calf.

Meanwhile, my boss is sayin', "Now, understand this, Fred . . . I ain't responsible, Fred . . . I got no part in this, Fred . . ." Dr. Bryan has confidence in me—up to a point—but he's never done a caesarean. So we make a deal: If the cow and calf both die, I owe Fred a hundred bucks. If the bull calf lives, he owes me a hundred bucks. If we save 'em *both*, he owes me two hundred bucks. Now, this is big goddamn money in 1951.

"All right," Fred says.

"Okay, you got a deal."

But, when I get my outfit out of the truck, we don't have a drop of procaine to anesthetize the cow. Then I see our bottle of Haig & Haig. I draw up seven cc's and give that heifer a shot of good scotch whiskey in the spine. Well, she jumps around but we get a nice bull calf, and the mother is almost ready to breed back.[25]

Now, I think nobody seen me do this, but the story beats me to town: I come out drunk, use good scotch whiskey as a spinal block, and do a caesarean section. Some kind of reputation! But the operation was successful, and it wasn't long till I was offered a good practice in Bridger, Montana, where we stayed for twenty-three years.

Now, farmers had row cropped the Clark Fork of the Yellowstone Valley to death by the 1950s. The county agent was tellin' the farmers, "Gotta get some cattle on that ground. Rejuvenate it before it starts eroding," and all the farmers believed him and got cattle, but they had no facilities or know-how.

Back in the hills there was well-equipped cow outfits, but most of my business was down in the valley, where animals had to be roped and snubbed to a

John Deere tractor. It wasn't unusual to be called to a cow with a beet crown stuck in her throat.

"What kinda corrals ya got?" I'd ask.

"Why, none. Can't ya rope her, Doc?"

And it got so I just expected to rope and trip such a case, and push the beet crown down with a piece of hose.

If she was calving, I expected to be told, "She's outside, Doc, but she's pretty sick; she won't go nowhere." I always hauled my horse along—just in case.

I'll never forget one call soon after I got to Bridger: Here's a guy tryin' to calve a little ol' heifer. He's got her tied to a post; there's legs stickin' out, and he's got 'em tied hard-and-fast to his old white Chevy pickup (I even remember the color). Well, he ain't goin' nowhere fast, so I crawl up on the fence and watch until, finally, he backs off and says, "Are ya gonna help me, Doc? Or ya just gonna sit up there all day?"

"Well, get that goddam riggin' off," I says. "Get outta my way, and I'll see what I can do."

Right away I see the calf is dead, so I take a piece of OB wire and cut through the calf's pelvis, and it comes out slick as a whistle. The cow is pretty bruised and will probably prolapse, so I give her a spinal, suture her up, give her some antibiotics. And danged if she don't get up and stagger over and take a mouthful of feed.

And, just about then the guy says, "I forgot to tell ya, Doc: I can't pay ya till Monday. But whadda I owe ya, anyway?"

Now, I know this guy has never paid anybody in the valley a cent if he could help it, so I says, "Let's see . . . I drove out thirty-five miles; I gave her a spinal block; I did an embryotomy; I sutured her vagina; I used some sulfa and penicillin . . . I guess that comes to a dollar thirty-five"—which turned out to be one of my better deals, because on Sunday the guy drops dead of an aneurysm, and I thought, "Well, at least the son of a bitch didn't chisel me outta *everything* I had comin'. He only got me for a buck thirty-five."

Well, there were more than a few things like that, but looking back, I'm glad I became a vet. I'm thankful for the many friends I've made in more than forty years in practice. I loved the rowdy freedom of the past—the freedom from rules and regulation, the freedom from litigation!

Those days are gone; I'm about to retire. But I'm thankful to still be around, as the century closes, to see all the marvels of modern medicine and all the wonderful new techniques. Especially in veterinary surgery.

ONE UP-TO-DATE specialization is theriogenology—unusual word; unusual technique—but state of the art for many food animal practitioners.

DR. JIM SCOTT

The study of bull fertility was a new and exciting field in 1958, when I returned to CSU after working in private practice in Montana. My old professor, Harold Hill, had kept a position open, and, along with instructing students in skills like pregnancy testing, I was put in charge of the "bull lab," designed by Hill himself a few years earlier.

DR. HAROLD HILL

Actually, the Weld County extension agent was behind it. There's a place called the Crow Valley Cooperative Range on the prairie east of Fort Collins; it belonged to a tribe of Indians who leased it to local ranchers, and the county agent supervised it for them.

Well, we had a hell of a blizzard in the spring of '49—I hope to never see the likes of it again—and a few weeks later the county agent noticed some frostbitten scrotums.

"Collecting" with an electro-ejaculator.

You've seen those big old bulls, I'm sure, just turn their butts to the wind—just stand there and take it for hours during a blizzard. They pull their nuts up tight, and later you notice their bags are all scabbed over, and you think, "By God, I'll bet the sperm got frozen—those bulls will be infertile." Bill Farr and the other Weld County ranchers thought like that in 1949 and figured they'd have to replace all their bulls that spring. The county agent wondered if we could test them.

We could, we would, and we did. We built a mobile laboratory and pulled it around and examined semen from all the bulls on those ranches. And, surprise! We found *no correlation at all* between frostbite and infertility.

What we did find was a heck of a lot of very infertile bulls—bulls that were never exposed to the blizzard! About 10 percent of the bulls we tested were duds.

The problem was genetic: a weakness in the cells that produced the sperm. That was logical because the genetic base was narrow; the bulls on that small public range came from one or two breeders and were related to many of the cows. There seemed to be a need for ongoing testing, and out of that grew the science of theriogenology.[26]

Dr. Hill's mobile lab in the 1950s.—Colorado State University Photo Archives

DR. JIM SCOTT

Dr. Dave Bartlett of ABS coined the word from *therio*, Greek for "beast," and the Latin root *gen*, for "beginning." By 1960 there was a whole group of interested scientists, and the CSU staff was given the task of training vets from around the world in the new techniques.

First we taught ourselves to make sure of uniform procedures; then we wrote the journals, talked at scores of meetings, and put on training clinics for practitioners as far away as Calgary. (When we put on our demonstration at the prestigious Calgary Bull Sale, we didn't publicize results because we wanted to get home alive.)

At first, we were the Rocky Mountain Society for the Study of the Breeding Soundness of Bulls, but in '66 we included females and other species and became the American Veterinary Society for the Study of Breeding Soundness, and, finally, the Society for Theriogenology in 1974. I served as executive secretary of one of the early groups when I was young and building a reputation.

Equipment used in assessing breeding soundness in bulls includes a variometer, dyes, a cell counter, and a microscope. —Colorado State University Photo Archives

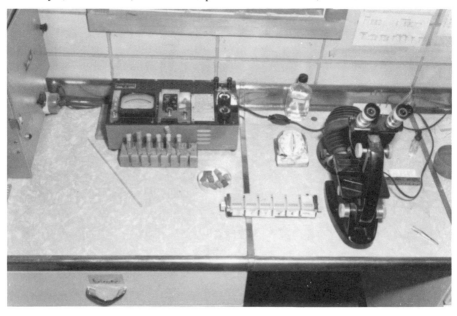

LOU SCOTT

Jim took me to Hawaii on our honeymoon—just a few days, short but sweet. I was a young airline stewardess ("flight attendants" were still unheard of) looking to sun and swim in the warm Pacific; I didn't expect a working honeymoon. But fame had preceded Jim, and a classmate with a new vet practice asked him to help test bulls on the beautiful Hana ranch on Maui.

"Sure," said Jim. So, while I toured the ranch with the foreman, seeing the many wonderful sights, Jim saw Hana through the working end of a microscope.

And that's exactly how he got his "handle" thirty years later, still testing bulls on the CL ranch in Alberta. Every time six-year-old Jennifer Copithorne saw Jim, he was squinting into a 'scope. Naturally, she called him "Dr. Peeker."

11 Genetics

ON A BEAUTIFUL, CRISP MORNING *in the fall of 1969, with the hay in the stack, the cows in the hills, and everything just marking time until weaning, I cranked up my Stinson flying machine for a bird's-eye view of the world.*

"Breadbasket," it's been called, and how apt that cliché seemed as we climbed over fields of yellow oats and barley and headed southeast across Alberta where combines spouted golden rivers of grain; then, on over eastern Montana's sea of grass streaked with wheat and durum stubble. Hour after hour, my smooth old Franklin engine rumbled along as townships of Dakota rangeland and acres of sorghum, corn, and beans slipped beneath my wings.

No bureaucracy, I thought—however well equipped with electronic wizardry— could replace the market wisdom of thousands of farmers whose land rolled out beneath me. No hardware yet developed could compete with all those gigawatts of brainpower in computing supply and demand. Or so I thought, back in 1969.

Now, I'm not so sure. I hear of computer programs designed to factor in government interference—all kinds of it—distorting signals from both sides of the border. But on that bright fall day, I chopped my power and settled into the grass airstrip of a lovely Iowa town full of faith in an open market.

The harvest was still a month away, and fields of seed corn trimmed to various heights in alternate banks of rows surrounded Coon Rapids, Iowa. This was hybrid corn country. That evening I asked Steve Garst about it.

STEVE GARST

The first hybrid corn was grown commercially in 1928 or 1929 by Henry Wallace and partners in the Pioneer Seed Company. My father, Roswell, tried it and decided to get in the business, and we've been at it ever since, here at Coon Rapids.

When inbred lines of corn are crossed, you get a kick of as much as 15 percent from something called *hybrid vigor*. That advantage disappears in later generations, so seed customers must come back every year, and my father knew a market when he saw one.

In those days, two-row horse planters were in style and, seeding in rows, you went back and forth instead of 'round and 'round. So, to get his business started, Father would provide a farmer with a bushel of hybrid seed to be run from one side of his planter, while the other side would be filled with old-style corn. When the crop came up, there'd be two rows of new and two rows of old, and it would be easy to make a comparison.

Father's bushel was gratis and good for seven acres (at 12,000 plants per acre), and the farmer had to agree to pay for half the increase—maybe twenty-five bushels per acre. Well, about the time he realized that he owed my dad a hell of a lot of money, Dad would tell him, "Let's just settle for the price of the seed," and the guy would become a believer and a customer.

I WAS HEARING ABOUT THE GENETIC BASE of the world food supply. People starving around the world? Certainly. But not because food can't be grown, and not because it's expensive; as a percentage of total living costs, food is probably cheaper everywhere than ever before in history. Farmers around the world can grow four times as much twice as efficiently as they could a short half century ago, thanks mostly to the science of genetics. Steve continues:

In the old days there was Yellow Dent corn and a few other varieties, and there was some degree of selection, but most of the reproduction was *open pollinated*—uncontrolled.

You see, a corn plant is bisexual: Each plant has a tassel, which we refer to as "male," and a number of shoots, which are "female." The familiar, thread-like silks extend from each individual kernel on a shoot, and when the pollen from a tassel lands on a silk, it impregnates or "breeds" its kernel of corn. At certain times, the air around a cornfield is full of floating pollen, so each of the hundreds of kernels on an open-pollinated shoot may have a different "father."

Now, consider inbred strains. To get your corn genetically uniform or pure, you put a sack over each tassel to catch its pollen, and you put another sack over the silks to prevent "unplanned pregnancies." Then, when the time is right, you shake the tassels, remove their sacks, and put them on the silks. In other words, you make each plant breed itself.

The bagging takes place on little plots, each a few yards square, and you do this repeatedly, reaching 50, 75, 87 percent purity as generations pass. After seven generations, each kernel of corn on each carefully isolated little plot is genetically identical, for all intents and purposes. You then have inbred seed.

Two rows of "male" corn, with tassels intact, alternate with several rows of detasseled "female" plants. —Iowa State University Library Archives

You continue to isolate your seed plot so that no outside pollen gets in. Your goal, now, is to raise a *field* of "inbred," with every kernel identical to every other, and that means a half-mile buffer zone where no other corn is grown. A mile or so away, there may be another field of inbred, and another and another, with plenty of separation in between.

As inbreeding progresses, plants *regress*: they get smaller; they yield less; their weaknesses show up—but their seeds are genetically pure. Now, you are ready to make "hybrid."

Now, you plant two rows of inbred on which you *leave* the tassels (male), and four rows of a different inbred on which you *pull* the tassels. The four rows of detasseled "female" plants produce your crossbred seed.

Theoretically, when you cross two inbred lines, you end up with *hybrid vigor,* a phenomenon also known as *heterosis.* You get the same effect by crossing Hereford and Angus cattle, except that cattle breeds are certainly far from "pure."

HERE ARE A FEW geneticists to talk about their science.

ROY BERG

I remember a lecture in 1950 by Professor Curt Stern, who developed much human genetic theory at the University of California. He said, "I really don't know very much about teaching the science of genetics; I never took a course in it, myself."[27] Genetics, as a science, was that new. It only goes back to 1909, when Mendel's laws of heredity, which he deduced from working with peas in the 1860s, were rediscovered.

One of the first mammalian geneticists was a guy by the name of Castle, who showed, with rabbits and guinea pigs, how simple one-gene characteristics such as color are passed on in a logical, predictable manner. But thinkers of Castle's era didn't talk of "heritabilities." The modern quantitative, mathematical heritabilities known to animal breeders today came from the study of traits that don't follow simple inheritance; the modern concept came from Jay

Population geneticist Jay L. Lush (1896–1982). —Iowa State University Library Archives

L. Lush, who followed the work of mathematician Sewell Wright at Wisconsin and Chicago. Most of today's "heritability freaks" are sons or grandsons of Lush, metaphorically speaking.[28]

ONE OF LUSH'S STUDENTS, Howard Fredeen, grew up on a Saskatchewan homestead where he hoped to spend his life raising cattle. As on most family farms, however, there wasn't room for all, so Howard left for an illustrious career at the Lacombe research station.[29]

HOWARD FREDEEN

Robert Bakewell, the eighteenth-century English farmer who started several breeds, talked of selection within individual herds. Today we look at genetic variation within entire populations and find performance characteristics distributed in predictable bell-shaped curves. We use performance testing to find superior individuals. Such things—so familiar to modern breeders—came to light with the Jay Lush school of population genetics.

By the time Dr. Lush came along, it was well established that crosses had a "luxuriance of growth" known as hybrid vigor, and he advanced a theory to explain it.[30] Many of his students were deeply involved in the development of hybrid corn.

ANOTHER of Lush's students, H. H. "Stony" Stonaker, influenced generations of practical ranchers at Colorado State. He was already very familiar with the development of hybrid lines of corn, swine, and poultry when he arrived at Fort Collins in 1946.

H. H. "STONY" STONAKER

Looking back, it was a whale of a time to be associated with agriculture. The hybrid concept, stemming from earlier work in Connecticut and Illinois, was in vogue. Henry Wallace had popularized hybrid corn in Iowa, where he and Lush had known each other well. Landrace swine had been brought from Denmark at the beginning of World War Two, and I always heard that Lush had been sent to select them. I had tremendous respect for my mentor, who was unsurpassed as a teacher of graduate students. He was a modest person who knew his own capabilities; he never held a grudge, but in a knock-down-drag-out battle with his peers he never came out beaten. I always thought Lush should have had a Nobel Prize; he probably would have, too, if he'd been in nuclear physics instead of genetics.

ROY BERG

And then there was *my* old mentor, Dr. Winters, who had an entirely different approach; his was *what you see is what you get*, not mathematical.

Winters began his career with a summer job with the pigs at Lacombe, Alberta, where the Experimental Farm Service was conducting one of the largest studies of crossbreeding up to that time. After graduation from Minnesota, he taught at Saskatchewan through the 1920s; then, he went on to Wisconsin and Harvard before returning to Minnesota to take charge of animal breeding and earn his Ph.D. in zoology in 1932.[31]

For the next twenty years he conducted pioneer research into crossbreeding, performance, and breed formation. He wasn't often quoted because he wasn't part of the Wright-Lush school, but he published before their classic work appeared.

Practical geneticist Laurence M. Winters (1891–1958).
—University of Minnesota Archives

I believe I was Winters's last student, and I remember him as a keen, hardworking, dedicated guy in his middle sixties, with plenty of everyday savvy. His warm, personal relationships with farmers helped spread the influence of his thought, and he was constantly on the run, often in trouble with department heads who had trouble keeping up with his many projects.

Winters believed in animals rather than systems, and his philosophy of teaching was consistent. Some teachers think their job is to bring students part way up to the great peak on which they sit. Winters would say, "If my best students don't surpass me, I have failed," and he'd quote a guy named Andrew Moss who had influenced him greatly.[32] "Give a young man enough rope," Moss would say, "and he'll hang himself or build a ladder with it." Many leading animal scientists of the 1970s and 1980s were those who climbed Dr. Winters's ladder.

HOWARD FREDEEN

You could say that all modern livestock breeding programs go back to Lush at Iowa State and Winters at Minnesota. Interestingly enough, a story has grown up that they disliked each other intensely. That's a myth. They were different in approach—Lush theorized, Winters practiced—but they ended up close together.

For example, I remember Lush's lecture on the limits of theory: People get so hung up on translating ideas into mathematics, he taught, that they forget biological limits. Lush, theoretician though he was, emphasized those limits—a very important aspect of scientific training.

Dr. Lush was a very gentle person and a true gentleman; he and his assistant, Dr. Lanoy Hazel, made an ideal team. They would even schedule classes at the convenience of their students; for example, thirty of us took Advanced Animal Breeding at six o'clock in the morning while the rest of the campus slept. Lush was never late, and the class was always full.

As for human interest, I remember one hot, hot Saturday night when I was working with a classmate, Andy Wyatt, in the lab. "I can't take this any longer," Andy said. "Let's go have a beer." So we hiked the mile or so to the town of Ames, bought a couple of six-packs, and headed back to the lab.

Meanwhile, someone had locked the door; we climbed a tree, crawled in through a window, and went on working on our project through that sweltering, hot evening. The cold beer tasted great!

Suddenly, in came another grad student who was working as assistant dean of men. This fellow knew us well; his wife had often drafted us as baby-sitters. Now, he looked at the beer, and Andy did the only reasonable thing: he offered him a bottle. It was refused. End of conversation.

Monday morning, Dr. Hazel hailed us after class and took us to his office where Dr. Lush was working quietly at his desk. "You fellows know the rules about alcohol?" Hazel asked.

113

We did.

"Well, they're pretty archaic, but students can still be fired for consuming alcohol on campus. Just thought you'd like to know. You can tell your friends, just in case they haven't heard." End of interview.

Dr. Lush continued working, pretending not to hear. But we knew that our fellow student had snitched and that Lush and Hazel were bending over backwards to help us. No disciplinary action taken, but we got the message!

M ANY YEARS LATER: 1969. Iowa farmers Steve and Mary Garst and hundreds of other American and Canadian cattlemen were playing a kind of game, and the stakes were high. They were beginning to make "inbreds," starting with European cattle seed, which was in very short supply and therefore dear. European cattle had been excluded from our continent for most of the century.

Not until 1966 had the first full-French Charolais arrived on our shores (as will be discussed in part four). Parisien, a "Pie Rouge," as the French Simmentals were known, came ashore in 1967. In 1968 it was Castor, a red bull from the Limousin district of France, and it was Castor's seed at $40 a shot that had brought Steve and me together.

As a master breeder, Steve recognized the potential value of heterosis. As a businessman, he saw opportunity in a restricted seed supply. The rush was on for 50 percent, 75 percent, and the grand prize, 87.5 percent "exotic full-bloods." Steve's father was not the only Garst who could spot a market.

But the Garst Company had been big in cattle for years and would continue to ride the cycles. Steve as president and Mary as "cow boss" think of cows more as scavengers than as chips in a poker game. Mary Garst is a director of large corporations and serves on a number of boards. I asked her about her job as cow boss.

MARY GARST

It's a typical ranch story. I'm an Iowa girl . . . married Steve knowing his family was big in the seed-corn business.

When I got to Coon Rapids, I found that they also kept a hell of a lot of cows, and that's when I learned that cows are, basically, scavengers. I learned that seed corn must be picked on the cob to keep germination up, so tons of cobs as well as stover are available as cow feed after each harvest. I also learned that seed-corn growers use cows to keep their seed fields pure; cows are pretty good gleaners, and every kernel gleaned by a cow this winter is one less volunteer plant to be chopped next spring.

Well, a few years later I found myself in desperate need of a challenge, so I approached my father-in-law, Roswell Garst.

"I've been watching you run cattle managers through like a revolving door," I said. "I know you don't need a trained historian like me, but I could be a helluva manager. How about a shot at the job?"

Roswell was one of the few men I ever met who never treated me like a woman. "Okay, Mary," he said, "I'll give you a try. But remember! I have just two rules: *Never lie*! and *Always close the gates*!"

STEVE GARST

And we would have saved $100,000, if only people had closed the gates. One time the crew went home and didn't secure a gate, and six hundred cows roamed the neighbors' cornfields on top of a three-inch rain. By the time we got there: Chaos! That one time cost us $6,000–$8,000.

In my youth, pure terror came with a three-inch rain. That's when cattle got out. Once, two bulls had a head-to-head in the middle of Mother's garden—that was known as *terror*! We heard about her peonies and tulips for an entire year.

Another time, a bunch of cows got loose on the Coon Rapids golf course right after a heavy rain; then they ran east down the railroad tracks till they met a west-bound freight. How many cows did we lose, Mary? Fourteen, fifteen head?

Mary always says twenty, but that's counting legs and dividing by four. Anyway, the cows tried to run down a freight, and the freight train won!

If only people would remember to close those gates!

*T*HAT BRINGS US BACK *to the infrastructure: roads, gates, trains, even golf courses—with a little heterosis thrown in.*

12   Performance

IN THE LATE 1950s—with the science of population genetics getting exposure— prestigious bull sales were finally goaded into posting weights and "average daily gains" on animals offered.

Naturally, they would still be shown at their very best, all washed and combed— nothing wrong with that. On the other hand, some buyers thought that the data posted misrepresented the facts. It would have been more appropriate, some thought, to have posted caveat emptor: "buyers [believing that like begets like] beware!"

The reasons: Bulls raised on foster mothers, creep feeders, exotic rations, and the like, might not be what you needed on Poverty Flats; seed stock clipped and combed to disguise weaknesses, fattened to simulate meatiness, pedicured for soundness, even implanted to enhance conformation, might not be the kind that "breed true" in Hard Luck Coulee.

Yet, such things are still dear to the showman's heart that beats in the breast of a breeder—even today. Been to Denver lately?[33]

*D*R. BOB de Baca *spent many years on staff at Iowa State, the fount of population genetics, and a perfect place to watch for progress in agriculture.*

BOB de BACA

I saw that it took twenty years for pioneer seed man Henry Wallace to bring hybrid corn from perception to production. And, that it took another twenty to get product to the people—a normal lag for innovations in agriculture. For example: by 1930, Dr. Lush had identified the basic genetic problems in livestock production; by 1950, answers in the form of heritability estimates had appeared.

But, even by 1960, purebred cattle breeders did not have the slightest interest in the "performance nonsense." And by 1990, after sixty years of hybrid corn and swine and poultry, the cattle trade is still infected with "purebredism."

A ND THE TROUBLE *with "purebredism," much glorified in the public eye, is that bulls (unlike "inbreds" of hybrid corn) are selected as much for* appearance *as for* yield.

H. H. "STONY" STONAKER

I taught the new performance philosophy for years at Colorado State. The breed associations dragged their feet, and quite naturally so, at first. They were reflecting the interests of members with big investments in a different kind of cattle.

We, on the other side of the fence, made life miserable for the establishment—also naturally so. We were teaching their kids population genetics; we were teaching heritabilities, correlations, and such, and we were proud to be onto something new and different. As a young professor I know I was intolerant; I spent weeks expounding the poor relationship between the show ring and performance.

But I never said that a cattleman need not look at what he bought. The show ring can be good training for the sale barn, where *shrink* and *dressing percentage* and *general health* are important—all visible to the naked eye, all related to "performance."

That great old educator Ralph "Bull" Durham used to put on seminars where kids were encouraged to look for oddballs in the sale ring; he would show how to spot a problem, buy it cheap, straighten it out, and bring it back at a profit. He taught that it paid to be a sharp observer! Observation was one form of judging he approved of.[34]

But the new concepts were complex and not easily understood. Lush used to find it difficult to explain "heritability." Most people thought, inheritance: "I'm going bald like my father"; and environment: "Worry made Mother's hair gray." That was *not* what Dr. Lush meant. He was simply saying that some traits respond to selection, and that such a response should be measured and put to use. He *quantified* the old debate on heredity vs. environment.

And, oh, how I used to love to argue such things with Tom Lasater. "Tom," I'd say, "you include fertility among your essentials, yet you know as well as I do that the heritability of fertility is low. Fertility *must* depend on environment."

"I leave such things to Nature," Tom would say. "Fertility always takes care of itself."

YOU MAY REMEMBER *Tom Lasater as the founder of the Beefmaster breed, and you may recall from* The Range *how Farrington Carpenter, an ambitious, young lawyer, "wise as Solomon," allocated grazing rights on the public domain in 1935.*

Lasater and Carpenter were longtime friends and like-minded thinkers on "performance" in breeding cattle. In fact, Carpenter, who died in 1980, has been called by Dr. Stonaker "the greatest spokesman, ever, for performance testing."

"Of course," says Stony, "we didn't all agree on every detail. But Ferry was a dramatic speaker whose attorney's nose could quickly find a weak spot in any argument; and—with his great sense of humor—he could finish you off quickly and make you like it. And he practiced what he preached: He built a productive Hereford herd in the Colorado high country."

TOM LASATER *reminisces*:

Mary and I had just moved to eastern Colorado from south Texas and were beginning to get some publicity on our Beefmasters when a big limousine pulled into our ranch one day, and a man got out, and I rushed up to see who was calling.

This man stuck out his hand. "My name is Farrington Carpenter," he said, "and I just read about your cattle in the *Denver Post* and thought I'd drive out and see what the hell you are up to with this new mongrel breed."

"Why, thank you very much," I said, "I'd be very happy to show you."

So, we drove around and looked at our Beefmaster cattle, and pretty soon Ferry said, "That will be enough; thank you very much," and he got into his limousine and left. And that was my first introduction to a great man who began his career as a cowboy on the New Mexico range back about 1900.

Later, we became great friends. We often appeared together on programs, preaching performance, and we took lots of flack from breeders but were always saved by Ferry's sense of humor.

One day we walked into a hall somewhere in South Dakota, and Ferry, looking around, said, "In churches they always put the sinners right up front, over on that side, right over *there* . . . Now, Tom, since you and I are about to be declared sinners, let's take those seats right now and save 'em the trouble."

PERFORMANCE TESTING was a sinful subject.

119

"Performance" pioneer Ferry Carpenter (1886—1980).

A S A VETERAN with the GI Bill, I could winter wherever I chose, and I chose to spend the winter of 1949–50 at the Cornell College of Agriculture. That was a biological—not intellectual—decision, having to do with courting a girl in nearby Buffalo, New York. And it was the best choice I ever made, for by spring Claire was persuaded to partnership.

Meanwhile, the college provided some basic animal science: It was home to Frank B. Morrison, author of the classic Feeds and Feeding, still a standard reference on nutrition; welding and blacksmithing sharpened some useful skills; slaughtering and butchering taught what was under the hide.

But I'm afraid I was a failure at formal stock judging: "I place this class of Rambouillet ewes, or Duroc boars, or Belgian fillies 4–2–5–3–1 because . . ." I could guess the weight of a chicken within a couple of pounds, but I couldn't see the practical value of judging. The instructors tried to reach me, but they must have lacked the skills of "greats" like Stony Stonaker and Bull Durham.

Once I queried Professor Miller on the genetics of weight-for-age (I'm proud to have asked the question so long ago). At the time, the best Miller could do was refer me to a scientist in Montana, and that was the first I ever heard of R. T. "Scotty"

Clark, the man said to have coined the term "performance testing." His name is still on the flyleaf of the animal husbandry textbook where I scribbled it that day in 1950.[35]

Some important things were under way at Bozeman:

JOE URICK

In 1946 or 1947 Fred Willson, the chairman of the Animal Science department at Bozeman, aided and abetted by Scotty Clark, talked fifteen well-known breeders into a cooperative program: They would each contribute two representative calves, and the college would feed and test their capabilities.

I was hired as feeder, right off the bat, and Montana breeders like Walter and Ross Higgins, Eaton Becker, Con Warren, and Wib Harrar sent us the kind of cattle they were breeding for the industry. We found out right away that some of the very best, in terms of show-ring winnings, couldn't compete in the real world of the feedlot. I'll never forget the disappointment when a guy like Con Warren's bulls turned up at the bottom of the heap.

I'd come from a 4-H background, and the well-known breeders were my heroes; I was just as disappointed as they were when their cattle didn't prove out, but my scientific training led me to say to Con or Wib or Ross, "You know, it's now been proved conclusively that performance is inheritable; why

Fred S. Willson (b. 1899).
—Montana State University Library Archives

E. Paul Orcutt (1900—1981).
—Montana State University Library Archives

121

not give it a try in making selections?" I hope I had some influence, but nothing came of it for awhile.

After graduation I was hired as herd manager at the northern Montana experiment station at Havre. We worked closely with the college in comparing inbreds from Miles City with conventional purebred bulls, and we watched performance-selected animals outweigh old-style calves by thirty or forty pounds at weaning and three-tenths of a pound a day on feed; it was obvious what this meant to the industry. But traditions die hard; most breeders had already committed to smaller-type cattle—often with color preference, such as "meller yeller," and so forth.

Slowly, however, we were able to show that performance testing paid, and the forward-looking breeders who had participated in Willson's original program were ready to follow through. In 1956, Eaton Becker and seven or eight others met with Willson and Paul Orcutt, the state livestock extension specialist, in Great Falls and founded the Montana Beef Performance Program. I'm proud to have helped write the rules, but it was years before *performance* was accepted.

Fred Willson used to get discouraged with the nit-picking.

"Give 'em thirty years," I said. "They'll come around."

I CALL 1950 to 1980 the "age of growth," when the aim of all good cowmen was to grow more pounds of calf. Growth was easy to measure. Today we want efficiency; that's tough to define. But I spent my ranching years searching for growth.

In November 1954 I delivered whitefaced calves to the Blackfoot, Montana, railroad pens, where buyer "Swede" Nelson had contracted to buy them at fifty cents a pound, with a "slide" over 400 pounds. Meanwhile, the market had taken a dive, and Nelson wouldn't take a calf that was one pound overweight. We only had one! The milk cow's calf—a crossbred—weighed 500 pounds.[36]

In 1956, in Canada, our whitefaced SN calves averaged 320 pounds. Obviously, we'd need growth to stay in business. The Miles City work told us progress could be made. But how? We didn't know Tom Lasater then, so we improvised. We sorted cow-calf pairs by calf size, then ran the cows through the chute and hung colored aluminum ear tags on them accordingly. Was nursing performance repeatable on our ranch? In time, we learned it was.

In 1958 we numbered our cows with a hot-iron brand on the hip, ear tagged their calves at birth, and went high tech with a homemade single-calf scale and a hand-cranked adding machine; "performance" was to become a way of life. When the crew cleared out after supper, our kitchen became a data center cluttered with slide rules, weight lists, and homegrown "performance cards"—records of each cow's production—a system we used for twenty years. It was a pound-producing plan, and extra pounds were money in the bank. And you could run a ranch pretty cheap in the 1950s.

SN Ranch
Claresholm, Alberta

16 December 1957

C. B. Thomas—Manager,
Canadian Bank of Commerce, Claresholm

Dear Charlie:
Here's my application for $15,000 operating credit for 1958.

Livestock on hand:
    245 cows to calve in April & May
    14 bulls
    116 steer and 117 heifer calves
    60 long yearlings to be sold mid-Jan.
    14 work and saddle horses
    30 chickens, 4 geese, 5 turkeys, and 2 ewes

Feed:
    8,000 round bales @ 50# per bale (200 tons)
    About 5,000 oat bundles
    100 bu feed oats

Note: In 1955, 300 cows weaned 180 calves (60% calf crop).
    In 1957, 260 cows weaned 233 calves (89%); all drys were sold.
    Future culling should increase per-head production.

Estimated Income for 1958:

110 yearling steers @ 700# @ 17¢	$13,090	
80 yearling heifers @ 600# @ 13¢	6,240	
60 2 yr old steers @ 785# @ 19¢	8,949	
20 cull cows @ $100	2,000	$30,279

Estimated Expense for 1958:

Wages	$3,300	
Buildng & Corral repairs	800	
Machinery repairs	1,000	
Gas & Oil	1,000	
Feed & Salt	3,000	
Veterinarian	200	
Insurance	125	
Miscellaneous	600	
Interest on Op Loan & Mortgage	3,500	
Land & School Taxes	1,057	
Living Expenses	4,000	$18,582

Surplus for Land and Cattle Debt: $11,697

Wow! With $11,697 left for long-term debt, I'd be cutting a fat hog in the butt in 1958! Or so I thought.

NOT FAR AWAY, on the Glenbow ranch near Calgary, a friend was building a similar program with home-raised bulls.

NEIL HARVIE

I came home to Glenbow after college and commenced a breeding program adapted to my area. We'd been buying traditional bulls and were raising tidy little black Angus feeder calves for the Ontario market. They didn't weigh much, and I decided to track weaning weights and try to improve performance.

The more I learned about my cows, the less I liked my bulls. Why was I castrating bull calves when, for all I knew, they were just as good as the registered bulls I was buying? Why not leave them entire and use the best?

Tradition—that was why! And so, in the early sixties I threw away my knife and began selecting my own bull calves as herd sires.

After ten years, was I on the right track? I really wanted to know. So, in 1970, I introduced (artificially) my top-producing cows to the most prestigious Angus bulls in North America. Their purebred genes had every chance to infiltrate my herd, and, amazingly, not one calf from those matings ever surfaced as a herd sire—which proved, to me at least, that my unregistered home-raised bulls would be very hard to beat.[37]

Then I faced another problem. In order to get the best measure of genetic ability, I made my selections as late in the fall as possible. So, what to do with my string of half-grown surplus bulls? Traditional feeders wanted steers, castrated in the spring. I could alter mine at weaning, but by then they'd be six months old; I decided to use their natural male growth hormones to produce beef more efficiently. That was a real break with tradition! Nobody ate bull meat; everybody knew that bull meat was tough and stringy.

Of course, bulls are larger muscled and slower to put on fat. Wasn't red meat what everybody wanted? Even in the sixties?

But steers were easier to manage. Moreover, packer-buyers wouldn't pay top dollar for bulls, no matter how young and fat they happened to be. They called them "stags," and the graders rebelled at "rolling" [roller-stamping] them Canada Choice. Tradition again.

So, each time I shipped bulls to the plant, I went out on the kill floor personally (at management's invitation) and, with a knife, "let down" the neck muscles to reduce the "crestiness" that characterizes a bull. I cut the erector muscles, too—all of this right under the noses of the graders, who could see perfectly well what I was doing but had now been instructed to grade for age, conformation, and fat rather than sex.

Soon the buyers were bidding my bulls "on the hoof," and I even heard of packinghouse workers buying sides of Glenbow bulls for family consumption. End of tradition.[38]

Eventually, my Glenbow herd became the cornerstone of a system known as "Beefbooster." The best one-fifth of my bull calves still go "on test" each fall; I keep the tops as my herd sires, and the rest of the best are sold to commercial ranchers—the finest young bulls, I think, that money can buy.

Importantly, 80 percent of our bull calves still go to slaughter. There's no such thing as a "Beefbooster" steer. Tradition!

W*HILE NEIL WAS BLAZING his bull trail, I was casting in other pools, but performance-tested herds were hard to find.*

Don and Charles Codding, of Foraker, Oklahoma, were promoting tested bulls for artificial breeding: "From Sperm to Steak the Wineglass Way," ran their ads—a wineglass being their brand. I wasn't ready for AI in 1956, but I ordered two living Wineglass calves at $325 a head, delivered. Though committed to performance, the Codding Brothers continued showing their cattle, and my bulls arrived with heads clipped as for the show ring.

A Codding ranch steer at 1955 Chicago International.

They were delivered by Don himself, in his pickup, and Don, a tall, flamboyant, cigar-smoking Oklahoman stayed a spell and greatly impressed our five-year-old daughter, Nina (the illustrator of this book), who memorialized his visit in crayon. Ranching, then as now, was a family business.

B Y 1958 performance-tested bulls began trickling into the Porcupine Hills from the Hughes ranch in Montana. These were the "Newfords"—pure but unregistered sons of Miles City Line One Herefords, weaned off their own dams and wintered under typical ranch conditions, then sold as yearlings, unfattened and unfitted.

And such was the Hughes reputation that ranchers often bought without visiting the ranch: "Just save us a bull," they'd write, while those so inclined would attend the annual auction with their families. No high-pressure stuff, no glitz; just very good bulls and a barbecue—always well attended by Canadians.

I N THE 1950s, the Canadian government was sponsoring ROP or "Record of Performance" for beef cattle, the same as they did for poultry, swine, and dairy cattle. In 1957, a quarter of the beef ROP participants were commercial ranchers who contributed half the bull calves. J. D. "Doug" Baird was director of that program.

DOUG BAIRD

In starting Canada's beef ROP, I spent a good deal of time in the States. I visited Dr. Winters on several occasions, and I especially liked his approach; a number of times I went to see Ferry Carpenter, a founder of PRI.[39]

Breeders everywhere were beginning to come under pressure to accept performance testing, but at first they were often attracted more by promotion than performance. In Alberta, a beef cattle performance association was started by commercial ranchers tired of looking to the breed associations for leadership. It sure wasn't coming from them, and it wasn't coming from ivory-tower scientists, most of whom were closely allied with government.

In 1959 I attended the first meeting of the Alberta Beef Cattle Performance Association (ABCPA), the "alphabet society." I helped them write their rules and regulations.

A S A FOUNDER and first president of ABCPA, I invited Doug Baird to that meeting and remember how we appreciated his help. Also very helpful was a leader in the Montana performance program, George Peterson, from Highwood. George brought the wisdom of Fred Willson and Paul Orcutt to our formative meetings.

One of my first duties to ABCPA was to write an article for the October 1959 issue of Canadian Cattlemen magazine that made a case for performance testing. It earned me an invitation to preach to a meeting of the Alberta Cattle Breeders Association, sponsors of the Calgary Bull Sale. I must have seemed a brash young upstart, new to the business and the province, and the established breeders were waiting in the gulch. After I laid my sermon on them—damning nurse cows, foot-trimming stocks, and calf creeps (and, I hoped, saying something convincing about performance)—a respected leader of the cattle-showing fraternity took the pulpit to denounce me as a "sinner."

The new "heritability" heresy was simply designed to cover the age-old truth that the eye is the tool of selection; scales were useless, numbers meaningless. Seated behind him, I saw his neck turn red with indignation, and I remember the rousing hand he got from the faithful.

But I had supporters, too. In the back of the "church" stood a brotherhood of ranchers who—smelling blood—had come to claim my corpse. I took heart from the grinning faces of McKinnons, Copithornes, Hargraves, Bergs, and Eatons and received the bureaucratic blessings of Baird and Lore. I'm proud to have been a member of the rancher end of the business, whence came the initial push for performance testing.

It wasn't long, however, until our movement had attracted three honest, genuine, purebred breeders: Orrin Hart, Matt Fraser, and Hans Ulrich. There were others, but I single them out to represent the forward-looking, open-minded segment of the Canadian cattle business.

Orrin Hart did as much, perhaps, as anyone on our continent to popularize performance testing with his Willabar Angus. But I will focus on Hans Ulrich because of his leading role in the importation of the sixties.

HANS ULRICH

I must have had an urge to see the world, but the *big* reason I left Switzerland was lack of opportunity. My dad's farm belonged to the bank, and nobody we ever knew got loose from the bank in Switzerland. I wanted a few acres of my own, so I spent a year in Denmark and learned there was more to the world than I could see from my valley in the Alps. Then I went home to find a wife and found, instead, a job—in Canada.

A Swiss lawyer, Dr. Ammann, owned an Alberta farm. In 1958 I got the job of running it. Of course the neighbors were just laughing when I got there; they just figured some dumb "furriner" had paid way too much money and wouldn't last very long, but Dr. Ammann knew what he was doing.

The former owner was an old man named Bud Williams, who had made his pile in farm machinery. He had invested wisely in land and purebred Herefords and had planted crested wheatgrass in the sandy soil, while most of his neighbors plowed and summer-fallowed. Dr. Amman studied the work of the Lethbridge Research Station, and three decades later we're still planting crested wheat and improving our soil with cattle.

Bud was as lucky as he was smart. In dwarfism days, he purchased a son of *Baca Duke the 2nd* at Denver, but he discovered just in time that *Duke* was "dirty" [had sired dwarfs] and backed out of the deal before the bull caused trouble. Bud was also one of the first to use "performance" in selling his cattle; by the time we arrived, his growthy Britisher Mischief line was much in demand. I think Bud learned about weighing cattle from Harry Hargrave.

ROY BERG

Harry Hargrave was the real instigator of the performance movement in Canada. He made a trip through Texas and came back talking crossbreeding and testing. He enthusiastically promoted Charolais. He introduced Ferry Carpenter and Tom Lasater to Alberta. And he brought the members of ABCPA together.

As for Bud Williams, I always figured he weighed his cattle simply to keep tabs on a younger brother who ran his ranch; he was making sure the feed was really going into the cattle—or so I thought from the use he made of his records. He was sure quick to learn their use in *selling*, but I was never sure he used them in *selection*.

HANS ULRICH

Well, Harry Hargrave told me about ABCPA as soon as I came to Canada, and I joined the outfit immediately, although I could hardly speak English at the time. A few other breeders joined, too: Orrin Hart, an Angus breeder from Claresholm; Matt Fraser, a Hereford breeder from Hussar; and Bill Hunt with Charolais from Endiang.

I managed for Dr. Ammann for about ten years. Then, with Canadian experience, I was able to buy his cows and a bit of his land. So, in 1990, with the help of those good cows and plenty of luck, I'm happy to say the bank doesn't own me yet!

*T*HERE ARE TIMES THAT SPARKLE *like points of light, and Bud Williams's dispersal sale was one of those times for me.*

Hans Ulrich and Dr. Ammann didn't buy all Bud Williams's cows. I don't remember all who did. But they were dispersed at auction at the Calgary Livestock

H. J. "Harry" Hargrave (1909–1984). —Alberta Archives

Pavilion. And while the auctioneer was crying the sale, Harry Hargrave led me along the benches and introduced me to Charlie and Neil McKinnon. A few weeks later we all met again at the Hargraves' house in Lethbridge, and ABCPA was hatched on their kitchen table.[40]

Charlie McKinnon died in 1982. He had ridden with the LK chuck wagon on the open range; later he built LK into the largest commercial ranch company in Alberta, while Neil, his son, will long be remembered as one of the best ranch managers ever.

For twenty-five years Neil ran LK from field headquarters at Bassano—sometimes it seemed that LK was Bassano. Neil knew cows. And he knew how to foster and maintain esprit de corps; in the 1960s and 1970s, it meant a lot to be an "LK hand."

Most LK hands had a handle: There was "Fud," whose real name was Elmer and who looked, I guess, like the famous cartoon character; there was "Taxi," a gofer when he wasn't fixing fence; and "Radar," who manned the CB radio—a near clone of the character on "M.A.S.H."

But they never got a handle on Bob Knight, an LK hand since before Neil McKinnon was born. Neil's Uncle Don had fired Bob once, back in the 1930s; forty years later, Bob was still there, "waiting for his laundry to dry" before packing up to go.

And there were cracking-good cowboys like the Hales—LK hands to the second and third generation. Bob Senior was corral boss at the Calgary Stampede for a quarter century; Bobby Junior managed a set of LK cows for decades.

LK's initial business was commercial beef production, and Charlie and Neil were always intent on finding the very best performance-tested bulls; that's what they were doing at Bud Williams's sale in 1957. They were also early buyers of Cooper-Holden Herefords in Montana and first to bid at Buddy Cobb's "silent" Charolais sale. And they blazed some trails in AI: Neil bred a thousand cows to Sally Forbes's famous Beckton bull in 1959.[41]

In 1960, in partnership with Master Feeds, the big Canadian millers, the McKinnons purchased and revamped a mammoth barn in the little town of Bassano. Inside, twelve pens became available for ration testing; eight were allocated to pure-bred bulls on Doug Baird's Record of Performance program; one held crossbred bulls from Dr. Berg's "Kinsella project," and fourteen pens held "progeny" steers for ABCPA under the watchful eye of provincial fieldman Sid Lore.

Much that was done for performance testing in Alberta came under the banner of ABCPA, and I had no greater privilege than to serve as its president through its formative years. It put me in touch with so many wonderful people.

But, enough of "performance." It's time to go to another tool of the trade: heterosis, or "hybrid vigor."

130

13   Hybrid Vigor

ON A VISIT TO MASSACHUSETTS in 1992, Claire and I walked Plimoth Plantation, a time warp restored to 1627. Outside the thatch-roofed village we watched a crew of shepherds erect a corral of wooden hurdles, much as ranchers set up portable pens with panels of steel today. Some things never change.

Others do. On a muddy street we passed Pilgrim leader "Myles Standish," directing a flock of sheep; then we stopped at a cottage where "Mistress Cooke" told of her two-month Atlantic crossing aboard the good ship Anne. In the yard, a small brown cow, waiting to be milked, chewed her cud while snuffling pigs rooted in a muddy sty. At Plimoth Plantation well-trained guides play seventeenth-century colonists whose names and origins, work and dress have been carefully researched.

"Tell me, ma'am; what breed of pig is this?" I asked, expecting the familiar name of an English county: Berkshire, Hampshire, Chester . . .

"We know naught of breeds at Plimoth, sir; these be sows and nothing more. Their young be the pigs," said goodwyfe Cooke in the "early-modern" dialect of the Pilgrims.

So it dawned on me: Breeds hadn't been invented in 1627.

A day's drive down the coast, Williamsburg, colonial capital of Virginia, is restored to the 1770s—a hundred and fifty years later than Plimoth Plantation. At Williamsburg, in the back yards of eighteenth-century wheelwrights, coopers, gunsmiths, potters, and politicians, Claire and I saw the food animals of the era: cattle, horses, swine, sheep, chickens, geese, and turkeys.

"How about these turkeys?" I asked our farmhand/guide.

"Well, sir, turkeys were discovered in Central America about the time of Columbus. Taken to Europe, domesticated and refined, they became popular farm birds and were carried back to the 'New World' with emigrant farmers."

"Here at Williamsburg, turkeys run free," our guide continued. "They are even encouraged to forage deep in the woods. Our farmers note a better hatch and more vigorous turkey poults when their hens go out and mate with the native toms."

Ha! Hybrid vigor in colonial days! Some things never change.

THREE HYBRIDS

a. A jack-mare cross produces a tough, smart, but almost always sterile mule.—Haynes Collection, Montana State Historical Society

b. A bison-Hereford hybrid cow is hardy and long-lived, but only marginally fertile.
—Agriculture Canada Research Archives

c. Holstein-Hereford-Brown Swiss crosses (as in the Hays Converter breed) should produce an extra fertile offspring.
—Ted Pritchett

*I*N THE 1990s it would be hard to find a straightbred pig, chicken, or turkey in any commercial farming operation, but, as one late Porcupine Hills rancher liked to say, crossbreeding isn't exactly a new idea.

JOHN CROSS

We've been crossing breeds on theA7 Ranche for a hundred years: Hereford, Shorthorn, Galloway . . . Hell! My father was bringing in different breeds of roosters for his hens in the 1890s. I like to say that "Cross" breeding was *invented* here [John grins].

*I*N THE 1800s most ranch cattle were mongrels—by chance if not by choice. But, gradually, through the 1920s and 1930s (as the Hugheses, Gilchrists, and Copithornes all point out), most herds were "graded up" with purebred bulls.

By the 1950s my SN cows were straightbred Hereford, and the ranch operation was geared for yearling production. We shipped SN yearlings to Waterloo, Iowa, where corn farmers simply enjoyed watching well-marked whitefaced cattle feeding at their troughs. On a visit in 1960, I got the impression that they didn't give a damn for performance testing, as long as our little cattle were turning their corn into money— and lookin' good!

*B*UT NOT ALL Corn Belt feeders were content with the uniform, slow-growing Herefords of the 1950s. Another friend from my later, Limousin days was well aware of the "luxuriance of growth" that comes with crossbreeding.

CARLTON NOYES

Well, see, I belong to the hybrid-corn generation. I grew up in eastern Nebraska helping Grampa hand pick the best ears for next year's seed, and when two big seed companies came to town, Dad grew seed for them. My very first paying job was detasselling inbred corn at twenty-five cents an hour— good wages for the 1930s. And I rose to foreman over a crew of girls in just three years—how's that for success for a teenage boy? Imagine!

Before the war we were happy with fifty-bushel corn crops. Later, with hybrids, seventy-five was good and a hundred exceptional. Today, with irrigation, we *expect* a hundred and seventy-five bushels to the acre. Incredible!

Likewise, thirty years ago most of our feeder cattle came out of Oklahoma, where producers didn't pay much attention to bulls. "Okies" came in all colors, shapes, and sizes, and that was where we first noticed *hybrid vigor*. We could use a shorter feeding period for those big crossbred steers. Two-year-olds came in weighing nine and a half [950 pounds]—big old raw-boned things, often with some 'ear' [Brahman influence], or roans [showing Shorthorn blood]. They'd go out in a hundred days at 1,200 pounds. What a difference in performance! You couldn't top the Omaha market with crossbreds, but you never paid top dollar for them either.

I DON'T KNOW WHY it took me so long to change. Tradition, I guess. I knew better; I had worked for Herb Lyttle in California in the 1950s and had seen that crossbreds did just as well as straights: They survived on the range, gained on feed, worked at the "plant," and produced just as much manure for the orange and grapefruit orchards—the primary job of cattle on that ranch.

Each fall, Herb Lyttle would travel the West, buying calves from Montana to New Mexico. Once they were assembled in sunny southern California, Dewey Culbert and I would feed them alfalfa hay until the rains came (and I'll never forget those heavy, three-wire "California" bales in the days before hydraulics).

With the rains, the calves grew to yearlings on lush "filaree" and burr clover; all we cowboys had to do was ride the pastures and doctor for foot rot and screwworm. Happy days!

HERB LYTTLE

Most of the cattle we bought were Herefords; even the *corrientes* showed English breeding. From our records we knew there was often more difference *within* the breeds than *between* 'em, but "performance" was hard to buy in the 1950s.

As our business grew, we reached farther east for replacements, and it was in Texas that we began to see the Brahma crosses and learn about hybrid vigor. I remember some exceptional Brangus [Brahman-Angus] steers; God, they were beautiful critters! Finished and ready for slaughter, they caused quite a stir at the plant. You could see they would yield like hell, and local ranchers began putting Brahma bulls on their good old Hereford cows, producing great big calves that fed like crazy! Good conformation, too. The packers loved 'em.

We sometimes bought calves from a rancher near Ashfork, Arizona, who would ship us a few pale, bleached-out individuals along with his straight Hereford calves—the influence of a neighbor's Charolais bulls.[42] We didn't know about Charolais, and we didn't care about color; we sold direct to the packer, and the right kind of cattle were good, whatever their breed. Those new Charolais made us realize that nutrition was only part of the feedlot formula; genetics was important, too.

Of course, off-color cattle never brought as much per pound from the packers—they were different, a novelty, and inconsistent in numbers. If a buyer could get 'em for less . . . well, that's what he was paid for. On the other hand, most crossbreds finished easy, marbled well, and netted more at the bank. They always made *me* look good; I liked 'em for that!

NOW, AS IF CROSSING beef *breeds wasn't enough, Lloyd and Alys Jane Schmitt, of Stanford, Montana, went a step further.*

LLOYD AND ALYS JANE ("AJ") SCHMITT

LLOYD: I grew up with Hereford cattle and was aware of the trend toward dwarfism in the 1940s, so when AJ and I went ranching, we went off on a track of our own—complete outbreeding. We were crossing Angus on Shorthorn cows in 1946.

Now in those days any crossbred, even a black one, was bad news on the market, so we made up our minds to feed 'em out and sell 'em "on the rail." We figured once the hide was off, there would be no discrimination; the meat was all the same. And we were right! We sold on the rail for years at the Great Falls Meat Company, where crossbred steers were perfectly acceptable, while their "f1" sisters grew into excellent cows for use on the ranch.

ALYS JANE: And we had another little project. We proved the value of dairy crosses for beef—a couple of heretics, we were.

We found that Angus bulls worked better on Holstein cows—even better with a little Brown Swiss thrown in. Soon we were getting 650-pound calves when the norm was under 400, and we knew we were doing right since we followed them through to slaughter. Crossbreeding at that time, of course, was definitely out of favor, and we made quite a splash with carcass data showing dairy breeds to be just as efficient as beef.

Well, the neighbors weren't impressed. We were about as welcome as cows in the corn at local ranchers' meetings. Ranchers don't like hearing about dairy cattle for meat—except when they eat their own, which is almost always.

And another myth of "purebredism" explodes.

ONE GREAT EXPLODER OF MYTHS *is Laurence M. "Laurie" Lasater, of San Angelo, Texas. Laurie doesn't own a ranch (he was raised on one and owned one, once, in Mexico); nor does he intend to own another, except, he says, "as a place to picnic on Sunday afternoons." Land ownership, to Laurie, is an inefficient use of capital. He's happy and proud to be developing, brokering, and distributing Beefmaster cattle around the world. Let others own the ranches; Laurie will provide expert advice on investment, breeding, and management—a talent he comes by naturally.*[43]

LAURIE LASATER

My family and I are not in the crossbreeding business. We sell cattle of a consistent, predictable breed—the Beefmaster breed: the second recognized, purely American breed, as my father told you.

Our family was short of cash in 1931, so Dad threw together the remains of his father's Brahman and Hereford herds and, remembering the Brahman-Durham crosses he'd seen as a kid, bought two Shorthorn bulls for less than $500 and turned 'em loose with the bunch. That's how he discovered, quite by accident (and because he couldn't afford to do things right), that a three-way cross is the best possible foundation for a breed. That's where he applied his "six essentials."

So crossbreeding, for us, is ancient history. Selection is an ongoing, every-day thing, but the actual selection of livestock starts with the individual instincts of a stockman; that was true of race horses and camels in Mesopotamia two thousand years ago and is just as true today in North America.

Tom Lasater with a Beefmaster range cow.

Strange to say, but Dad's success in Colorado is best explained by Roy Berg's work in Alberta, begun twenty years after Dad had finished crossing. I know Roy Berg well and have heard him expound his theories on several occasions. Of course, he casts the whole idea of "purebredism" in doubt by showing that purity is nothing compared with the productivity and genetic diversity of the parents.

M Y OWN CONVERSION *to crossbreeding came on a TransCanada Airlines flight between Winnipeg and Calgary in 1962. I had been attending a cattle meeting and was lucky to get a seat, since the extended Berg family of Millicent, Alberta, was returning from a wedding. I already knew several members of the family through ABCPA, and I sat with Roy and Margaret as our Viscount skimmed the prairie.*

Roy Berg lecturing at a stockmen's short course: "Gotcha!"

The talk soon turned to selection on my ranch, still purely Hereford at the time. "Suppose you keep selecting within one breed till you have the fastest growing Herefords in the country? Whaddaya gonna do then?" Roy wanted to know. He thought, with my limited gene pool, that I was missing opportunities, and he used the words "Kinsella" and "hybrid populations."

Roy had been teaching at Alberta for about ten years when his employers were persuaded to set up a research ranch near the little town of Kinsella, a hundred miles or so east of Edmonton. With his solid farm background plus a doctorate in genetics, Roy very properly was chosen to run it and soon had in motion a project known to detractors (and there were many) as "Berg's Great Crisscross Gamble."[44]

As popular as he was with the ranching crowd, Roy Berg was persona non grata to the purebred establishment, and they sponsored radio spots and newspaper columns directed against him. It is to the university's credit that he was steadily promoted in spite of such opposition. In a more politically sensitive environment, he could not have lasted.

I ASKED Roy about events leading up to Kinsella—events that should be of interest to animal breeders anywhere.

ROY BERG

My mentor at the University of Minnesota, Laurence Winters, published his landmark crossbreeding paper in 1936, but, by 1952 when I knew him, he was long past simple crossbreeding and into *lines* of crossbred swine. Here's what happened:

Winters had made the [line known as] Minnesota #1 pig, a cross between the Tamworth and the Landrace. The Landrace, an efficient bacon-type pig, had been hustled out of Denmark just before the Nazi occupation in 1940; I always heard that Agriculture secretary Henry Wallace saved the breed by arranging passage on a U.S. warship [highly illegal, considering the foot-and-mouth embargo passed fewer than ten years earlier]. Such is the importance of food in time of war.[45]

Anyway, by agreement with the Danes, the Landrace breed could be used only for research and only for crossing—never bred straight, which explains why it was crossed with everything imaginable. There were several Landrace crosses made at Beltsville [the USDA research station in Maryland], while the Montana #1 was a cross of Landrace on Black Hampshire, and the Palouse Pig in Idaho was Landrace on Chester White. In Alberta, the Lacombe BW was Berkshire on Landrace-Chester White. Most important to research, though, was Dr. Winters's Minnesota "Line One" pig.

Winters's idea from the start was to combine the traits of several breeds into one superior strain. He believed that inbreeding was required to "fix type," and he wasn't worried about "inbreeding depression," although it was well known at the time. Instead, he was happy to let inbreeding take place so long as he could be selective—a very important point.

Next, he took a Canadian Yorkshire boar and crossed him on Poland China sows and inbred and made the Minnesota #2. Now, the trouble with all the lines was that they didn't have much "bottom"; there was even an inbred registry for a while, but the lines became so inbred that there wasn't enough variation for selection.

When Dr. Winters was selecting for growth and litter size, carcass merit was not a consideration. And the way things sorted out, the Minnesota #1 was a very fat line and the #2 was none too lean, and, with lines so narrow based, there wasn't much he could do about it. In any case, Dr. Winters knew by the end of the 1940s that inbred lines were not the way to go; instead, he took an entirely new direction.

In making the Minnesota #3, he put ten or a dozen breeds together—a great mess, really—and selected for the traits he considered important, including carcass characteristics. This was a new and different concept, an intensely practical approach. Dr. Winters let the pigs sort themselves out, and, by the time he retired in 1955, the future was looking good for his #3 pig.

Laurence Winters in a pen of Minnesota #3 pigs. —University of Minnesota Archives

Now, the thing is, back in the 1930s Winters's brother-in-law, Scotty Clark, and researchers at Miles City began building on what Winters had started with pigs. Theoretically, inbreeding was important; so, even though Winters's results from inbreeding were proving unsatisfactory, here came the beef men doing the same thing. They didn't seem to notice that it wasn't working with pigs.

Dr. Winters felt that if you inbred *slowly* and applied enough selection, you could avoid inbred depression. Perhaps he was fooled. Perhaps he never really had much homozygosity. Perhaps his heavy selection encouraged heterozygotes. Actually, I'm quite sure, now, that's what happened.

So, Line One Herefords were inbred, but I don't believe their success—and they have been very successful—had much to do with inbreeding. More likely, performance testing and steady selection for growth retained the heterozygotes over the years.

Real inbreeding comes with sire-daughter and sire-granddaughter matings, which would certainly soon result in inbred depression. In Line One's case,

Laird W. McElroy (1911–1988), chairman in the 1960s of the department of Animal Sciences, University of Alberta. —University of Alberta Archives

A Kinsella hybrid pair.

the foundation bulls were speedily replaced by sons and grandsons, with each generation further removed from the first. With fast generation turnover, inbreeding isn't a problem.

So, on to Kinsella. With all the research, heterosis or hybrid vigor had become well understood by the 1950s. Not only was it known to be important in poultry and swine, but the role of crossbreeding in beef cattle was under study at many stations. At Miles City, for instance, the British breeds were being crossed under Ray Woodward's supervision, and at Manyberries, Alberta, Hobart Peters, another Winters protégé, was studying "cattalo," a bison-British breed cross.[46]

Now, the advantage of using crossbreds, as with Dr. Winters's pigs, was reinforced by success stories such as Tom Lasater's. But hard, institutionalized evidence was lacking. So, into that gap in 1955 stepped Dr. L. W. McElroy, my department head at the University of Alberta.

For me, there followed five years of writing proposals and drumming support for his project. Finally, a 5,400-acre ranch was found and 170 suitable cows were purchased with a $200,000 grant from the university. By 1962 we were ready for business and, for starters, compared the production of purebred Herefords against that of a Charolais-Angus-Galloway cross which became the Kinsella #1. That so-called synthetic strain is still going strong, although closed [no new genes added] for thirty years.

141

So, what did we learn? In a nutshell, whatever a breeder's goals (and they are varied), they can best be reached starting from a crossbred base—a theory confirmed again and again and again in many places.

*F*OLLOWING MY CONVERSION *in the skies over Manitoba, I went home and began adding Red Angus and Charolais genes to my Hereford base. Then, inspired by Neil Harvie, I "threw away my knife" and began selecting yearling bulls to carry a registered trademark—the word "HYTESTER"—tattooed in qualified ears.*[47]

I advertised that every bull with such a tattoo had been picked on comparative yearling weight (top 10–20 percent) in an economically significant environment of at least one hundred herd-mates. Furthermore, I claimed that Hytester bulls had attained breeding age with no genetic defects. And no females need apply; there would be no Hytester cows—only the cream of the bull calves could achieve such elite status. Hytesters would never become a breed!

I used Hytester bulls on the SN herd for about ten years and sold quite a few to other ranchers. Their effects are still around, and I'm still on friendly terms with many old customers. I'm kind of proud of my Hytester bulls of the sixties.

But our herd has come a long way since then: Weaning weights have almost doubled; weaned calf to bred cow ratio, up 15 percent; calving season, cut in half to 45 days; better udders; better feet; over a hundred qualified bulls produced each year. Only now, in the 1990s, we call them "M4" bulls. M4 being the fourth maternal strain in the Beefbooster system.

We had lots of luck along the way to Beefbooster status. Consider this: In breeding cattle, it takes three years just to learn of a mistake; another three years to correct it. Crossbreeding was one step along the way.

I remember showing my first crop of multicolored calves to Sid Lore, the livestock fieldman.

"Not uniform no more," I muttered, kind of ashamed.

"Not uniformly bad no more, at least," said Sid, with his usual candor. And, compared with ten years earlier, he was right. These "mongrels" weighed 100 pounds more than my 1955 Herefords.

*N*OW IT'S TIME TO LOOK *at a wonderful tool that helped bring genetic diversity and performance to the ranch. That tool was artificial breeding with frozen semen.*

14   Frozen Seed

ALBERTA FIELDMAN *in charge of performance, J. S. "Sid" Lore, was not your typical "man from the government, come to help." Sid really came to visit.*

And he was such good company, so widely traveled, and knew so much about what was happening in so many places, that he was always a welcome visitor. What's more, with his farm-ranch background, he made a useful hand on any occasion.

SID LORE

My job in the fifties and sixties required visits to hundreds of ranches, and I don't recall anything that got the kids and their parents as excited as going off to school to learn AI.

Almost every outfit in the country sent somebody off to the Graham School, if not to a local college. AI was becoming popular as a tool in fighting diseases like vibriosis; it also made "clean," high-performance bulls accessible to commercial ranchers. But it really took hold with the "exotic" boom of the sixties, when bulls of the many "new" breeds started bringing $50,000 and more per head.

I REMEMBER THE DAY in 1962 when I waved goodbye to my family and headed for Colorado with Neil and Dan McKinnon, and Elmer Rutske, an LK hand. We were going to learn about artificial insemination.[48]

Elmer and Stuart and Danny were enrolled at the Hedrick School at Fort Collins, whose proprietor, Jack Hedrick, delighted in teaching artificial insemination, pregnancy testing, and other "classified" subjects to do-it-yourself practitioners like us.

Neil and I were enrolled in an AI short course at nearby Colorado State, where they didn't teach preg-testing and didn't approve of Hedrick doing so, either. Such skills were reserved for the veterinary profession.

*Sid Lore checking
performance on Hans Ulrich's
ranch in the early 1960s.*

So Neil and I got the theory; our pals got the practice, but each night we compared notes at bull sessions presided over by Professor Jim Scott, our friend and
adviser ever since.

And we all went home "ready to breed cows." It just took Neil and me a little
longer.

PROFESSOR SCOTT

In the 1930s and 1940s bull semen was collected, diluted, and shipped
"fresh" to nearby users by train or bus. Technicians handled it carefully, protecting it from sunlight and keeping it at the proper temperature of 40 degrees
F. If that was done, fresh semen could be used for four or five days with good
success on dairy herds, and on the occasional beef herd with an innovative
owner.

Semen was collected once or twice a week at the Colorado State University bull stud, where we students were trained in handling Holstein and Guernsey bulls—a dangerous business. Bulls were controlled with a pole snapped
into the nose ring and "collected" with an artificial vagina (AV), simply a
length of radiator hose with a latex liner funneled into a test tube. A water
bath kept the AV at body temperature, and the device was put in place by a
student-technician standing alongside the bull as he mounted a teaser cow or
steer. It's a wonder we weren't all killed!

The western colleges, though, were generally slow to include AI in their
curricula. That was because artificially sired calves were not accepted for reg-

144

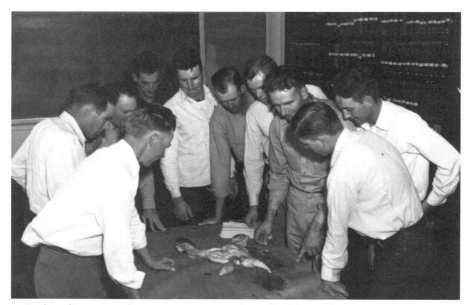

Studying bovine reproductive organs at a typical AI school for ranchers. —Colorado State University Photo Archives

istration by any beef breed and because professors—dependent as they were on politics for salaries, research, and retirement—looked pretty close at their hole card before teaching anything as politically incorrect as beef AI.

ONE PROFESSOR *who was not always politically correct was theriogenologist Harold J. Hill.*

PROFESSOR HILL

I'd been taking care of bulls since high school days in New Hampshire; I'd worked my way through Michigan State with the bulls. As a third-year vet student at CSU, I'd taught seniors the art of collecting, evaluating, diluting, and shipping semen. So right after graduation the dean says, "Hill, if you stick around, we'll give you $250 a month and three nice, big titles."

So I signed on as "veterinarian in charge" of the bull stud, "assistant professor of surgery and clinics" at the college, and "agent of extension" for the state. But, what the hell! $3,000 a year was big, big bucks in 1946, and they agreed to a twenty-cent bonus per cow inseminated, which, at $4,800 a year, gave me the second highest salary on the faculty.

But our bull farm had the lowest budget in the country. Ten dairy bulls ran out on long steel cables; a heavy chain attached to a large steel roller ran

*Until the mid-1950s,
semen was shipped
"fresh" by rail or bus and
had to be used promptly.*
—Colorado State University
Photo Archives

through a heavy halter and hooked to each bull's nose ring, and of course those bulls bellered and roared and charged, making the cables zing and occasionally turning one of the flimsy fences into kindling. Folks came from miles around to watch the excitement.

We had two big dogs and one hard and fast rule: Nobody goes to the bulls without a dog! But one of my guys forgot; he went out in the dark, and a Guernsey bull was loose in one of the alleys. Somehow the man must have fallen, must have been going backwards watching the bull. By the time I got there the bull was on him, rolling him, crushing him, using his short, nubby horns.

I crawled out on the rafters, onto the bull's neck, kicking his face until I could reach his nose ring. The guy rolled under the fence, but what a disaster! He lived about three days in terrible misery, ribs broken off at the spine. When he died, the state paid his widow $10,000. Life was cheap in the 1940s.

Guernsey bull on cable with a dog. —Colorado State University Photo Archives

*A*RTIFICIAL INSEMINATION—*so, what's new? Some people had been us-ing AI for decades.*

JONATHAN FOX

Heck! Dad was artificially impregnating mares before I was born. He trav-eled the rich Minnesota Valley, driving one stallion on a cart and leading another; when business was good, even two stallions weren't enough.

Each horse was allowed to breed only two mares at a "stand"; if more showed up, the extras were serviced with fresh [collected] semen. Dad taught me the technique later, in Saskatchewan, where we once had thirty stallions on the road.

When a stallion dismounted after breeding, we'd catch the surplus semen in a pail, set it in a tub of warm water, cover it with a hat to keep out the sun, and that was all there was to it. If an extra mare showed up, we'd impregnate her with a kind of homemade syringe. We could breed five or six mares with the one service of a stallion and expect terrific success.

Of course, customers were skeptical: "Okay, put that junk in there, but we don't pay till we get a colt!"

But, like as not, when we came back three weeks later the mare would have "missed," and we'd collect the $5 service fee. Next spring she'd have a good live foal, and we'd collect the stud fee in full—$15 or $20 was standard, when the horse business was good; AI made it even better in those days.

147

*F*ARM BOY James H. Clark *graduated from the University of Manitoba in 1950, went with the extension service, and quickly rose to provincial livestock commissioner. Ten years later he was hired by American Breeders Service (ABS), the AI giant, to manage their Canadian operations.*

JIM CLARK

The first I ever heard of AI was with Clydesdale horses at the experimental farm at Brandon, Manitoba; that was back in the 1930s. In recent years, the people at ABS have learned to process horse semen quite successfully, but horses are an infertile species, at best; a mare's reproductive tract slopes *in*, as if designed by nature to contaminate easily. I'd say Jonathan and his dad were extremely lucky.

The earliest AI studs in America, of course, were set up as dairy co-ops. There were one or two in Canada in the thirties, and the first technician registered in the United States was a fellow Manitoban named Jim Henderson; he was employed by a New Jersey dairy co-op in 1938.

When Canada went to war in 1939, Jim came home and joined the RCAF and became a pilot. He didn't do much flying; when the Brits discovered his expertise, they seconded him to the food ministry where he would have a bigger impact by breeding cows and making food than by flying "Spits." After the war, he helped develop artificial insemination in Canada.

I went with American Breeders Service in 1960 and stayed with them twenty-five years. Now, to know about ABS, you must know about its founder,

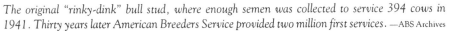

The original "rinky-dink" bull stud, where enough semen was collected to service 394 cows in 1941. Thirty years later American Breeders Service provided two million first services. —ABS Archives

148

Rockefeller Prentice. "Rock" inherited a fortune from his mother, and an intense interest in genetics from his father, Parmalee Prentice, a corporate lawyer who began experimenting with cattle, sheep, and poultry on his Massachusetts farm in early 1900s. Rock combined his father's passion for genetics with family capital and invested it, along with his own drive and ambition, to found a business that grew into ABS.[49]

It was 1946, the fresh semen era, when Rock established his first bull stud with three Guernsey bulls in a little rinky-dink barn outside Chicago. Fresh semen was viable for three or four days, which meant restricting operations to areas of dense population. By 1950 Rock had collection centers called "bull studs" at Madison (Wisconsin, where he had to buy a co-op to be legal), Carmel (Indiana), Asheville (North Carolina), Duluth, Kansas City, and Palo Alto—six bull studs in all, in fresh semen days.

MONTANA FARM BOY *Clair C. Willits went to work for Rockefeller Prentice's Palo Alto bull stud in 1953.*

CLAIR WILLITS

I was raised on a seventy-acre farm in the Sun River valley, near Great Falls, but when I came home from the Navy, an officer and gentleman, married and finished college, well, a few milk cows, some sheep and hogs, and rows and rows of sugar beets were not for Dorothy and me and our young family. So in 1950 we headed for California.

I got a job as a county agent/dairy adviser in the San Francisco milk shed, where I became acquainted with ABS, which had been shipping in semen from Illinois and, in 1953, decided to establish a bull stud. I was hired as manager, and when people ask if I ever knew Rock Prentice, I say, "Know him? Hell! He fired me three times."

All stud managers were called to Chicago headquarters for an annual five-day conference and, on one such occasion, Rock took us all to dinner at the Pump Room. When we got up to leave, he, as usual, had no money—never carried any—so somebody else paid the bill. Then, as we strolled down the avenue, Rock began talking about one of his kids who was having trouble—a personal matter; he was more than a little drunk.

Just trying to be friendly, I said, "Heck, Mr. Prentice, we can't always be responsible for our children. Can't force 'em into a mold, ya know."

"That's the trouble with you, Willits," Rock exploded. "Always willing to settle for second best! You're fired!"

Then, hailing a cab he says, "Here, take these gentlemen back to their hotel. They're *all* fired!" And of course he fished around for a bill to pay the

J. Rockefeller Prentice
(1902–1972).

cabby and didn't have one, so we paid the fare ourselves and went to bed chuckling over another good story on Rock Prentice.

Next morning we turned up at our conference unconcerned—these things happened. Rock said nothing about it either, but later he spoke to each of us alone: "I understand we had a little trouble last night; let's just forget it." That was okay with us. We young managers liked and admired Rock; we talked like him and even copied his dress: gray flannel suit, dark tie, button-down collar. We were proud to be part of his team.

Rock Prentice was a rather slight man, probably not more than five foot five, but the thing that struck you immediately was his energy; he was full of nervous energy—always doing something, found it difficult to sleep or even rest. He had a well-known drinking problem and went on *sobriety* binges as well as occasional drunks. I thought he was slightly paranoid—never sure whether friends were friends or simply after his money; when he hired his friends, as he often did, he paid them handsomely but could terminate their services just as quickly.

We thought he was brilliant. He would pick up a Dictaphone and fire off a detailed technical bulletin complete with facts, apostrophes, periods, quotation marks, and spellings of difficult words. One of his famous letters instructed us that "Alright is not all right," and he insisted on proper grammar and spelling in all correspondence.

But Rock was also a businessman. When I knew him, he was in middle age, and his great concern was profit; he needed to establish—as much for himself as the IRS—that ABS was a business, not a hobby. Of course, the Palo Alto stud was a great success. Thirty or forty dairy bulls were kept busy producing semen for processing in our lab and shipment to technicians across the West.

That was the situation in 1956, when our industry was becoming thoroughly "frozen."

RESEARCH HAS A GLOBAL MARKET, and a momentous discovery at Cambridge by E. J. Christopher Polge and his team of English scientists changed the North American beef business overnight.

CHRISTOPHER POLGE

I was born in England in 1926. My father had a small farm, but farming didn't seem right for me, and I left college in the forties still not knowing what to do. For a short time I worked in economics; then one day I heard, quite by chance, of an opportunity at the National Institute for Medical Research in London and was soon involved with low-temperature biology.

It's surprising how you get these breaks in life; within a year I was working with somebody called Professor Sir Alan Parkes, who had been having a squint through the literature and found reference to freezing human sperm in the 1800s. Way back then some people had exposed semen to very low temperatures and observed that, under certain conditions, the sperm survived.

Of course, we had known for a very long time that dehydrated plant seeds could be preserved by freezing, and there was a body of literature suggesting that frozen bacteria and protozoa could be stored for long periods of time, but there weren't any good examples of preserving mammalian cells. Such cells were usually killed by internal ice.

In 1942 a very interesting person in America, a Jesuit monk called Father Luyet, made a study of all the literature and published a book called *Life and Death at Low Temperatures*. Next, came reports from other Americans—Shaffner and Henderson, I think—who had tried freezing chicken sperm in a sugar solution, which, they theorized, dehydrated the cells. The sperm had not survived, but Sir Alan Parkes was fascinated, and he repeated the experiments with just enough success to keep him pursuing the subject in earnest. Imagine! Living cells in suspended animation—perhaps forever!

I came and saw Sir Alan one day in 1948, and we got on quite well from the start. Nowadays, you'd need all sorts of degrees before you could even speak with a fellow like that, but we had a couple of beers, and I was immediately appointed to his staff. I was assigned to work with Aubrey Smith, a very good colleague ever since, and we began by repeating the experiments of Shaffner and Henderson—including the use of sugar. (We used fructose, which we acquired with great difficulty because such chemicals were scarce in post-war England.)

And we got no success at all! The sperm cells did not survive. So, after a few weeks—much discouraged—we stored our valuable fructose, put the work aside, and went on to other things.

Aubrey Smith, it should be said, stayed on in London, experimenting with low-temperature preservation of red blood cells, endocrine organs, corneas, and other mammalian tissue, which eventually led to successful applications in blood transfusion and the grafting of human organs. I moved out to Mill Hill, a laboratory near Cambridge, and made ready to continue with my chickens.

I had our bottle of fructose sent down from London, and this time it worked magnificently! I actually got one chick! But then, I ran short of fructose and, finding more, made up a fresh brew—which didn't work at all! Something was very wrong!

There was a very small remnant of the successful solution left—the one sent down from London that had worked—and I sent it off to the laboratory for analysis. Word came back: "No fructose here! What we have is a mixture of glycerol and protein!"

What? My one success had come with an entirely new solution! One that contained no sugar at all! Somehow, back in London, the labels had got muddled, bottles were switched and the wrong solution sent. By purest chance we had stumbled upon glycerol, the dilutor that protects through freezing and thawing.

We still had a long way to go. The sperm came through alive, but a number of difficulties had to be overcome before we consistently produced live chicks. Clues came with discoveries made by Aubrey Smith and our "freezing" colleagues in London, and gradually the fertility of our fowl semen improved. The chicks we hatched were the first warm-blooded creatures ever produced from frozen sperm. Our methods were clearly defined and very repeatable.

The next step was to experiment with cattle. We knew that Father Luyet was working on rapid *cooling*, rather than freezing—which set us back a bit as a pioneer's first probings often will. And so it was with semen. Finally, after much experimentation and some inspired thinking by my colleagues, we found that cells, including bull sperm cells, require slower cooling to achieve the necessary dehydration. That was part of the answer. Then chance came to our aid again.

I was in the laboratory late one evening, preparing semen for freezing and pondering problems, when it seemed a good idea to go out for refreshment. One thing led to another, and I stayed somewhat longer than expected; the semen never got frozen that night at all. And that's how we discovered (with the aid of a few beers) the value of a long equilibration period—an important factor to this very day.

Soon, we were achieving satisfactory laboratory results, and Dr. Parkes decided to send me off to the Cambridge AI Centre for practical trials in the field. I fitted up a trailer, slept on the job, and traveled many miles with the head inseminator, persuading farmers to try our frozen semen. Of the first thirty or forty cows inseminated, more than 60 percent did not return to heat. Ah, what joy and excitement! And when Tim Rowson did the pregnancy diagnoses and declared the cows in-calf, I immediately telephoned Parkes, to announce our success.

"This is it!" Sir Alan said. And a few months later *Frosty the First*, a little black calf, was born—the first mammal ever produced from frozen semen. That was 1952.

In the United States, a very keen chap called J. Rockefeller Prentice was quick to see how frozen semen could transform cattle breeding. Within months he had set up a research lab in Wisconsin and tantalized Father Luyet into coming to work. I came over from England. Frozen semen was off to a very good start.

One of the Rockefeller Prentice's old associates continues the story:

DAVE BARTLETT, DVM

Immediately after the announcement of the success of frozen semen, Mr. Prentice hosted a seminar featuring Dr. Luyet, the scientist and author, and invited the entire AI industry to attend. He hoped it would stimulate research into freezing semen.

He invited Dr. Polge to come from England, and all of his exciting new principles were restudied by the American Foundation for the Study of Genetics, a Prentice organization, which evolved into ABS.

To give you an idea how quickly Mr. Prentice acted, the first calf from frozen semen in North America was born May 29, 1953. And within five years our team had perfected packaging and thawing, and ABS had converted entirely to frozen semen.

Quick work! Frosty the Second was born to this cow in Wisconsin just a year after Frosty the First, in England. —ABS Archives

MEANWHILE, *Dr. Harold Hill watched what was going on from his mobile lab at the foot of the Colorado Rockies.*

HAROLD HILL

Polge, Smith, and Parkes: Perfectionists! Dedicated to research! They produced the first mammal, ever, from frozen semen, and they published their momentous work in the little journal *Nature*, sometimes only five or six pages long, but what prestigious pages—read all over the world!

Real ivory tower guys, those British scientists. Their world revolved around chemistry, protein molecules, salts, pH; they had made one of the great technological breakthroughs of the century, and they gave it away! They just *gave* it to the world—no patents, royalties, licenses, nothin'! I don't know if they grasped the true significance of their discovery.

154

*A*PPARENTLY, *they did. In the 1990s Dr. Polge is still a director of Animal Biotechnology Cambridge Ltd., which has been making genetic breakthroughs ever since. Dr. Hill continues:*

In any case, if those scientists didn't recognize the real potential, neither did a lot of other people. Hearing that Polge was scheduled to attend a conference at Cornell, my mentor, Dr. Gassner, invited him to CSU. Dr. F. X. Gassner was a very intelligent German-style veterinarian with a *thorough* education. And, my God! Did he have drive! He was a workaholic, and something like frozen semen set him on fire! So Gassner, on a college professor's salary, personally paid Polge's way from New York to Colorado. He thought it was worth it just to get the great man cornered and learn about his work, and he invited all the M.D.s in the Denver area to hear him, too.

And, you know what? Very few M.D.s came. Here was a phenomenon ready to change the world—not just birds and cattle, but the world. And nobody gave a damn. Gassner was disgusted! He'd invited all the big shots, and they hadn't bothered to come. God, he was disappointed!

In the next few months we spent thousands of hours working out the commercial applications. We kept it simple; we found an old refrigerator, removed the guts, and kept a sludge of crushed dry ice and alcohol in the bottom. We filled long glass tubes with concentrated sperm and fire-closed the ends. At that point, we didn't dilute because the kill rate was too high; instead, we concentrated the semen and immersed the tubes in freezing alcohol for various lengths of time. Then, after careful thawing, we counted the live and dead sperm to learn about optimum freeze rates. Weeks were spent on such experiments.

Much was still to be learned about buffers and extenders. An early favorite was egg-yolk citrate, the simplest thing in the world. All you needed was four or five hen's eggs and a solution of sodium citrate; you dumped the yolks in the citrate and added sperm—no antibiotics, no enzymes, nothing else. Egg-yolk citrate is still the most practical semen extender going, but it took months to work out the details. Our first commercial frozen semen was ready in 1953, about a year after Polge spoke.

CSU got a grant from Lafayette Hughes, of Childress, Texas, one of the largest Hereford breeders in the world (and that was odd, because it was years before the Hereford establishment would recognize AI). So the Hughes grant financed a mechanical freezer designed by Dr. Gassner and built from scratch by engineers at the college. I didn't know doodley-dip about mechanics, but I was fascinated. That machine was six feet high, with solenoids and thermostats and coils of Freon gas and nozzles for alcohol, all designed to bring the temperature down to –110 degrees F (–79 degrees C) at a predetermined rate. The whole thing cost us $30,000.

*Dr. Hill ponders the
workings of his freezer.*
—Colorado State University
Photo Archives

Well, we stayed with alcohol right through the 1950s for the simple reason that they didn't deliver nitrogen to Fort Collins. And we couldn't have stored it anyway; all the rights to the "superfreeze" system belonged to Rockefeller Prentice. He kept it to himself, and who could blame him? Except, perhaps, the Brits who made the breakthrough.

But DAVE BARTLETT, *an ABS official, begs to differ.*

That's what all our competitors thought, and I hope I can clear the record, once and for all.

Despite his name, Rockefeller Prentice was not the very rich man that people assumed him to be. In the tough, development years of frozen semen, most of what he accomplished was done on borrowed money—and usually under duress.

156

Take the "reefers"—those ubiquitous nitrogen refrigerators thought of as secret weapons by our competitors: Rock had to come up with $200,000 cash to get the Linde division of Union Carbide to make the first 450 reefers. That was *risk* money. No guarantees. No one had prior experience. The precedent was the classic, narrow-necked Dewarr flask designed to keep things cold for just a few days. Rock required a rugged tank, wide mouthed for easy access to frozen inventory under remote ranch conditions. He wanted a field time of fourteen to twenty-one days.

It was widely believed—and absolutely false—that ABS controlled those reefers. Once developed by Linde, Rock reserved the right to have his orders filled first; that was all. Then he *gave* the nitrogen system to his competitors. Deliberately, he did not apply for a patent.

The only secret was Linde's. They developed a plastic powder for insulating the tanks; we found out later that each grain had a hollow center like a miniature Ping-Pong ball. But there was nothing to stop other companies from designing their own.

A Linde "reefer" first designed for storing bull semen; now they are used in hospitals and labs the world over for all conceivable (no pun intended) frozen substances. —ABS Archives

I knew Rock Prentice well and admired him much. He was a very tough competitor who believed wholeheartedly in the universal values of competition. His competitors had trouble understanding him and his motives, and I think that was mostly because of his name.

*I*T ALWAYS SEEMED *to me that ABS was a model American company—tough, aggressive, competitive—that grew and survived because it provided a very good service at a very fair price. Another longtime employee adds some history.*

JIM CLARK

With frozen semen, we were ready to move from dairy into beef. All practical restrictions were removed, and our refrigerators were easy to ship. We could send one out to any ranch, no matter how remote.

Actually, the airlines didn't like those reefers at first; they were uneasy when a top came off and filled the airliner with "smoke." They got over that when they learned that liquid nitrogen is a safe, noncorrosive, nonflammable element that boils off into an inert gas at –196 degrees C. Really, those refrigerators revolutionized the industry; soon you could ship semen anywhere in the world by airplane, train, or bus.

My ABS career began in Canada just as the company was moving into beef. Most Canadian units were still organized as co-ops and ruled by a committee of dairymen armed with a very big stick. ABS, as a profit-oriented company, didn't quite fit; listen to a rule adopted by the industry just as we were coming onstream in 1963:

> Privately owned semen-producing businesses operating primarily for profit shall not be allowed to . . . upset the efficient system that has been built up in Canada, nor to siphon off profits needed for further improvement of the system.[50]

So much for competition. That regulation hamstrung our Canadian operation until rancher-training programs changed the ball game. Meanwhile, we carried on business through distributors like Keith Robson, at Selkirk, Manitoba. I was transferred to Billings as ABS regional manager for Montana, Wyoming, North Dakota, and western Canada. This was a new position; we were in position for the "exotic" importation coming later.

ONE EARLY ABS CUSTOMER in Canada was my friend Wes Alm. He and his wife, Dixie, were our predecessors on the SN ranch and, later, neighbors down the coulee on the Bar 15. Our children shared the one-room "44" school. We have worked together at brandings and seen eye to eye on politics and family values for almost forty years. What more need be said?

Well, this: In the 1960s I was selecting commercial cattle with the care others used on purebreds; Wes was using ranch sense in selecting purebreds. I learned a lot from him; he may have learned a little from me. We shared an early interest in performance. To obtain it, Wes was one of the first Canadian ranchers to "go AI."

WES ALM

I told you in *The Range* how my dad came to the prairies to break the sod—first with oxen, then with steam. In 1927 he moved to Alberta and after a couple of good years was ready for cattle.

In 1934 he got a good deal on ten cows and calves at $10 a pair, but when he went to the bank the manager said, "You're wastin' your time, Albert! Cattle will never be worth nothin' ever again." But he lent Dad $100 anyway, and the next spring calves were worth a cent and a half a pound. But Dad loved cattle and stuck with 'em, and all through the war he saved to buy fifty head of purebred Hereford cows—his heart's desire.

In '48 we moved to the Porcupine Hills, where our Herefords gave us trouble. For one thing, they didn't wean big enough calves. . . . Well, all the breeds were small in the 1950s, and anyone selling "pounds" was in big trouble.

L4 Mischief 91, the Miles City Line Four bull purchased by ABS and widely used on ranches in the 1960s. —ABS Archives

159

In 1955, Dix and I bought a part of the old 44 [ranch] on Trout Creek and built the Bar 15 from the ground up: house, barn, sheds, corrals, feedlot, fences—everything sawed from logs we cut in the hills—which kept us busy when the kids were small.

In 1962, ABS distributor Doc Robson was promoting AI in Alberta; I started with *L4 Mischief*, a Miles City Line Four bull, and used him heavy in building our herd. The older kids did the "detecting"; our daughter Anne [Stevic] became one of the first rancher-technicians in our area.[51]

L4 and the other great performance-tested domestic bulls were a help, but we wanted more: more milk, more growth. For that we had to wait for the exotics.

Now, back across the border to CLAIR WILLITS

The ease of shipping frozen semen was making local AI studs redundant, and, as my job at Palo Alto began to fold in 1956, I told Rock Prentice I'd take my know-how back to Montana.

He thought I was out of my mind but said, "Willits, if you are sold on it, go ahead; I'll keep you on the payroll. Beat the Montana bushes, but keep your eyeballs skinned for beef bulls." Rock offered me a loan of $4,000—substantial for those days—at 4 percent interest, and I came home and chose some partners and organized Montana Proved Sires Service with exclusive rights to ABS products in Montana.

Business was slow in the summer of 1956, and I was in Miles City on a weekly basis "collecting" Line One bulls at the station. For the scientists, it was much like storing "heirloom" seed against some future need; for me, it was a source of extra income. Anyway, one day I went to Ray Woodward, the director of the station, and asked him where I could find a proven beef sire.

"Well," said Ray, "I know of a polled bull that just might suit. He's a station bull that we used in developing Line Nine, our Polled Hereford strain. When we replaced him, we peddled him off to a rancher."[52]

That was *L9 Domino 7*. When the rancher showed him to me, he was lousy and thin and didn't look the part of an ABS sire. I had to grit my teeth and think of the great records on his offspring. Here was a tested, proven product. Finally, we made a deal, and *L9* soon shaped up quite nicely with care and feed; now, with the new freezing, we were ready to make high-quality, high-performance beef bulls available to ranchers everywhere. To the best of my knowledge, *L9* was the first proven beef bull in any stud, and he went on to sire more calves than any other bull in history.

L9 Domino 7, *ABS's famous Miles City Line Nine bull.* —ABS Archives

But, in dealing with ranchers, my partners and I were faced with a new set of problems: Montana ranches can be so remote that they need their own tomcat, we say. Also ranchers, unlike dairymen, must get their cows bred in sixty days or less. It wasn't practical to bring in professional technicians for such a short time.

So somebody said, "We'll teach the ranchers to breed their own cows." Good idea. Cache Valley Breeders in Utah was already doing it. So we encouraged five or six prominent Montana cattlemen to attend our ABS school: Jim McDonald and Hank Goldhan, from the Highwoods; Louis Petri, Jerry Hould, and one of the Pancake brothers, from Malta; Rol Mosher, from the T Bar ranch at Augusta—they all went through the ten-day course in Wisconsin, came home, ordered semen, and began breeding their own cows.

THAT WAS THE START of many new ranch skills and traditions.

ROL AND CAROL MOSHER

ROL: It was 1960 when Clair Willits talked us into trying AI, and we were among the first in this part of the country. I went to the ABS school at Madison, Wisconsin, and learned on big old dairy cows, while my brother Jerry attended a course at Fort Collins. He and I did the breeding on our ranch for many years.

   The day I got home from school, all the bulls were out with the cows. "Oh, oh!" I thought. "Dad lost his nerve; he's decided not to go AI." Of course, the bulls had knocked down a gate; we run 'em out real quick and went to breeding, hoping there was a few cows left to do.

CAROL: And we've AI'd ever since—every year since 1960.

ROL: We used L9 and were well pleased with the results. Our calves had been weaning off at 450 pounds, which was average for our area. The L9s did better than 500, and we thought we'd really caught a fat hog.

CAROL: Our L9 steers went to Watkins in the Corn Belt, and they really liked 'em! They were all half brothers, see, like peas in a pod, and gentle! The heifers grew into the gentlest cows we ever had.

ROL: But we still had lots to learn about AI. Take heat detection; that was all new to us. First thing we learned was to take a pair of binoculars to the field. Later, we got "gomers"—eager bulls, but fixed so they couldn't breed; I don't know who first called them "gomers," but it soon spread through the country. Next, it was chin-ball halters; when a gomer mounted a cow, a big roller bearing under his chin left a smear of thick, bright paint to help in spotting cows that had been standing at night. We didn't go much for such gimmicks.

   When you go for AI, you're in for long days in the saddle; you're out as soon as it's light and spend two or three hours watching for "standing heat." Now, a cow that's "coming on" will be mounting—or, as we say, "riding"— other cows; she's beginning to show some interest but not quite ready to release an egg.

   After a few hours of "riding," you'll see her standing still, waiting to be mounted by other cows, and that's what you're looking for—"standing heat." Now ovulation will occur in the next few hours, and a sperm will find an egg. Your job as an AI technician is to thaw that one-in-a-million sperm and release it with the others in the vicinity of that egg. Timing is everything.

   So, after the morning ride, the cows picked up the previous night are put through the chute, inseminated, marked, and released to find their calves, which have likely been ignored for a day or two. The rest of the morning you're in the saddle, penning cows that are "on," and pairing out cows that are "off" with their hungry calves. You're home at noon and back by 4 P.M. to go through it all again: picking up cows that are "on," breeding the ones that were "on" this morning, and so forth and so on—daylight to dark, seven days a week through breeding season.

CAROL: And, without fail, just as you're starting home, you'll spot another cow and have to saddle up and pen her in the dark.

ROL: I remember once it rained all day, and we couldn't get anything done. The cows were bunched in a corner, tails to the wind; we'd been through 'em two or three times without spotting anything "on." Then, just at dark, we went for one last look, and there they were, about twenty cows milling around in the fence corner. So, back to the barn; saddle up and corral the bunch in the dark. Next morning it would be easy to tell which ones had been "on"; they'd be covered with mud from the mounting.

CAROL: And another thing: Spotting and penning cows and pairing them out is a great family project; the wives like to help with the riding and, even when they are little, kids are great help in AI. It made great stories for show-and-tell at school!

ROL: I remember years ago when our Jeff was five or six; we had shut the AI program down and dumped the "cleanup" bulls in the pasture. Those bulls were roaring around, bellering, riding, looking for cows that would stand, and Jeff says, "Dad, what's those bulls doin', jumping on those cows?"

"Why, they're breeding them," I says. "That's where babies come from."

"Huh!" says Jeff, "I never seen you jumpin' on Mommy's back." Good old Jeff! Now grandchildren are helping on the ranch.

"WORDS ARE THE DAUGHTERS OF EARTH," *Sam Johnson said. I was chewing the fat with my learned friend Frank Jacobs (a man of livestock as well as letters), and we dallied with some daughters of The Ranch. Frank observed that a townsman wouldn't know a "bobtail" from a "possum," or a "sidewinder" from a "gomer" if one bit him. Well, even an old-time Lasater, Gilchrist, Hughes, de Baca, or Berg might have trouble talking cows on the ranch today:*[53]

"After you were gone, Grandad, we went *exotic*, like, you know: *Simmental, Limo, Fleckvieh, Pie Rouge, Tarentaise, Saler*. We even imported a "*Kee,*" and he froze so good that we quartered him at a *stud* to be *drawn* and *frozen*. That's frozen semen, Grampa, for *insemination*, not the old-fashioned "impregnation" of your day.

"Like, tanks of steaming "N" to keep *straws* and *ampules* cold. Like, *gomers* fitted with *aprons* (your old binder canvases hanging in the shed came in handy for aprons); like, *breeding chutes*, plastic *pipettes* and *sleeves*.

"And what a *gene pool*, Grandad! *Exotic imports, domestic exotics, composites, synthetic strains* . . .

"Know what I mean? You don't? Let me explain . . ."

So, now, to "domestics," "exotics," and "synthetics."
But first take time to consider the "low-tech cow."

THE LOW-TECH COW

MY FRIEND Roy Berg likes to talk of the "low-tech cow."[54] The beef cow of the twenty-first century, he says, will be a low-tech beast—unlike the dairy cow, the chicken, or the pig.

Pigs and chickens used to be scavengers; now the beef cow (along with the ewe) is the only scavenger left. She subsists on anything from dry range grass to crop aftermath to cull potatoes, while the others require the very best feed, the very best land, the very best management, the very best housing—all of which is very, very, very expensive.

So, with all the talk of modern high-tech discoveries, and with all the exciting, exotic things to come, I hope you won't forget the low-tech cow, who nurtures the grass that builds the soil that grows the food we eat.

"A cubic inch of lean, they tell us, weighs twice as much as a cubic inch of fat. Since we sell pounds, we need as much red meat as we can get."

—Wayne Malmberg, rancher, 1960

PART THREE

THE INVASION

Part Three: The Invasion

THE SCOUTS

MANY VETERANS CAME HOME *from the wars in Europe with memo-ries of large cattle in "exotic" places. In gathering stories for this book, I heard several accounts of "liberated" livestock.*

Alberta rancher BERT HARGRAVE

I went ashore on D-Day with a tank-retrieval unit, and over the next few months as we crossed the lowlands the food supply was pitiful. Belgium and Holland had been occupied for years, and many cattle were rotting in the fields. Cow carcasses! Bad news to a rancher at the best of times!

I remember, though, one living critter that served our company well. We had set up shop in what was left of an orchard, when here came a scrawny horse, scrounging apples under the trees. He had saddle marks so I caught him, fixed a thong around his jaw, and rode him Indian-style in mock review of the rows of tanks.

Well, seeing my flashy "parade horse," the men sprang to attention and laughed and cheered "Old Skin-and-bones" as he slowly stumbled by. I think we scrounged up something from the mess tent; he was the only *live* stock we'd seen and worth his weight in gold in morale alone.

Montana rancher BILLY BIG SPRING

Hell, yes! I saw some cattle. I went overseas with the 35th in January '45 and fought there till the end. I remember one dark afternoon soon after cross-ing the Rhine; we got in a hell of a fight, and I took cover in a Charlie Russell-type barn: small, plastered with mud, and roofed with some kind of straw.

Something moved in the dark. I kept it covered while I inched around. There! A big cow tied to a manger! But just then—Damn!—a bullet come a-whistlin' through the walls. I ducked. The dust flew, and that old cow stood there, wild-eyed, scared to death. Well, it scared the hell out of me, too.

As soon as the fight was over, I cut the old girl loose and kicked her out on what was left of the grass. And that's when I saw how big she was; that's where I saw all those big white and yellow cattle, a whole lot bigger than ours at home in Montana.

Right then I talked to myself: "Boy! I wish I could get some of these cattle home." Of course, our buyers docked ya if a calf weighed a little too much or had a little red on its face, but I thought, "Boy! I don't care what color; these calves will easy go 600 pounds at six months old! Give me some calves like that, and I'll have a ranch!"

169

And my neighbor, JIM GRAY, *in the Porcupine Hills*

In August 1943 we invaded Sicily; then it was Italy and the Appennines. I didn't see all that much fighting but, sure, I remember cattle: Monte Cassino—six white heifers hooked two-and-two in-line to a Massey binder, with an old guy walking along, hoppin' 'em up with a stick.

And, I'm kind of ashamed to tell ya, but we shot one! Ate her! They made us pay for her, which didn't replace her for her owner, of course, who'd had trouble enough with Germans and Canadians, both, living off his land.

Nope! There was just no excuse for shooting that farmer's cow; it was a terrible thing to do. But, I'll tell ya something else: That big white heifer sure tasted *good* after living all those months on mutton stew! Even now, listenin' to cow talk forty years later, they can't tell me anything new about Chianina beef! How good it was!

*B*UT IT IS ANOTHER *breed of large white cattle, named for the ancient district of Charolles in central France, that draws attention in the following chapters. Hundreds of thousands of North Americans slogged through two world wars in central France, where the Charolais breed originated.*[55]

In World War One, a Franco-Mexican army officer named Jean (or Juan) Pugibet was impressed by these cattle. And it was he who actually opened the "invasion" discussed in part three.

The cattle he brought to Mexico in the 1930s advanced north in droves from their beachhead at Veracruz, into the states of northern Mexico and across the Rio Grande into Texas. Twenty years later, it was the memory of some "big ol' white cattle layin' where an artillery shell had killed 'em" that led ex-artilleryman Mack Braly off to Texas, where he found his Charolais bull "Seguter" and launched the final wave I call "The Importation" of the 1960s and 1970s, which infiltrated the cow population of North America with new bovine genes. But I'm getting ahead of myself; we'll save that for part four.

170

15   Ashore in Mexico

REPORTS OF GROWTHIER CATTLE OVERSEAS! As a matter of fact, by World War Two, French cattle were already established in North America. Remember Blanco *and* Plato *from chapter 6?*

Manuel Garza, a third-generation Mexican rancher, explains.

MANUEL GARZA ELIZONDO

Northern Mexico is where most American ranching traditions start. The northern states of Sonora, Chihuahua, Coahuila, Nuevo Leon, and Tamaulipas have most of the cattle and, traditionally, the people there have been ranchers—cattle people.

Those Texas longhorns are descendants of the cattle imported from Spain in 1519 or 1520 that wound up in northern Mexico—no cattle on this continent before that. Later, besides the criollos, we had the Hereford, Brahma, Aberdeen Angus, and Shorthorn, the same as Texas, but it was not till the last fifty years that Mexican ranchers realized they had to be more efficient.

Why? Because of the agrarian situation. Every year the government was expropriating land, so every year the ranchers had to live on smaller pieces. This forced them to look for more productive genes, which brings us to Charolais.

There are rumors that a few head of Charolais cattle were brought to Mexico—perhaps to the states of Tabasco or Veracruz around 1924. If so, these cattle must have come from Brazil or Uruguay, which imported Charolais from France in 1922, but no significant progeny was noticeable. Then, in 1930, two yearling bulls, *Iroquois* and *Image*, and ten yearling heifers were imported from France. In 1931 came six yearling bulls and twelve heifers, followed in 1937 by seven heifers already bred in France. Credit for this must be given to the Frenchman, Pugibet, who had the support of both General Marqués de la Guiche, head of the Sindicato de Exportation in France, and the approval of the Mexican government.

Not all these cattle were kept by Juan Pugibet. Around 1933, General Manuel Perez Treviño, secretary of Agriculture of Mexico, bought *Iroquois* and ten cows, which he kept at La Candelaría, his ranch in northern Mexico, until 1937 when he traded them off to Señor Gudelio Garza Gomez at Villa Acuña, Coahuila, for a bunch of good mares. Don Gudelio, whom I personally knew, didn't know what Charolais was, but he thought his ranch was overstocked with horses so he decided to trade some off for Perez Treviño's herd of big white cattle.

At the same time, six of Pugibet's cows and a few bulls went to Colonel Serrano and Colonel Daniel Breen at Rancho El Canelo in Tamaulipas. So, then, there were three main Charolais breeders: Gudelio Garza Gomez at El Olno ranch, Max Michaelis at El Fortín, and Colonel Breen at El Conelo. Those three ranchers kept the breed going for the next few years.

Max Michaelis Jr., Manuel Garza Elizondo, and Col. Dan Breen, circa 1963.

KEEPER OF CHAROLAIS FOLKLORE Dick Goff asserts that when Breen crossed the border, southbound, riding a horse with a "US" brand on its thigh, he was Sergeant Dan Breen of the U.S. Cavalry. By the time he appeared at Rancho El Conelo with a Mexican wife and an interest in a herd of Charolais cattle, he had somehow been promoted to colonel.

M. G. "MAXIMO" MICHAELIS

Dan Breen was one of those colorful Mexican breeders—very flamboyant, the type who dominates meetings. His ranch was on the Tamaulipas coast between Brownsville and Tampico, and he had a very influential partner, Colonel Serrano, in Mexico City. Somehow, the Breen-Serrano cattle had been liberated from a government experiment station, and later my father swapped bulls with Colonel Breen; that's how we got *Quiriño*, and I've already told you about *Blanco* and *Plato*, the two bulls given us by our neighbor, General Acosta. As you can see, the early Charolais business was full of colonels and generals.

Another colorful character was General Alejo Gonzalez, who often claimed to have defeated Pancho Villa. One of Gonzalez's neighbors owned a Hereford bull that weighed a thousand pounds at a year of age; he proudly invited the general over to see him. Not to be outdone, Gonzalez said he had bigger bulls at home, but when the neighbor came to see them, they rode all day to find one old *corriente*.

"General," the neighbor said, "that bull does look like he might weigh a thousand pounds, but he must be ten years old. My bull was only a yearling."

"So?" said General Gonzalez. "What's time to a bull?"

GENERAL ALEJO GONZALEZ often claimed to have defeated famous guerrilla fighter Francisco "Pancho" Villa. Dick Goff met him many years later in San Antonio, Texas, and the old man told of "mechanizing" his cavalry on twenty-seven freight trains, thereby outmaneuvering Villa and catching him single-handed.

In fact, Pancho Villa was defeated several times, most notably in 1915 by General Älvaro Obregón. General Alejo Gonzalez was only one of dozens of generals under Obregón's command, but he was still, no doubt, a very colorful character.

To quote another character,

Montana rancher BUDDY COBB

They was all characters! General Gonzalez was a character! Max Michaelis was a character! I found out to be a Charolais breeder you *had* to be a character!

And, as for Max Michaelis and his Rancho El Fortín,

RODNEY JAMES *remembers:*

Some of us, back about 1960, went to Texas a few days early for the Houston show, and Max Michaelis invited us to his ranch in Coahuila. What an experience!

We flew down in Max's little airplane and found the ranch to be a little town in itself—school, store, church, and all; in fact, it had once been a fortress. The master bedroom was something else! A holstered, loaded revolver slung on each bedpost; an assortment of rifles and shotguns hung over Max's head where he could reach one at any time. One whole evening was spent entertaining the "cops" who collected the rent.

The fortified old Rancho El Fortín.
—Watt M. Casey Jr.

When it was time to leave for Houston, Rancho El Fortín was zero-zero in fog, so there we sat—a fine place to be stranded. About four days later, "How about driving out?" I asked.

"Not on your life," said Max. "There's fifty-six gates, eighty-five mudholes, and hundreds of hostile Injuns; I've never driven out and don't intend to." So we missed the Houston show, but it was worth it.

MANUEL GARZA ELIZONDO

That's a slightly exaggerated story; Max was a great storyteller who sometimes got carried away. It's true, though, that all of those Mexican ranches were interesting places.

Max Michaelis was a very fine man who really liked the Mexican people, and it was he who pushed Charolais across the continent. You remember that Max's father took two young Pugibet bulls to Texas in the 1930s. Others did the same, but as far as I know no Pugibet heifers ever left the country. They stayed in Mexico, multiplying, until 1946.

Then foot-and-mouth! When the *aftosa* was discovered, we lost our markets. It did a terrible impact on our business, and a lot of cattle were dead before it ended!

16   Dripping with Germs

*D*ISEASE CONTROL *is a time-honored function of government. One of the very first laws enacted by the Parliament of Canada was designed to control the importation of livestock.*

And I like this American legend told by my friend Tom Lasater. Tom wasn't there when the historic event took place, but he told it to me as his father told it to him: the folklore of a simpler time when a rancher might have a direct line to the president, and the president had a line on the roots of government. So they say.

TOM LASATER

The old Texas rancher "Shanghai" Pierce sent his foreman over to India in about 1905 or 1906 to study the herds and breeds and varieties of cattle. He finally selected some Brahmans and loaded them onto a ship bound for New York harbor, but when they got to Ellis Island the customs people pulled out their machine guns and started mowin' 'em down.

Well, Shanghai finally talked 'em into turning off their machine guns while he telephoned Teddy Roosevelt down in Washington and explained how he'd spent billions selecting Brahma cattle, and now these stupid people were killin' them off.

"All right," the president said, "I'll talk to the customs people just as soon as you hang up, and I'll tell 'em to stop the killin' for at least twelve months. Then, if your cattle haven't developed diseases of any variety, you can load 'em up and take 'em on down to Galveston."[56]

So that's what Shanghai did, and he began crossing 'em on his native Texas cattle, and back in the brush near our ranch at Falfurrias, people like my father saw how good they were and tried 'em. Later I used their offspring in founding the Beefmaster breed.

*I*F IT AIN'T ALL TRUE, IT SHOULD BE *(to paraphrase Winston Churchill on King Arthur). Maybe Tom does swap a tad of color for some fact. The zebu or*

Shanghai Pierce. —Western History Collections, University of Oklahoma Library

Brahman breeds of the Indian subcontinent have proved their worth, consistently, in hotter parts of the world, but—in fact—by the time the first "Bremmers" arrived in Texas, old "Shang" was dead, and the project was under the management of his nephew, Able Pierce Borden.

According to Chris Emmett in a book on the subject, the debarkation point was Simonsons Island (not Ellis), and the story (much condensed), goes like this:[57]

Finally on the fifth and sixth of July [1906], a number of rabbits were taken to Simonsons Island and inoculated with the blood of individual Brahmans under extreme sanitary conditions. A few days later rabbits 16, 39, and 42 showed a marked rise in temperature. The blood of each was then examined microscopically, and *Trypanosoma evansi*, the causative agent of the dreaded surra was found.[58]

The gravity of introducing surra into the [country] was, of course, known to John R. Mohler, Chief of the Pathological Division of the Bureau of Animal Industry [and his inspectors, and] it was decided that the infected animals should be killed [while] repeated tests were made on the other animals.

The Pierce attorneys, Proctor and Vandenburg of Victoria, Texas, received word of the approaching execution and relayed the news to Borden who was en route . . . to take delivery of his cattle. Telegrams were sent to every official in Washington . . . to no avail. Finally, Vandenburg said, "We have wired everybody except the president."

"That," said V. B. Proctor, "would be an idea."

"He ain't God," Vandenburg observed, "but let's go." [So they sent Teddy Roosevelt] a two-hundred word telegram with the assertion that, "It would be a calamity . . . if all those cattle were slaughtered just because one rabbit caught the sniffles."

The infected Brahmans were killed and their bodies destroyed with unslaked lime and pure sulfuric acid. On November 14, 1906, the Secretary of Agriculture issued a permit releasing the thirty-three surviving cattle from quarantine, and they went direct to the Pierce Ranch and became the foundation stock for the Brahman breed in the United States.

*F*OUR YEARS LATER *Robert J. Anderson was born on an east Texas farm. When he graduated from Texas A&M as a doctor of veterinary medicine, he went right to work for the Bureau of Animal Industry (BAI). It was 1935. His salary was $2,000 a year.*

Over the course of a long career, Bob rose to become chief of USDA's Disease Regulatory Service, now APHIS.

ROBERT ANDERSON, DVM

There used to be a saying that disease spreads as fast as man and his livestock move. Think about it. In covered-wagon days a disease only moved as fast as a yoke of oxen. Today we go from Moscow to Washington in something like six hours—the risks are frightening. Four years after I went to work for the BAI the Germans invaded France; nine years later the Russians blockaded Berlin, and it's been Cold War ever since [or, at least until 1991]. I retired in 1970, so throughout my long career my prime responsibility was the protection of our country's food supply.

The Bureau of Animal Industry was established back in 1884 to deal with contagious bovine pleuropneumonia, brought ashore by a ship's milk cow in New York harbor. Britain, our big trading partner, prohibited cattle from infected countries, so BAI was organized to eradicate the disease in the interests of commerce.

In the years since, many other diseases have been brought under control: tuberculosis in poultry and cattle; brucellosis [known as undulant fever, in humans]; anthrax, one of the most virulent diseases known [for man or beast]; and foot-and-mouth disease [FMD], another great threat to production. FMD has broken out in the United States, been eradicated, and reintroduced fourteen times in the last 150 years. FMD is a continuing problem.

Now, let's say an enemy agent introduced a disease like foot-and-mouth or anthrax or rinderpest! How quickly it could spread! As a check, we simulated infection at each of three main terminal markets: Chicago, East St. Louis, Omaha. Seventy-two hours later "exposed" animals had been traced to every state in the Union, so a mechanism for rapid response, rapid diagnosis, swift containment, and sure elimination had to be developed. We want to be ready—now!—before a disease becomes unmanageable.

Up to 1928, the chief of the BAI wrote his own regulations to protect the industry. Finally, after two serious FMD outbreaks in the twenties, it was decided that regulations were inadequate; pressure from interest groups often caused "misjudgment." So the powers that be decided: "Prohibit! Don't just regulate. Accept nothing [no animal material] from any country where foot-and-mouth is tolerated, unless it has been processed to destroy the organism."

In 1931 such a law was passed: Importation prohibited! Hands off! No provision for adapting to special circumstance. At the same time, a tripartite agreement was struck with Canada and Mexico by which all parties undertook to protect our continent.

In the 1950s and 1960s I was "the fellow in the black hat," charged with enforcement, keeping foreign livestock out. The people we were regulating didn't like me much, and those we were protecting didn't care for me, either. Just the other day a friend said, "Bob, it's four or five years since I've heard a bad word about you. You don't seem to have an enemy left!"

"That's right," I said. "It's simple. I've outlived 'em."

A DICHOTOMY EXISTS, *worldwide, between those who would keep cattle out and those who would bring them in. Both sides have the highest—if generally unappreciated—motives.*

ROY BERG

In 1955 I came home to Canada after my stint with Dr. Winters in Minnesota and applied for permission to import pigs. Pigs! I wanted to bring in Minnesota #3 pigs for continuing research, and all I got was a very polite "Impossible!"

"We can't let you import pigs," said Health of Animals; "American pigs have diseases." No interest in finding a way, and that was the mentality of official veterinarians everywhere. You remember Peter H——, the government vet at Edmonton? His mother brought a beautiful stuffed pheasant home from England. "It is my duty as a Canadian veterinary officer," said Peter, "to confiscate that bird." And he did!

The Australians were even more paranoid. I went to Brisbane to study in 1964, and I remember the lurid mural in the vet college: a mob of cattle dripping, dripping, dripping germs of pleuropneumonia across the continent.

The lesson: Don't move livestock!

S O, COME WITH ME *on a side trip to Australia. Meet Gordon Burcher, a man driven more by adventure than by profit—maybe.*

Anyway, his story illustrates the international flavor of the game, the aggressiveness of the center, the ferocity of the defense. He shoots! He (almost) scores!

—School of Veterinary Science, University of Queensland

181

By way of background, my father was a stock and station agent and a partner in a 12,000-square-mile property where buffalo were harvested for hides. Dad bought in when hides were almost worthless; his plan was to upgrade "scrubbers," cattle that had been running wild for years.

I was in Brisbane trading cattle in 1966 but felt my forte was in management and breeding, so I had made a small down payment on a property near Ipswich when I read about Charolais in Canada. "Cracky!" I thought; "I must see what's going on."

Dad had been in Alberta after the war and had made contact with Ed McKinnon, a prominent rancher.[59] A job was arranged, and I was absolutely astounded by what I learned! Australia was fifteen years behind in every way. Feedlotting wasn't practical; there was no established market between grass- and grain-fed stock; AI wasn't accepted by the established cattle industry. It was an eye-opener, what they were doing in Alberta.

The first season, Ed and Harriet McKinnon gave me a job and treated me like a son at their feedlot north of Calgary, but when winter came I found I hated the cold, so back to Calgary I went to learn the boilermaker's [welder's] trade.

The following spring, I went to work for Ed's nephew, Neil, on the LK ranch at Bassano and, Cracky! How I loved that! It was all I'd ever hoped for—just what I enjoyed—a riding job on a large, well-managed ranch with 2,000 cows to breed. Everything was new. I learned AI; I bought an old car; I traveled around. But when winter came I got cold feet, again [Gordon laughs]. I thought, "To hell with this bloody weather; I'm goin' home."

Now, there was a test station at Bassano [the ABCPA test station], where Neil was comparing breeds for the Alberta government. And as I studied the data, I became convinced that Charolais was exactly what we needed in Australia. I thought, "I'll take some home."

I wrote the Australian high commissioner in Ottawa; I wrote him twice. No answer. I wrote the high commissioner in Canberra. Still no answer. "Well, stuff it!" I thought. "I'm bringin' some Charolais home; if you take me for a whirl, it's just too bad." And I obtained 300 ampules of frozen semen.

I filled a half gallon thermos with dry ice and spirits, drilled a hole in the top to let off steam, and the whole thing fitted neatly into a portmanteau or suitcase. Airline inspection was easy; funnily enough, I went from Calgary to Vancouver to Hawaii without anyone ever looking in my luggage. I missed a connecting flight in Honolulu and panicked—thought I'd lose the lot. But, in the end, I found dry ice at a nearby hospital and all was sweet when we "set sail" for Australia.

But the toughest part lay ahead; I was sure they'd check my suitcases at Sydney. Funnily enough, again, I was just coming down the line when somebody paged me. "Look," I shouted to the customs man, "d'ya mind if I leave me port' while I go to the phone?"

"Okay," the inspector said. "Go ahead." And when I came back my luggage was covered with stickers: Pass, Pass, Pass. They hadn't even looked, just cleared me through. That was fine; I'd been traveling 48 hours and was only in Sydney. I still had to make it to Brisbane with my brew boiling off all the time.

Once home, I could start breeding cows—implant the evidence, so to speak. I hadn't been challenged; customs had cleared me; others were too bloody busy to answer letters. Now, all I had to do was troop down to Brisbane every few days to top up my dry-ice cocktail.

And it was on one such trip that I came a cropper. I braked sharply at a corner, and the whole bloody lot fell off the seat and smashed to the floor of the car. The bloody stuff went everywhere; I hurried back to Brisbane to top up. But what of the sperm? Were they dead? I had to know.

Just before going to America, I'd worked at the university and come to know some scientists fairly well. I rang one up: "Look, I've got some semen here that may be spoiled; would you stick it under a mike' and check it out?"

What a mistake! My friend said something to somebody, who said it to somebody else, who eventually told a professor, who tipped the bucket on me. I admitted what I'd done, of course—no use denying. I only hoped they'd see the sense, but what they saw was a nightmare. They panicked! Soon a story spread of bull semen full of bluetongue, which drove the sheepmen crazy.[60]

"Look," I said; "be reasonable. It's not possible. There's no bluetongue in Canada" (which was true, as far as I knew; Canadian authorities had been saying so for years).

But no! The pig-headed beggars saw a chance to practice eradicating a serious disease like rinderpest or foot-and-mouth or something. Soon the press got hold, and I was headlines, accused of wiping out Australia's flocks with bluetongue.

What *was* wiped out was my father's herd and every cow for five miles 'round. The officials went berserk! They seized my Charolais semen and sent it to South Africa for testing. Results negative, but too late to save the neighbors' cattle. A thousand head lay dead in just a few minutes.

Of course, the neighbors did okay; compensation was based on pretty good prices. Later, prices would fall and they'd buy back cheap. But as for me, I was wiped out: No thanks; no kiss-me-foot! I was excluded from compensation by a special bill in Parliament and fined $500, but it cost me thousands. My place was quarantined for months, my cattle slaughtered. Fortunately, I had the boilermaker's trade to help me pay me debts.

Still, I don't regret a bit of it. No bluetongue or other disease came in. Actually, I helped set things afire. Before you knew it: Aah! They were bringin' in live horses, live pigs, live cattle. Now it's simple, bringing livestock from abroad.

I'M GRATEFUL to Gordon for sharing his tale of chances taken and prices paid. I should add, however, that some Australians don't think he paid enough. One stockman friend in Queensland with whom I checked faxed back: "They should have hung young Burcher by his thumbs for a good long while . . . let him consider the risk he put us all in."

The risk of foot-and-mouth disease—fiebre aftosa in Spanish, fievre afteuse in French, "FMD" in officialese—is a terror to stockmen, everywhere, who have seen it.

CATTLE DISEASE SAID LOCATED NEAR REGINA

CATTLE DISEASE BRINGS QUARANTINE DECISION

EVIDENCE SEEN THAT DISEASE *NOT* FOOT-AND-MOUTH

. . . so read the headlines in the Regina Leader-Post *in February 1952. A Canadian vet remembers:*

KENNETH WELLS, DVM

Winter of 1951–52: A disease outbreak in Saskatchewan; it could be foot-and-mouth, or it could be vesicular stomatitis, a less severe endemic disease with similar symptoms.[61]

We hoped it was stomatitis, but there was a delay in diagnosis because of an international understanding that suspect material would not be transported. Rather, diagnosis would be attempted on the site. Unlike foot-and-mouth, stomatitis affects horses, so we made up a vaccine from the tongues of sick animals and inoculated horses as well as the cloven-hoofed animals on premises. When results were not conclusive, we moved the material to Grosse Ile—taking a bit of flak for doing so, I might add.

Once diagnosis for foot-and-mouth was firm, Dr. Childs, the veterinary director general at the time, sent for me and packed me off to Regina to eradicate the disease. Having spent four months in Mexico, I was one of the few Canadians with experience.

It was a cold and desperate winter, which did nothing to inhibit the virus but *did* curtail the movement of livestock. That made our job much easier and, in the end, only forty-four Saskatchewan farms were infected.

The Americans immediately prohibited Canadian livestock and livestock products, of course, as we expected them to do; such restrictions were accepted on a worldwide basis. But of course the market fell, and the cost was high: According to notes I kept, direct expense was over a million dollars while the true cost was even higher—perhaps $100 million in loss of exports.

EMBARGO ON CATTLE CLARIFIED BY U.S.

ONTARIO BANS CATTLE SHIPMENTS FROM WEST

FARMERS WATCH AS CATTLE PIT DUG

. . . more headlines from the Regina Leader-Post in February 1952. J. D. "Doug" Baird was one of the people in the field.

Mountie posting a premises near Regina.
—Saskatchewan Archives Board

DOUG BAIRD

My office was in Regina, not many miles from the heartbreak. When the Americans slammed the gate, that fixed cattle prices; they had been going up since the end of World War Two and had just reached fifty cents. Now—boom!—they were back in the thirties and took a long time to recover, as you may remember.

We looked for contact herds. Any farmer who happened onto an infected farm became a "contact"; his own herd was condemned—not that his cattle had the disease, but they were suspect. I was the evaluator; after my visit, that was the end. The cattle were shot and buried in the dead of winter.

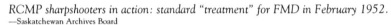
RCMP sharpshooters in action: standard "treatment" for FMD in February 1952.
—Saskatchewan Archives Board

POLITICS: Canada's Liberal Party was in power when foot-and-mouth broke out in 1952. Alvin Hamilton (not yet a Member of Parliament) was leader of the Conservative Party of Saskatchewan and, as such, relayed farmers' problems to John Diefenbaker, leader of Her Majesty's loyal opposition in Ottawa.

ALVIN HAMILTON

The policy was to shoot all animals exposed to FMD; the question was what compensation to pay. Minister of Agriculture Jimmy Gardiner [a Liberal] was not reporting the full story to the House, and the debate turned into a clash of credibility. John Diefenbaker [a Progressive Conservative] used my information; Gardiner went by the book.

In 1952 the suspect cattle (many of them purebreds) were worth several hundred dollars a head and, as I remember, seventy farmers were affected—perhaps 700 cattle in all. The legal rate for compensation was $20 or $30, and the farmers—my constituents—were hurting.

As a provincial politician visiting Ottawa, I could sit in the House gallery as an observer, going down occasionally to brief the members. Diefenbaker made a dramatic opening challenge, calling for reasonable compensation for the good people of Saskatchewan, whose cattle were being shot.

Prime Minister Louis St. Laurent called Diefenbaker off the floor, waved me down from the gallery, and met us outside the House where Diefenbaker said, "Prime Minister, don't ask me for details; Hamilton, here, has just come from Regina and has talked with Health of Animals and all the farmers there. Let him tell you what's going on."

St. Laurent listened to me for probably ten minutes; then he walked back into the House and overruled his own minister, saying, "When there is a clash between my ministers and the Conservative member [Diefenbaker] from Prince Albert, I usually find it wise to accept the advice of that member."

Not much later, compensation was set at $75 a head—a very important victory for Saskatchewan cattlemen.

U.S. OFFICIALS STUDY FOOT-AND-MOUTH IN CANADA
Regina Leader-Post, April 1, 1952

DR. FRANK MULHERN—USDA

I had just returned from fighting foot-and-mouth in Mexico when Washington sent me to North Dakota to liaise with Dr. Wells in Regina. I remember one North Dakota cattleman who proposed to fence the international boundary, and when I told him that would not be necessary, he said, "It may not seem necessary to you, but I've got a million dollars invested along this border, and it keeps me awake at night." Disease control is always political, and it seems to go through stages: panic, cooperation, apathy. In the panic stage, producers will stop at nothing.

There's no doubt the disease was foot-and-mouth, unlikely though it seemed in the face of the continental embargo then in force. I know of no more quali-

187

fied, ethical scientist anywhere in the world than Charlie Mitchell, the virologist who diagnosed it at Grosse Ile. And there was nothing wrong with moving the stuff to Grosse Ile; that island had been quarantined for generations. In my opinion, the Canadians went beyond the call of duty.

Actually, in the 1952 outbreak, the virus is believed to have arrived with a piece of sausage in the pocket of a German farmworker. We in the United States still confiscate tons of meat from tourists every year, and it wouldn't surprise me if the virus was hiding here, right now, waiting for the right conditions to break out.

U.S. EMBARGO HITS WINNIPEG
Cattle Feeders Face Big Loss
Regina Leader-Post, February 28, 1952

ALTHOUGH THE 1952 foot-and-mouth "break" never spread far from Regina, it affected people right across Canada, including one young Albertan who was just getting started in business.

KEN HURLBURT

I grew up in Milk River and was always at the shipping pens when old-timers from the west country, like Joe Snow and George L. Stringham, trailed their three-year-old steers to town.

One summer I worked on the "Quarantine," an unfenced range, and did I love that! Back to town with thirty bucks in my pocket from just two months of riding. What a life![62]

After the war I worked for Colburn Johnson, who shipped thousands of steers to the Corn Belt every fall. Before they could go to the States, those cattle had to be tested for TB and brucellosis, and if just one went down, the whole shipment was canceled, so Colburn had a feedlot, just in case. Soon I became manager, and one of my jobs was looking after that feedlot; you had to get out and hustle if you worked for Colburn.

When I was twenty years old I went out on my own as an order buyer. I was pretty smart. Nothing to it! I bought lots of cattle and bought 'em high. The market was up, up, up! I was makin' nothin' but money with my own little feedlot when foot-and-mouth broke near Regina. The border closed with a crash!

I had 600 two-year-old steers on feed at thirty-four cents a pound. Now they were worth twenty, and I was broke. I sold my equipment. I sold my feedlot. I was twenty-four years old and owed the bank $24,000! //

So, in I went to see Harry Hutchison, the banker (and one of the greatest! Gilchrists, Hargraves, all the ranchers in the south country knew him). Harry knew my story: "What do you plan to do, young man?" he asked.

"I aim to keep goin'," I said.

"Well, I have another suggestion," he said. "Bankruptcy."

I jumped to my feet and looked him straight in the eye: "I'll tell you one thing, Mr. Hutchison," I said, "at age twenty-four I'm *not* takin' bankruptcy! You'll get every penny you got comin'!"

Harry grabbed my hand. "Good luck, Ken! Now get outta here. I'll back ya!"

First thing was to go and see Rube Gilchrist on the Whitemud ranch. After Gilchrist Brothers sold in '45, Rube had bought himself a place near Waterton Park, but he hadn't liked the winters that close to the mountains, so now he was back on the Whitemud where he started. But the interim owner had brought in a lot of new cows and, with them, brucellosis; I'd heard that Rube was stuck with 300 drys.

I went to the ranch. "Mr. Gilchrist," I said, "I'm here to buy your cows." We drove around in his old black Chrysler and soon had a deal. There was just one problem:

"How do you plan to pay for these cows, young feller?"

"By cheque," I said.

"You got that much money in the bank?"

"No sir, I'm broke," I said. "But we can trail 'em in to Maple Creek on Friday; ship 'em to Burns in Calgary on Saturday; and I'll have money in the bank on Monday morning."

"I'll do a little checkin'," said Rube, and of course he phoned his buddy, Hutchison, and when he came back it was, "Okay, you bought some cows."

Well, I made a few bucks on those Gilchrist cows, and I took 'em right to the bank, and the banker told his customers who continued to sell me cattle; four years later I had paid back every cent, and I never looked back. As you can see, it was foot-and-mouth put me out of business, and Bangs disease put me back. Funny, how success often starts with failure.

AND KEN—*one of the greatest free enterprisers ever—went on to build his dream: a sale barn where a ranch family, kids and all, could sit in comfort and see their livestock sold. And meet their friends. And eat in a nice clean restaurant. And many a pleasant day I've spent at one of the Hurlburt markets at Fort Macleod or High River, the crossroads of Alberta cattle country.*

*N*OW, BACK TO *a former director of disease eradication for the USDA, a man who knows a few things about viruses.*

FRANK MULHERN, DVM

I have been fortunate from a career standpoint, to have worked on all the important eradications in my time: foot-and-mouth in Mexico and Canada; vesicular exanthema; sheep scabies; hog cholera; Venezuelan equine encephalitis, a viral disease of humans as well as horses; a virulent form of Newcastle disease in poultry; and lastly, with the Inter-American Institute for Cooperation on Agriculture, on the eradication of African swine fever in Haiti.

So I've been involved, directly or indirectly, with all the animal disease eradications in North America in modern times, and there's just one problem—that vesicular exanthema.

In 1931 or 1932, ves-ex or VES, a disease of swine that looks like foot-and-mouth, was found in California, where it stayed for twenty years. In 1952 it popped up across the country, and we traced it to a Cheyenne, Wyoming, hog producer who was feeding garbage from the transcontinental trains—including trimmings of uncooked pork from California.

That producer sold apparently healthy hogs to a plant at Lincoln, Nebraska, where they made hog cholera serum. He shipped others through the Omaha Stockyards, contaminating resting places everywhere with an incubating virus; vesicular exanthema soon appeared in forty-one states. It was diagnosed for the last time in New Jersey in 1956 and formally declared "eradicated" in 1959, after a direct expenditure of $39 million.

Now, here's what keeps me humble. I'm joking with a researcher: "Man, you know what I've done? I've eradicated the ves-ex virus from the face of the earth—the world!"

"You haven't eradicated nothing!" the researcher said. "It's around."

"If I can't find it, it's gone," I said—I'm cocky.

Thirteen years later my friend called up: "Ahem! Mulhern, I told you VES was still around, and now we've found it."

"You're kiddin'."

"Nope. We identified it in a dead sea lion on a California beach."

Hmm . . . That was 1972, and it's since appeared in several saltwater fish. So, eradicated? Hey, the seas are full of the stuff.[63]

So, how about "the face of the earth?" Years ago I was visiting with Richard Shope, discoverer of the flu virus, and—proud of my accomplishments—I told him we were eradicating hog cholera.

"Wait till you see what I've got here," said Shope, pointing to some plots of earth.

"What's that?" I asked.

"Your virus."

"Whaddaya mean?"

"I've been feeding some of your viruses to my earthworms. I can retrieve them anytime I want."

So . . . eradicated from the face of the earth? Hmm . . . Hog cholera has been recurrent since the 1830s. What happens to the viruses in the interim? Do they just go underground?

A SON FOLLOWS ON in Dr. Richard Shope's footsteps. He is an epidemiologist with a special interest in animal diseases, some of which, like rabies, also affect humans.

ROBERT SHOPE, MD

The swine flu story is interesting. In the old days, it used to break out every spring, costing farmers millions of dollars, and Dad, who discovered the flu virus, wondered where it wintered.

Well, there's a swine parasite called the lungworm, and Dad [Dr. Richard Shope] theorized that pigs cough up the lungworm, which goes to ground carrying the virus with it. There, one of the parasite's stages is ingested by earthworms, and pigs love earthworms. So, in spring, young piglets root out the worms, retrieving the virus, and starting another outbreak. Dad was able to demonstrate this in his lab.

I like to use a classic story to show the interrelationship between human and animal disease. Smallpox has been one of the most dreaded human diseases until recent times; it disfigured whole populations; large percentages died. Well, cows get a kind of "pox" on their teats and udders, and somebody back in eighteenth-century England observed that milkmaids often had pocklike nodes on their hands. But milkmaids seldom got smallpox. Interesting observation![64]

Putting two and two together, they wondered: If we purposely gave people cowpox, would it protect them from smallpox? They tried. It did. And a primitive "live vaccine" was developed.

So, today, we protect against smallpox, influenza, and many other viral diseases [including foot-and-mouth] with vaccination. But, before we produce a vaccine, we must first identify the type or subtype of the virus. That's where we epidemiologists come in.

I work at the Yale School of Medicine's Arbovirus Research Center, where we have the proper USDA permits to accept infected materials from around the world. We get stuff from Australia, Asia, Egypt . . . and, if a viral disease is suspected, our job is to identify it *fast*, so that safe vaccines and diagnostic sera can be produced in a timely fashion.[65]

191

Now, a virus consists of a protein plus a nucleic acid, the genetic material that tells a cell what protein to produce. We call virus proteins "antigens"; we call proteins found in the blood serum of recovered animals "antibodies."

Now, antibodies fight off associated viruses and protect from reinfection, and such a fight helps identify a virus. With reaction comes identification, so you can see that introducing a known antibody is the key. Our unique collection of reagents and antisera provides the keys to over 500 viruses. We strive for good, safe vaccines for all diseases from around the world.

Just think for a moment. If foot-and-mouth broke out in this country today, with modern highways and trucking, it could spread like wildfire; it was bad enough in the past.

Relying on test and slaughter only, we couldn't dig a deep enough pit to hold all the carcasses.

17   The *Aftosa!*

A S DIRECTOR *of USDA's Plum Island Animal Disease Center from its in-*
ception until his retirement in 1988, Jerry Callis knows foot-and-mouth well.

JERRY CALLIS, DVM

Foot-and-mouth, FMD, *aftosa,* is one of the most dreaded animal diseases in the world. First reported by an Italian monk in 1514, it was the first disease of any kind proved to be caused by a virus.[66]

Foot-and-mouth affects cloven-hoofed animals, or ungulates, by producing blisters around the crown of the hoof and the vesicles of the mouth. One of the last big outbreaks in the United States occurred in the early 1920s in one of the national forests in California. Once the disease gets started, it spreads quickly and insidiously, and in that instance military, USDA, and civilian hunters killed 22,000 deer and, once again, eradicated the disease.[67]

Each of the seven known types of the virus has subtypes so unique that immunity to one does not guarantee immunity to the others. The United States has had many battles with FMD, and when it appeared in Mexico in 1946, Uncle Sam responded with manpower and money: 2,000 men and, eventually, $132 million in cold, hard cash.

ROBERT ANDERSON, DVM
codirected the Mexican campaign

We found that the Mexican government had authorized two importations of zebu cattle from Brazil in violation of the tripartite agreement signed in 1931, and it was the second shipment that got 'em in trouble. The cattle were quarantined on Sacrificial Island off the city of Veracruz, then moved to Colonel Serrano's ranch—the same Serrano, I believe, who was in cahoots with Colonel Breen.

With foot-and-mouth, the first thing you see is strings of saliva droolin' from the mouth; eventually the whole mucous membrane of the tongue will pull right off in your hand. Pigs slough off their hooves. And there are associated chronic problems: heart disease, chronic mastitis, severely decreased milk production—any kind of production. Death loss is greatest among the young, but adult animals never totally recover, what with heart problems and all. An FMD outbreak is serious business.[68]

The first principle of any disease eradication—human, animal, whatever— is discovery and diagnosis; next is containment; third is elimination; and fourth is cleanup. In Mexico, the process involved inspection, quarantine, slaughter, and disinfection of premises; finally, test animals were collected and observed for any signs of a lingering virus.

As I recall, the Mexicans asked for diagnostic help in late November 1946. I went there in April but, with diplomacy and all, nothing was done till May

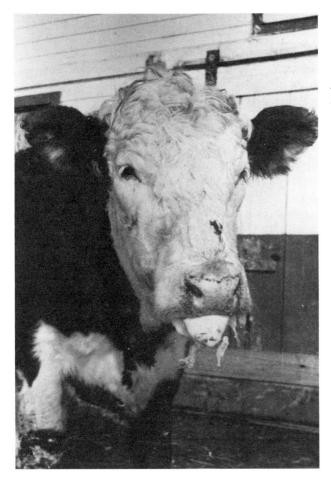

Cow with typical FMD symptoms. —Saskatchewan Archives Board

194

of 1947. The *aftosa* had a six-month lead between Sacrificial Island and Colonel Serrano's ranch.

Range scientist MARTÍN GONZALEZ, Ph.D.,
of El Paso, grew up in Coahuila and Nuevo León.

Right away the International Sanitary Commission—a joint effort between Mexico and the United States—was set up to control the *fiebre aftosa*. First job was to establish "sanitary barriers"—east-west transcontinental stop lines—north and south of the subtropical infected zone. Between those lines, all animals with symptoms would be killed, and you can imagine the social problems; you had to be very strict, very firm, to eradicate the disease.

Martín Gonzalez.

195

Within the infected zone there were many *ejidos* [rural communities], where the only money the people had came from one or two animals. Then, some people thought they did unnecessary killings in many places, and the natives were very, very angry. Sometimes they shot soldiers or even veterinarians, because they didn't understand the sanitary measures. As you can imagine, some officials were very "show-off" with their guns and uniforms and credentials; they thought they could do what they wanted. Even when they paid, the money couldn't buy more animals, which were the only patrimony in those villages.

Now, the ten northern states of Mexico were always free of foot-and-mouth, so here they didn't use the "sanitary rifle" [to put down the cattle], but we couldn't move our cattle, either. Immediately, the exportation of stocker cattle and weaner calves was suspended until the disease could be eradicated, and you might not understand what that meant to the ranchers here.

Northern Mexico is a semiarid region with millions of acres best suited to raising livestock. There's a potential domestic market a thousand miles to the south, in the big population centers of central Mexico, but it never did pay to send weaners and stockers south. So close to the border, our natural advantage is to produce good feeder calves for the U.S. market.

Then, in 1947, with live cattle under quarantine, something had to be done. Our cattlemen's associations were forced to build a series of slaughter houses and *frigoríficos* [coolers] so that we could export processed meat; one was built in Chihuahua, one in Piedras Negras, others in Laredo and most of the border cities. More plants were built in Zacatecas, Aguascalientes, and Monterrey, in the quarantined zone.

In the old days, cattle exports was the number three source of foreign exchange in the northern states. Then sugar went down, tobacco went down, coffee went down; now, perhaps, live cattle is number one. I guess those sanitary measures were necessary to free our country of disease and, eventually, renew the exportation, but it was a very serious times for Mexico—the *aftosa*.

BOB ANDERSON

With such high stakes, we had to get right to work. Using the old tripartite agreement as a basis, we immediately built the FMD eradication commission through an exchange of diplomatic notes. This set a precedent: the first time in history that two nations had joined in eradicating an animal disease.

Here's something we considered right from the start: Livestock always get to market somewhere, somehow; if the price is right, quarantine lines be damned!

So, when the border closed, we knew we would have to provide alternate markets for the cattle in northern Mexico, and we financed canning plants and arranged sales as far away as Greece, through the Marshall Plan, while other plants turned out acceptable carcass beef. Then, with such things in mind, a line was drawn, south of which all meat traditionally went to Mexico City. Likewise, south of the infected area a line was cleared through the jungle, and a barbwire fence was built to prevent "mistakes."

FRANK MULHERN

In 1947 I went to work in Tabasco, the state south of Veracruz, which is about 50 percent wetlands; we were keen to establish a quarantine area quickly in the south, knowing we'd have real trouble if the virus got a foothold there.

I was twenty-five years old and just out of vet school. My team included a Mexican army lieutenant, a Mexican veterinarian, a Spanish-to-English interpreter, a Spanish-to-Indian interpreter, and an interpreter from one Indian dialect to another (as though we expected some lengthy conversations). I was authorized to hire five saddle horses and ten mules for transportation.

Frank Mulhern on the job in 1948.

Exchange at the time was eight and a half pesos to the dollar, and I began paying five pesos for each horse or mule per day. The first night it went to ten pesos, the next fifteen, then twenty, then twenty-five; I had to set some limits. We were in mountains 10,000 feet high when I made my ultimatum: "Okay, guys, twenty-five pesos per horse is as high as I go. From here to the Gulf of Mexico, that's the standard fee."

"Muy bién, señor . . . ," and I went to bed thinking, "Boy, you sure do know how to handle people." When I got up next morning, all the pack animals were gone, and we hiked for the next five days before finding more. Such was my initiation into business in southern Mexico.

We stayed in dirt-floored school houses; the teachers were barefooted; illiteracy was high. Most people still used gourds as water containers; empty cans were treasures. One little village had an extremely high incidence of blindness due to Onchocerciasis—a fly lays eggs on the back of the head; the larvae burrow into the optic nerve. I asked one mule skinner why he didn't squeeze the grubs out.

"Hurt too bad," he said.

"You'll go blind," I told him. He didn't believe me.

After the northern and southern lines were drawn, the sixteen central Mexican states were divided into sectors, each with one U.S. and one Mexican cowboy, small enough for every animal to be inspected once a month. Anything suspicious, the cowboys called the vets.

"So, what's so bad about the *aftosa?*" the campesinos asked.

Well, the type-A virus in Mexico was said to be "highly invasive but with little virulence." That meant that in one area, infected animals might be obvious; in another, a high percentage could be carriers showing few symptoms. It was this second form, with undetected carriers, that caused problems.

Compensation was part of the plan, of course, and we paid in cash on the spot. Just as there were Mexican and American cowboys and veterinarians, there were Mexican and American paymasters; the American would count the money and give it to his counterpart who counted the money again and paid the campesino whose animal was condemned. Psychologically, it was a very good policy and something the locals had never seen before; I think we were paying $40 a head.

And what variety! Holstein milk cows in the settled areas, criollo cattle everywhere, and everyone had an ox—oxen were what you plowed with in central Mexico. Somebody in Missouri got the great idea of exchanging mules for the oxen, and the campesinos were given the choice of money or a mule. Some of the mules came back as fast as we delivered them.

"*Por qué* you don't want this mule?" we'd ask.

"He walks too fast," they'd say.

"Perhaps, if you plow deeper, the mule can't walk so fast."

"I do not wish to plow deeper; I will plow the same as with *el buey* [the ox]."

198

But some did not return their mules; some saw the benefits of deeper plowing—that's progress. I look back on our *aftosa* team as a forerunner of the Peace Corps.

The Mexican campaign was a brand new ball game, completely beyond our experience. On the advice of veterans of the foot-and-mouth campaigns in California in 1924 and 1929, we began to slaughter every sick animal; we slaughtered a million cattle, sheep, goats, and hogs in the very first year, and we didn't make a dent in the *aftosa*. Of course, many animals were moved before we found them. Resentment raged. Even with a military escort, some of our people got killed.

One of our Texas cowboys, a fellow named Proctor, was "dry gulched"—stoned to death in a little gully. A Mexican veterinarian and six soldiers were shot and stabbed. A short time later, I went into the village of Huahuapán, Oaxaca, with a Mexican colonel (tough as nails, but only five foot four), and our arrival was announced by the church bells. We were quickly surrounded by a crowd of unfriendly Indians who had no use for "sanitary rifles." Momentum built. Anxiety grew. We were in a very delicate situation: outnumbered fifty to one, and under the strictest orders not to carry guns in any circumstance.

Well, the colonel filled a big syringe with strychnine, waved it in front of the crowd, and injected it into a nearby cow. The cow went into paralysis; the crowd dispersed, staying clear of that "big medicine." We quickly inspected and killed the infected animals, paid compensation to the *presidente municipal*, and drove away with our big syringe taped to the hood of the jeep—in clear sight of anyone who might be watching.

I never told that story around headquarters. They would have canned me had they known how we did business in the boonies.

BOB ANDERSON

Unforgettable poverty! People begged for meat, but in the early days we didn't allow them to eat the animals we killed. Instead, carcasses were slashed and covered with slack lime with a bit of phenol added to make the meat, well, less attractive. Even so, people sometimes dug up the carcasses. Later, we learned that natural acids destroy the virus in twenty-four hours; after that we sold the meat locally, especially in districts that were already infected.

The spread of disease was never attributed to meat handled in that fashion, I'm happy to add.

FRANK MULHERN

There was a mesa in my district inhabited by Indians, isolated and hostile; even the army was afraid to go there on patrol. But there were cattle on that mesa, and they had to be inspected, so I sent a Mexican employee to make the arrangements. He came back naked, with a warning: "No gringos *aquí*."

Bert, a big ol' lanky cowboy from New Mexico, was with us for the challenge. "I'm lookin' for the roughest places you got," he said, "like in my grandad's time."

"By God, here's his chance," I thought, as I called him in and told him about the mesa.

Three days later Bert was back, thoroughly shaken, skunked. "When I got to the top," he said, "the chief was waiting in a clearing armed with a bow and arrow. I went through all the friendly greetings, and he never changed his expression. I offered him a cigarette; he didn't smoke. I rolled one for myself, acting friendly as could be—surrounded by hostile Injuns—and kept on talking. Finally, I flipped my butt to the ground, and the chief put an arrow through it. And he was glarin' as he notched another arrow. I got the message: 'Adiós, señor.'"

"Well," I said, "forget it. There's plenty to do down here. We'll find a key to the mesa sooner or later."

A few days later Bert came to see me; he was drawn and nervous, smoking one cigarette after another, short of sleep for thinkin' about that mesa. "Gotta go back!" he said

A mule skinner who spoke the dialect went along. Three days later the skinner was back with a message: "Bring the team."

Bert had offered to break the toughest bronc they had, and they'd brought him every outlaw on the mesa. By God, he had rode 'em all and won their respect. Finally, it was, "Okay, bring your gringos," and we completed a successful mission on the mesa.

JERRY CALLIS

"Quarantine, slaughter, and cleanup" had been the British policy in eradicating pleuropneumonia in the 1880s. USDA had followed suit, and by 1946 it was a time-tested, proven procedure. But one that didn't work in Mexico.

The method had never been tried in a place where livestock were like members of the family. In central Mexico in the forties, take away a fellow's ox, and you'd taken away his tractor, food, friend, and everything else. So the campesinos fought the veterinarians, and the Indians hid their cattle, and by the second year it was obvious that slaughter, alone, wouldn't work. It would have to be followed by a vaccination regime.

BOB ANDERSON

After eight months we had killed so many animals that we feared the economy of Mexico couldn't stand it. The people depended on oxen for "horsepower"; they depended on milk and cheese and meat for food. We had to find a way to break the chain.

We accomplished this by establishing an outer quarantine line, parallel to the first, and setting about to vaccinate every susceptible young animal in the buffer zone between them. The northern buffer was divided into ten districts, each with a head veterinarian responsible for six or seven areas subdivided into sectors. Finally, an inspector was assigned to inspect all cattle in each sector once a month. Each premises had a signed notice on the door, with the date of last inspection.

It was quite a campaign. Over the next few years sixty million cloven hoofed animals were vaccinated: five cc's for cattle; two and a half for sheep, goats, and swine. The first vaccines came from Switzerland, Denmark, and Argentina, while we were crankin' up production labs of our own. The procedure was to buy hundreds of clean but highly susceptible northern yearling cattle, bring them south to central Mexico, and there inject their tongues with infected material. Twenty-four hours later the cattle were slaughtered, their tongues removed, and viruses harvested for use in making vaccine.

FRANK MULHERN

So, having destroyed a million head of livestock in a little over a year, we stopped the killing in July 1948; then, by vaccinating all animals in the buffer zones, we hoped to solidly immunize the population.

Twelve months was the longest the virus was known to live outside the body and, since our vaccine gave four months protection, the plan was to vaccinate everything three times a year.

The old-timers said, "Forget it. Language barriers. Climate's different. Culture's different. You'll never do it here." But we did! In one year we immunized 99 percent of the populations of those zones—verifiable because our nonabsorbable vaccine left a clearly-visible nodule from each injection on the neck.

The real key to our success, though, was the public cooperation. Without it we could not have achieved complete coverage between those lines. If we had missed some animals, with pockets of infection smoldering, the disease could have burst into flame at any time.

BOB ANDERSON

We announced Mexico free of FMD in September of 1952 but maintained our northernmost line for a few years yet. It was just an imaginary line, but we had a verbal understanding with local authorities that animals *would not be allowed to cross it*—just in case of pockets of infection. But the virus never appeared in northern Mexico.

201

Well, I'm the oldest living member of the Commission for Eradication. Some fellow workers stayed on with the Commission for Prevention and made their careers in surveillance, providing a nucleus should disaster strike again. We formed many long-lasting friendships in Mexico, and we have reunions still.

But in 1953 I was kicked "upstairs," to assistant chief of regulatory programs, and I went to Washington, taking my black hat with me.

18 The Pugibet Herd

MANUEL GARZA ELIZONDO

My grandfather founded La Rosita ranch about twenty miles upriver from Nuevo Laredo in 1907; it's in the family since, and now my son, Manuel Garza Jr., is to follow the family tradition, which makes me glad. An animal science graduate of Texas A&M, Manuel loves ranching, as I do, and we try hard to be the best in this business of raising top-quality cattle.

In the late 1950s I was raising Herefords and Brahma-Hereford crosses when my father saw some Charolais at the Gudelio Garza Gomez ranch at Villa Acuña, Coahuila. "Son," he said, "you should try this cattle; they're big and heavy boned, and I heard they adapt well to the range. I'm gonna send you a couple of bulls to La Rosita; I hope you try them."

"Okay, Dad," I said, "I'll turn 'em loose with the others and wait what happens." These were not top Charolais bulls from Don Gudelio, but they left big, light-colored calves, and—sure enough—when I weaned 'em, they out-weighed the others by forty or fifty pounds. From then, I fell in love with Charolais cattle.

Well, as soon as I saw how good it was, I went back to Don Gudelio and bought more bulls. The next year I went to Max Michaelis: "Max," I said, "I want the best. What you got to sell?"

"I'm not selling any full-bloods now," Max said; but, finally, because we were very good friends and, perhaps, because he saw how enthusiastic I was about Charolais, he agreed to sell me five heifers and a bull calf. And I don't mind saying what I paid: $5,000 a head—a lot of money in 1960—but they were "Pugibet" cattle, and that's what I was after.

Now, it might surprise you to know that the parents of those Mexican cattle had been in the USA; here's how it happened:

In 1946, some years after Pugibet's death, his herd was bought by the Gilly family and kept in the state of Puebla. Then, in 1952, the whole herd was taken up north and crossed by the Rio Grande into Texas, and on to Lafayette, Louisiana. There the party keeping them tried, perhaps, to pass them off as "domestic"—maybe as white Shorthorns—but since they were quite a different breed, the USDA soon learned and concluded they were smuggled from Mexico—which, in fact, they were. Now, the government confiscated them until final arrangements were made to return these cattle to Mexico.

Meanwhile, the USDA kept very tight custody, highly concerned as they were about disease; even then, no cattle could be brought from central Mexico—precisely the state where the Gilly cattle were.

Finally, in 1955, the herd was returned to Mexico—most to Max Michaelis at his Rancho El Fortín, but a small part to a government station at Ajuchitlán, southwest of Mexico City. It's worth mentioning, I think, that 27 percent of the Pugibet herd at El Fortín was registered in the name of H. M. Kimball, senator of Louisiana.[69]

M. G. "MAXIMO" MICHAELIS *adds details:*

I was a teenager in 1952, so I guess I know the story. First of all, Juan Pugibet was a dedicated cattleman. To give you an idea of his dedication: He asked that a newborn calf from a favorite cow be brought to him on his deathbed; he had his hands on that special calf within an hour of his death. After he died in 1942, his cattle were kept together by another Frenchman, Gilly.

Some say Pugibet worried that the Charolais herds in France might not survive the Nazi onslaught and believed he was preserving the breed in Mexico. Be that as it may, in 1952 his seed stock—what we call the "Pugibet herd"— was taken to the States.

Now, at that time, after many years of guarding against the *aftosa*, the U.S. border was open again, and feeder steers were coming across by the thousands—with appropriate permits, of course. But the Mexican government, it seems, had come to consider the Pugibet herd a national treasure, and they denied Gilly's application for an export permit.

Then, frustrated, Gilly and his American partner, Broussard, moved them across the Rio Grande "without permission" and arranged for their keep at a Catholic school, hoping not to attract attention. Well, how ya gonna hide fifty or sixty big white cattle back in the 1950s when Charolais were *really* an "exotic" breed? Soon they were reported and impounded and, while the Mexican government negotiated their return, Gilly fled to France, and Broussard got five years in the federal penitentiary.

I got to know Alphe Broussard very well, and he was one of the finest gentlemen you'll meet—not just a common smuggler, by any means.

Now, here's how we got involved. Our herd at Kyle was quite inbred, going back as it did to *Iroquois*, a "Perez Treviño" bull. So when Daddy learned of the Pugibet herd, which went back to different bulls, being close at hand in

Louisiana, he was interested. Soon, he and his partners, Henderson Coquat and H. M. Kimball, were making plans to buy the herd and return it across the border to northern Mexico.[70]

I was given two weeks off from school to go to Louisiana with my father, and that was an education in itself; I learned French waiting in a Louisiana law office, and I remember Daddy saying, "Never go to a lawyer, Son, when you want to settle something." Finally, he and his partners told their attorneys what to negotiate and reached an agreement with everyone concerned. The cattle would go to El Fortín, and the Gillys and Broussards would retain a silent interest. Many years later we paid 'em off in cattle.

So, in January or February 1955, two or three years after their illegal entry, the Pugibet herd, now caked with Louisiana mud, was loaded onto trucks and returned under bond to Mexico. I remember one old cow that was almost ready to calve; a trustworthy man was posted to keep an eye peeled and fish her calf out of the truck box before it was trampled. Next day, the herd arrived at El Fortín—with one extra head, and that one clean of mud.

The next crisis came on a morning in May, just as the cattle were slicking off after three good months on Coahuila grass. The *federales* stormed the ranch at dawn, seized our Pugibet herd at gunpoint, and trucked it off to Querétaro, 800 miles to the south across the buffer. There the cattle were impounded behind the locked gates of an old hacienda, and I went down with Daddy while he and Mr. Kimball fought to retrieve their property. I saw the excitement; I watched tempers flare until we finally got possession of our cattle and nursed them back to health, while negotiating their return to northern Mexico.

As you probably know, the embargo had been lifted in 1952, but the joint commission still maintained a buffer, in which cattle movements were restricted. But that wasn't enough, it seems, for one group of Texas cattlemen who had applied the pressure to have our herd moved south—never again, they thought, would they compete with Texas cattle. That is what we believed.

Daddy knew how much power and *dinero* would have to be applied in so many places to have his cattle moved so far south, across the buffer zone and all, and he blamed the U.S. government for complicity. Once, when he was in Washington, he shook his finger under Secretary of Agriculture Ezra Taft Benson's nose, saying, "You, sir, are the biggest cow thief in the business! You have tried to rustle a million dollars worth of cattle in just one pull!"

That is how I remember the Querétaro affair.

205

THE BEST OF MEMORIES dulls with time, and some of the details of the Querétaro affair have yet to be sorted out; I'm glad to leave some of that to further research.

But Dr. Bob Anderson, "the fellow with the black hat" who worked for the USDA, was in Washington in 1955, and he remembers the affair this way:

ROBERT J. ANDERSON, DVM

It's my recollection that some brothers by the name of Babb actually drove the Pugibet herd across the border, and we had all kinds of trouble getting Mexico to take 'em back; they didn't seem that sorry to be rid of 'em.

The point to be remembered is that the herd had originated south, in the state of Puebla, and we had that understanding that nothing would be allowed to cross the buffer where everything was vaccinated. FMD had never been found in northern Mexico—and wasn't welcome, either, after all the trouble we'd had.

But the Pugibet cattle had come north across the buffer, then across the international boundary, and when we caught up with them, we inspected 'em every week, accounting for each one by brands and ear tags. I want to think it took two or three years to get those cattle back across the border; then they crossed the buffer zone again, both ways—to Querétaro and back.

And don't you know how frustrating this must have been to the International Commission on Prevention, whose job it was to keep our cattle healthy!

BUT THE GENES of the Charolais imports of thirties were in the North to stay, poised on the Rio Grande in 50,000 head of "domestic" cattle.

19   The Rio Grande

YOU HAVE ALREADY READ HOW, in 1934, Max G. Michaelis (the younger) drove Blanco and Plato (sons of the French bull Iroquois) across the Rio Grande at Eagle Pass, quite legally, for use on his father's Texas ranch.

Many other Texans did the same. Manuel Garza Elizondo thinks the following deserve mention: Robert Kleberg, of the King Ranch; Joe Pate, of Hidalgo; Cap Yates, of Alpine; Turner and Thomas, of Weslaco; Hogue Poole, of Catulla, Texas; and J. A. Lawton, of Sulphur, Louisiana. There were others who imported the big white Mexican cattle with the full knowledge and consent of the border authorities. All this before 1946, when the aftosa closed the border.

Then there are all those stories—widely believed—of Mexican Charolais bull calves "dropped" by Cessna or Piper aircraft on Texas ranches. Grossly exaggerated? Maybe. But stranger things have happened. In any case, by 1952 there were thousands of percentage Charolais cattle north of the Rio Grande.

A S EXECUTIVE SECRETARY of two early Charolais breed associations, Dick Goff knew many of the early breeders and listened to their stories.

DICK GOFF

My information was that the King Ranch of south Texas got hold of two Pugibet imports, Neptune and Ortolón, as early as 1934, by which time it was already famous for its red Brahma-Shorthorn cattle. Sensing a conflict of interest with its developing Santa Gertrudis breed, it eventually sold its white herd to Pete Frost, another Texan, and there were other perfectly legal imports.

Still, by the early 1950s it was amazing how many big white cattle were to be seen in the southern United States. One way or another, Charolais genes had been crossing the border in numbers, and usually nobody knew—or was about to say—just how.

I remember asking Max Michaelis about it. A bunch of us were sitting around the fire at El Fortín, visiting, drinkin' whiskey, and I said, "Max, you're the only guy on earth who can tell me how so many Charolais got across the border so fast."

"I know of a couple of loads," Max said, and he mentioned a ford of the river.

"How come no one ever gets caught?" I asked.

"Maybe they do," Max said.

"What happens then?"

Nobody said a word. Max turned to another visitor, a Texan: "Know anything about that, Jim?"

"Yeah," Jim grinned. "I spent two years in jail for drivin' a truck."

A THOUSAND MILES TO THE NORTH, *a rancher on Ford Creek in Montana became the first Charolais breeder in the Treasure State. He's a "character," of course, and a top hand with a story.*

BUDDY COBB

I took over the ranch from my mother and sisters in 1952, payin' $300 a cow. By 1953 cows were worth $150, and I was out $50,000; I lost about fifty grand for the next three years.

We were running commercial Herefords—good 'uns; Father had been buying bulls in Canada, where a few breeders hadn't yet gone "comprest." But, even so, our calves were weaning small and finishing light, and I was goin' broke with "six-weight" [cattle weighing 600 and some pounds; see glossary] yearlings and thousand-pound, three-year-old spays.

We are grassmen first, on the Cobb ranch, and I had enough sense to know that we couldn't raise more *head*; what we needed was more *cow*! And I kept reading about improving British cows in terms of a 5 percent "kick."

That didn't interest me. Hell! The buyers docked you more than that on color. I needed all the kick I could get! Then I saw an ad: "Get ya two hundred pounds more calf with Charolais." I wired the guy: "Ship me a carload of heifers."

"Dear Mr. Cobb," a wire came back. "Doubt if carload of pure Charolais in whole United States. Happen to have cow due to calve six months. $5,000 down puts name in hat. (Signed) M. Cohon.".

Wow! *Only* $5,000 *down*, for a *chance* on a calf! That was the first I knew what Charolais were worth. I never answered, but I met Morris Cohon some years later, and we had a good laugh. He was a very wealthy man with a very good nose for a deal.

That winter I went to Arizona, where I came on hundreds of big white cattle grazing in a field. They appeared to be livin' on cactus—but fat!—and the sign said, "Oak Bar Ranch—Division of Spreckles Sugar." I drove in and met Peter Lewis, one of the heirs, who showed me two big bulls and gave me a lesson: "Which bull d'ya like the best?" he asked.[71]

"Why, *that* bull, there," I said, knowing nothing about it.

"You're right!" Peter said. "He's the best bull on the place. And let that be a lesson to ya! That other bull is a purebred; cost me $20,000 and ain't worth a damn. The one *you* picked is only ⅞, and I only give $800 for him; he's the better bull by far."

I got the message: *Never buy a bull on blood alone.*

Well, I sure was impressed with the Oak Bar, which by 1955 had 5,000 head of percentage Charolais, and their biggest market was back in Mexico. But when I asked about buying a bull, Peter Lewis referred me to a character closer to home: Clint Ferris, of Tie Siding, Wyoming.

Now, Clint was a hometown boy who had made his pile on Madison Avenue—wrote the ads for Carter's Little Liver Pills, Wheaties, and put Tarreytons on the map with "the thinking man's filter." I noticed that Clint smoked Camels, but he sure was a *record-keepin'* man; he had his bulls on "performance" at Fort Collins, Colorado—one of the first such tests around.

So, next spring, oh, we were havin' a hell of a time! I'd just got done with taxes and, again, had lost a hell of a lot of money. So, I went to the lower ranch one day where Hy Krebs, my foreman, lived, and I says, "Hy, go pack your suitcase."

"Why?"

"We're goin' to Colorado."

"Why?"

"Why, to buy a Charolais bull!"

"Oh!"

Hy still lives in Augusta; he's always been a Hereford man, but that day we got in the pickup and drove to Fort Collins, Colorado, and hunted up the test station, and there we found ol' *Snowball*, a ¹⁵⁄₁₆ Charolais and the top-gaining bull off test. We brought him home and turned him out, and Hy didn't have much to say; he loved his Herefords, but *Snowball* wasn't bad. In two years he sired 124 calves averaging ninety-three pounds over our Herefords at weaning.

Based on that performance at two bits a pound, it would take five Hereford bulls to replace him, and in those days you could buy a hell of a Hereford for $500. I could give $2,500 for a good Charolais and still make money.

But of course I'd never seen a "real" Charolais; all I'd ever seen was Charobray [Charolais-Brahma cross], so late that fall when Hy was gettin' "ouchy" again I says, "Hy, why don'cha get outta here? Go see what the rest of the country looks like."

Well, Hy had never taken a real vacation and didn't know where to go, so I said, "Why'n'cha go to Texas and look for a *good* Charolais?"

"Okay," says Hy; so him and his wife heads south, and pretty soon I get a call from Fort Worth, "Buddy, come down here quick! They got the biggest doggone cattle I ever seen!"

"Well, if they're that good," I says, "just buy five bulls."

"No, no; you gotta see 'em." So I got on an airplane, and they were *big* but owned by one of them Texans, and you know Texans! Right off the bat, this one's talkin' $20,000.

So we looked around the country. Cap Yates's cattle just up the road weren't no bigger than our own. So, finally, back to the first, a guy called Buck: "We ain't got your kind of money," I said. "We're just commercial cowmen. Most we can give is $2,500."

"Sold!" said Buck, and I shoulda been leery right then, with the price droppin' $18,000 overnight. But we picked five bulls at $2,500 each and—like in Montana—closed the deal with a handshake. "Ship 'em!" I said.

It was 10 below zero when those bulls come off the truck on Christmas Eve, and not a one was a bull we'd picked. One was so old he had to "gum" his feed. But, the ear tags were right! Now, how could the ear tags be *right* and the cattle *wrong*?

The only explanation was the ear tags had been switched. I called Buck: "Whatcha tryin' ta pull?" I asked him.

"Well, every bull you picked went down on Bang's," he said; "I didn't think you'd mind if I substituted."[72]

Mad! Was I ever mad! They was quarantining Texas cattle for Bang's. Maybe these had been tested; maybe they hadn't. "Folks up here," I said, "would do ya the courtesy of tellin' ya the facts," and I hung up and called my lawyer down in Billings. Art Lamey had run for governor, been UN ambassador, done a lot of business with the oil patch; when I told him about my deal he says, "Buddy, Buddy, Buddy! How many times do I hafta tell ya: 'Stay away from Texans!'"

He says, "I bet you went and threatened the guy!" And I had.

And he says, "Now, don't you go back down there, Buddy! Them Texans got funny laws. Right after Christmas you just load up and send those cattle back. Send Hy with 'em and keep in touch; I'll tell ya what to do."

So, Hy went back and supervised while a vet tested several hundred of old Buck's cattle and come up with just thirteen head that wasn't "Bangers." We took 'em all, and ol' Buck cried but couldn't do nothin' about it—even when Hy took *Samson*, another "$20,000 bull."

Of course, *Samson* wasn't papered so I couldn't register his calves; but later I sold a son to ol' Lloyd Schmitt at Stanford, who sold him to Carnation Farms, who proved him as one of the first Certified Meat Sires in the country.[73]

Nobody knew for sure where ol' Buck's cattle came from—whether he'd smuggled 'em, or what—but that "gummer" carried Michaelis's brand, and Max told me later he was one of the old originals out of France; had to be over twenty, but that was nothin'. I've had Charolais cows wean twenty-one, twenty-two calves.

Well, I was just tryin' to raise enough *pounds* to stay in business; didn't intend raisin' pure Charolais. I come to the conclusion that purebreds are a con man's game: one guy sells "the best in the world" for $800; another gets $20,000—he's a salesman! I learned another lesson from all this: *To hell with eyeballin' cattle; just be careful who you deal with!*

Charolais cows on the Cobb ranch in Montana. —J. E. Larcombe

AND ONE OF BUDDY'S closest and most trusted friends is this third-generation Texas Charolais breeder:

MAXIMO MICHAELIS

By 1949 enough Charolais had been crossed with Brahma that the American Charobray Association was formed as a stepping stone towards $^{31}/_{32}$—"pure." Next came the American Charolais Association and the International [Charolais Association] in 1951 and 1952. Later, they merged as American International [Charolais Association (AICA)] and accepted Charobray as a division.

There were conflicts. Grampa, as I told you, kept good records; others went by looks and color. Pedigrees were often based on eyeballing; many ¾ and ⅞ cows were appraised and registered as purebred in those days.

And purebred politics are the worst! Daddy and his partners had a tremendous investment in the Gilly-Broussard herd, whose success depended on the sale of *registered* seed stock. So, before they returned to Mexico, Daddy registered his cattle in the American International, of which he was a founder; but, once they were out of the country, the directors—in their wisdom—ruled that registry was only valid for cattle in the United States.

That made our cattle less attractive to U.S. buyers, and Daddy saw it as an attempt to cut competition. But he was a fighter and held his fire until 1958, when he and other breeders started the Herd Book International.

Then, they went AICA one better with five-generation pedigrees, gaining USDA recognition and World Bank eligibility for their customers' loans.[74]

MANUEL GARZA ELIZONDO

Once we saw the need for an official registry in Mexico, we organized the Charolais Herd Book International [CHBI]. Headquarters: Piedras Negras, Coahuila. First president: Max Michaelis Jr.

In 1962, with General Alejo Gonzalez as president, we held the first Charolais Congress of the Americas in Nuevo Laredo and had a very big success with visitors from Central America, the United States, France, England, and Canada. The guests of honor were Governor Norbert Treviño Zapata of Tamaulipas and Secretary Gilberto Flores Muñoz of the Mexican Department of Agriculture; even Canadian minister Alvin Hamilton was there. I had the honor on that occasion to be elected CHBI president to serve from 1963 to 1965.

And another thing, very important: It was announced right there at the congress that—for the first time, legally—Mexican breeders would be allowed to export Pugibet cattle. Max Michaelis, Gudelio Garza Gomez, and Dan Breen sold bulls on the spot.

BUDDY COBB

I attended that Congress, and by that time Max was treatin' me like a son. I couldn't buy nothin' from him. When I saw a bull I liked, he said, "Take him home; he's yours. Just don't sell him in case I want him back." That's how I got ol' *El Fortín*.

Now, there was nothin' some Americans wouldn't do to keep Mexican cattle out. Somehow, the dipping vat at Eagle Pass got mixed too heavy on arsenic—enough to "cook the nuts" on bulls.

El Fortín was dipped that day, but Max was right on the spot, saw what was going on, and washed him down. Other bulls was ruined, but *El Fortín* left lots of good calves on the Cobb ranch, so I put him out with ABS for collection.

I USED El Fortín semen on my SN cows in Alberta in 1964 and 1965 with good results: His calves came easy and grew like weeds. We still get good yellow "throwbacks," thirty years later.

We never knew, nor cared, if El Fortín was "papered" (although I suppose he was). Registration then, as now, was a political, devious process with no effect, whatever, on production. Buddy Cobb continues:

About the time of the congress, somebody put me up for AICA director. But just before the vote they called me in: "Say, Buddy, what's you and them other guys testin' for in Denver?"

"Why, for honest cattle," I said.

"Well, if word gets around that Charolais ain't honest—have to be tested—it'll give us all a bad name. We're taking your name off the ballot."

And they did, and I guess they were right. Performance testing has ruined many a reputation. In fact, the old American International would register anything *white*, but there was nothin' "international" about 'em. As one director said, "Stay away from Europe! We got a good thing goin'; that France'll break us."

And so it was that Clint Ferris and I and a few other performance-minded breeders got together with old Dick Goff in Denver and organized the Pan American Charolais Association [PACA]. We set it up for both performance record keeping and artificial insemination, and, with that kind of competition, the other associations were never the same again.[75]

DICK GOFF

And therein lies a tale. As the only association of any beef breed to accept calves from AI, it was perfectly logical that PACA should attract new breeders and threaten AICA's dominance.

Soon we were ready to take control and went to AICA with a proposal for merger—it wasn't automatically accepted, to say the least. The president was an overbearing fellow named Homer Peterson who had made millions in construction during World War Two, and when PACA began taking business away with performance and AI, why, he was just going to tromp us into the ground.

Now, in those days, the National Association of Animal Breeders (NAAB) served about 15,000 AI technicians and kept in touch with them through *A. I. Digest.* Of course, they were mostly involved in the dairy industry, but I—as an advertising and promotion man—was acquainted with the publishing world and knew the *Digest* editor well. So, one day I got to brainstorming and came up with an idea.

The AI business was very slow in winter. What if we offered every technician a chance to represent PACA—the only beef association that accepted AI calves? Wouldn't that get their attention? And what if we got them selling memberships by letting them keep half the fees? We could raise our PACA membership fee from $50 to $100 and split it fifty-fifty with the technician; in addition, we'd furnish a list of every PACA member in his state. It wouldn't be hard for a guy with real good contacts to make a couple of thousand dollars in his slack—that was a hell of a lot of money in the fifties.

So, we had all this worked out and were ready to go with an ad in the *A. I. Digest* when I went to AICA again and said, "Homer, let me show you what'll happen if you don't accept a merger."

Well, he was ready to start trompin', but I brought out my easel with a blowup of my ad and said, "This has all been discussed with the NAAB; all I have to do is pick up the phone and 15,000 salesmen will be on the road next month. If only one in ten sells a PACA membership, that's 1,500 members. Can you beat that?"

Old Homer got red in the face; I thought he might have a heart attack, but all he said was, "Gimme that agreement!"

So AICA decided AI was here to stay. And they decided there was no point in two associations competing for one breed. PACA had done its job; the name remained AICA. And I got the ad and promotion account for the combined operation.

Manuel Garza Elizondo (2nd from left) with representatives of fifteen national associations—at Vichy, France, September 1963.

MANUEL GARZA ELIZONDO

A great opportunity for the Mexican Charolais breed was lost in 1963, while I was CHBI president.

In September a gala was held in Vichy, France, on the hundredth anniversary of the Herd Book, and I was honored to represent Mexico among twenty-one other countries of the world. The newly appointed Canadian minister of Agriculture, Harry Hays, was a participant; he was a very nice person and a highly respected cattleman.

We visited several times, and Hays said, "Mr. Garza, it's been thirty years since the Pugibet importations; it's time Mexico had some new genetic material."

"I agree, Mr. Hays," I said. "But you know the hoof-and-mouth disease; we can't bring French cattle in."

Mr. Hays said to me, "My government is opening a quarantine in the St. Lawrence River, and we can let your government use it; you can import cattle from France, quarantine them in Canada, and fly them across the United States to Mexico."

215

I said, "Mr. Minister, I think that's a *great* idea. You are actually offering the use of your facilities?"

"You'll have to come and work out the details," Mr. Hays told me, "but you can count 100 percent on my support."

I was very glad to hear it—so happy, that I bought one very good bull in France, thinking I could get him home to Mexico. But when I went to officials in Mexico City, the answer was "No!"

I couldn't believe it! I begged. I explained the improvements we could achieve on the Charolais breed, but our secretary of Agriculture, a professor called Gil Preciado, was afraid of the hoof-and-mouth.

I went to President Lopez Mateos. He wasn't interested. He wasn't cattle people. He didn't understand.

Harry Hays was a cattleman. He was also said to have an interest in a Charolais bull, but—be that as it may—he did everything in his power to make things happen, and they happened! Canada has, today, some of the best Charolais in the world, and we had that same opportunity in Mexico.

So Mexico lost out; but, to this date, I personally appreciate that very nice gesture of good will by Canadian minister Harry Hays back in 1963.

It would be another ten years before Mexico imported, again, French Charolais.[76]

216

20   The Forty-ninth Parallel

IN 1949 THE CANADIAN *experimental farm service sent my friend Harry Hargrave off on a "tour of discovery" through the western United States, where he found a gold mine.*

After visiting land-grant colleges, research stations, and ranches across the country, Harry came home with a wealth of ideas on management, selection, and crossbreeding, among other things. And, so highly respected was Hargrave that the new ideas were soon being tried on many Alberta ranches—including the JH ranch near Medicine Hat, then owned by his brother Bert.

BERT HARGRAVE

Harry visited Frank Campbell, an Arizona rancher who had been using Charolais for several years, and Harry was so impressed with what Frank showed him that he kept talking up Charolais at home. A few years later, Campbell sent him a calf.

Well, the price was right, but of course Harry couldn't keep him, so he promptly phoned me up: "Bert, I'm shipping you a bull. He's different. But, whatever ya do, don't shoot him and don't send him to market till I get a chance to explain."

And a few days later, here comes this ⅝ Charolais calf with some Shorthorn and a shot of Brahma in him. He grew to be *huge*, and we used him on the JH for a number of years.

YOU MAY RECALL, *at this point, that the Hargraves and the Gilchrists were the very first customers for the growthy Line One Hughes bulls in Montana. The cow business, as always, is international.*

BILL GILCHRIST

By the time Dad rebought the Whitemud (brucellosis and all) in 1951 [see Ken Hurlburt's story, page 219], I was up and runnin'. And Dad, who was pushing seventy, liked to winter in Arizona, where he met Frank Campbell. No doubt, Harry Hargrave introduced them.

This Frank was quite a character, always giving away bull calves to promote the breed, and he offered Dad a couple of bulls as well; all we had to do was go get 'em.

So I went south in the spring of 1953 and trucked them home as yearlings, and they produced the first Charolais ever seen in Saskatchewan. We decided to feed 'em ourselves, because no buyer in those days wanted a crossbred calf, and they made us nothin' but money. I think those Campbell bulls were the first Charolais in Canada.

AN EARLY CONVERT to Charolais was eastern Canadian farmer Gerard Lalonde. When Claire and I visited his farm on the outskirts of Ottawa, he told us this story.

GERARD LALONDE

My first look at the breed was *Sir Alto*, imported by the Maple [Ontario insemination] unit in 1957 from the Turner ranch in Texas. I immediately bought some semen and bred six Hereford cows; the next year I bred more and, by 1959, had nine half-blood females on the ground.

By then, I had joined the new Canadian Charolais Association and had attended a meeting in Calgary where I was elected director for Ontario. I was enthused! It's easy to get enthused if you spend much time in the West.

Bill and Helen Gilchrist sent me notice of a meeting at their ranch. I didn't know how to get there, so I asked Fred Leslie [registrar of Canadian Livestock Records], "How the hell do you find the Cypress Hills?"

"First you have to find Maple Creek—a hell of a hole!" Fred said. [This is tough on a very friendly town.] "You want to fly to Regina and take a train that stops to pick up cream cans along the way. But be prepared! There's only one hotel at Maple Creek."

So I phoned up Bill: "I'm taking the late train Tuesday; get me a room," and I staggered off that goddamn train at four o'clock in the morning. "You got a bed for me?" I asked the clerk. "My name's Lalonde."

"Nope. Nothing at all."

"What? Not even a bench in the lobby?"

Nope. Just one room saved for a guy with a funny name."

"Oh, shit!" I said. ("Dese Anglos . . . ," I thought.) "That's me!" [And Gerry, a good-natured fellow, laughs.]

So I stayed a couple days at the Gilchrist ranch and got to know the western directors—friendly people; beautiful country. Bill Gilchrist always claimed the first Charolais in Canada—and I believe him, too—although, I think the first *real* Charolais in was the ⅞ bull imported by the Malmberg boys in 1955.

DENVER-BASED Dick Goff saw his first "true" member of the Charolais breed in Canada.

DICK GOFF

When I left my job with the Colorado Cattlemen, I piled my family into the "wagon" for a month-long trip to Canada: up the B.C. coast, over the Rockies, and home across the prairies.

That was the summer of 1957, and I'd heard of the Malmberg boys who were using a ⅞ Clint Ferris bull on their ranch near Waterton Park. I called from the Prince of Wales Hotel: ". . . Wonder if I could come out and shoot some pictures?"

"Sure," Wayne Malmberg said. "It ain't very far."

So, I got a story on ¹⁵⁄₁₆ Charolais calves produced on the northern plains, which I sold to the *Record-Stockman*, which featured it in their "Stockshow" edition in 1958—which made me an instant "expert" on Charolais.

THE MALMBERGS of Spring Coulee had a long tradition of crossbreeding, but Wayne and his brother Max were heavily into Herefords when they discovered Charolais on a trip to Texas.

Wayne had better luck with the Texans than Buddy Cobb; Harl Thomas, whose ranch he visited, thought it wrong to ship cattle all the way to Alberta. So, like Peter Lewis of the Oak Bar, he advised Wayne to visit Tie Siding, Wyoming. There, "thinking man" Clint Ferris must have seen Wayne coming, for he sold him a ⅞ bull for $1,100—the bull that really got the Charolais breed going in Canada.[77]

KEN HURLBURT

The Malmbergs had always been known for terrific cattle. And, boy! The comments that went around! "What're those Malmbergs doin'? Wrecking the greatest set of Herefords you ever saw!"

But I'll never forget the big, beautiful, yellow, whitefaced steers they brought to the yards a few years later; beautiful cattle—but they sold at a sharp discount because of color. The packers discounted them even when they were fat.

It took guts for pioneer ranchers like the Malmbergs to continue what they believed in, and they *really* believed in a future for Charolais. They never looked back. They didn't let up. And time has proven them right.

SID LORE

I used to travel Alberta in the sixties, explaining "performance" and weighing calves as part of my job as provincial livestock fieldman. Many ranchers were considering drastic changes in their cow herds, and the Charolais crosses I began to see were often flighty and hard to handle—partly, at least, because of hybrid vigor. Crossbreds tended to be more "alert" than purebreds, and in my business you wanted to be pretty alert, yourself! Or prepare to be trampled!

The Malmbergs are certainly remembered as the first real Charolais breeders in Canada, but it wasn't long till the Bennetts, Bargholzes, Branums, Rouses, Rudigers, and others, especially in the Red Deer area, began getting people excited about their breed.

HOWARD FREDEEN

Harry Hargrave and I set up many livestock meetings and brought in people like Scotty Clark from Montana to speak to our breeders, but I attribute the rapid acceptance of so many new ideas to the early Charolais breeders.

Scotty Clark was a great spokesman for "performance," but the established breeds weren't interested in performance testing. The founders of the Canadian Charolais Association, on the other hand, were underdogs who had to pull together; they filled their committees with commercial cowmen—beef men!—and the beef industry benefited greatly from their actions.

The people out for an easy buck came later—with "The Importation."

BUT, BEFORE THOSE "people out for an easy buck" came others I call "the adventurers." Some had money to burn; others had only the shirts on their backs to risk on a good idea.

Rodney James (no adventurer, he) was a down-to-earth founding member of the Canadian Charolais Association, its first executive secretary, and founding editor of the Charolais Banner.

ROD JAMES

Along about 1956 I read an article in *Cattlemen* about artificial breeding. Frank Jacobs, the author, had taught me animal science in high school, and I rang him: "Frank, you really think AI's got a future?"

"I surely do," said Frank; so, I hold him responsible for me being in the AI business when Roy Snyder brought *Sir Alto* into Canada.

In 1957, four or five thousand cows were bred to *Sir Alto*. I bred several hundred to him, myself, and when branding time rolled around in 1958, a lot of people were talking Charolais![78]

I was sitting in Harry Vold's auction at Ponoka when a customer asked what I knew about the breed.

"Not much," I said; ". . . new breed; some in the States; one in Ontario. I've been writing for information about Charolais." And a fellow sitting in front of me turned: "Did I hear you say 'Charolais'?"

"Yep. Ever hear of 'em?"

"Name's Rawe," he said, "from Strome. My brother Jim is in Texas buying Charolais right now."

That night I traced Jim Rawe to his hotel in Texas and asked him to buy me a couple of heifers sight unseen (you could get away with that sort of thing in those days). Jim agreed, and the heifers he bought got me off to a very good start.

*J*IM RAWE *was a controversial player in the Charolais business—a maverick; I had only met him once when I started this book. The year was 1964. The place, Calgary. The occasion, an early meeting of the Canadian Charolais Association.*

I had been attracted by the international panel of "experts": H. J. Hargrave, Roy T. Berg, Howard Fredeen, Scotty Clark, and Lloyd Schmitt among them. At lunch I sat near a rancher talking with a vestigial Kentucky drawl about a recent English adventure. He got my attention. It sounded pretty adventurous to me. Here, it turned out, was a Canadian rancher, who had served a hitch in the U.S. Army; later, he had stayed in the South working on the railroad.

JIM RAWE

In 1956 I was working as a Southern Pacific brakeman when my brother, back in Alberta, sent me a clipping about Charolais. That was the first I ever heard of the breed, but it wasn't long till I saw one at the Los Angeles stock show and couldn't believe my eyes!

Next spring I went to Roy Hislop's place at Phoenix and gave $1,000 for a $^{31}/_{32}$ "bred-up purebred" heifer. That was *Miss Julie*, AICA F627, first purebred Charolais in western Canada.[79]

Soon I was buying more percentage cattle and became so excited I decided to give up railroading and go ranching with my brother. All we could talk of was *real* Charolais—the ones in France. Just like a mountain bein' there: Some fool's gonna climb it, and I wanted to be first.

Then, from a copy of the English *Farmer-Stock Breeder*, I learned that the English Milk Marketing Board had imported French Charolais bulls to "freshen" Friesian milk cows and improve the English beef.[80]

That gave me an idea: Why not take a heifer to England, AI her to a Milk Board bull, and bring her home in-calf to a French Charolais? Oughta be easy—Canada and Britain both being Commonwealth countries. Or so I thought till I met two junketing English politicians, John Mackie of the British Labour Party and Peter Embry, a Conservative. I invited them to Strome and showed them our cattle. They were interested, but, Mackie said, "you'll never get 'em to England. The minister won't permit it."

Now, this is where I take my hat off to Canada's chief veterinarian, Dr. Ken Wells. When I inquired, Ken said, "Jim, you don't need a permit; you can take your cattle over on the English Importation Order of 1933.[81]

So, that took care of that. All I had to do was meet the health requirements, and the English ministry couldn't stop me. Pretty simple. There was just one little hitch: One section of the order read: "If, in the opinion of the Minister, such cattle fail to meet British standards . . . they may be slaughtered." Well, what the hell! I decided to try the system, ship one over, see what happened, and that's how my six-month-old Charolais heifer, *Bebe*, went to England in 1962.

That was the year of the Big Toronto Fog. That was the year they canceled the Grey Cup game with twenty-one seconds to play because they couldn't find the football. Hell, they couldn't find the *field*. Hell, airplanes couldn't find *Toronto*, where I had lined up overseas transportation for *Bebe*. I had to move her to Montreal.

GERARD LALONDE

We always remember that time when Toronto was fogged in, and the Grey Cup game was quit, and I became involved to find Jim a truck to bring his heifer to Montreal so they could fly to England. Jim stayed with us for a week, and of course I did find out—just by putting pieces together—that it was Andy Williams from the Turner ranch in Texas (the same that had raised *Sir Alto*) that was behind his big adventure. Jim Rawe, I guess, was only the front Canadian. Still, the venture took lots of guts and determination and was one of the events that prompted the "importation."

JIM RAWE

When a London-bound DC-6 freighter arrived in Montreal, I jumped on with my heifer.

"Sorry, sir, but our freighters don't haul passengers," the loadmaster said.

"You better call your office." I said, "You can tell 'em there's a passenger riding this one." No way was I gonna let my heifer beat me to London. She'd be hangin' in a cooler when I got there.

Pretty soon he came back: "We can't believe it, Mr. Rawe; you're authorized to ride with the freight."

But just before takeoff I received a wire from the British high commissioner in Ottawa. Mr. Christopher Soames, the minister responsible for the Milk Board, had stood in the English Parliament and stated a new regulation:

Henceforth, Charolais semen would *not* be authorized for use on a Charolais female; it would be used for crossbreeding only.

"Recommend you cancel plans," warned the high commissioner.

Well, there wasn't no other Charolais females in Britain, so this was aimed at me. But things had gone too far; I wired back, "Advise Mr. Soames we're comin'."

There must have been fifty reporters at Heathrow when we arrived! My heifer went to the quarters of the Royal SPCA, where they let her out of her crate and held a thirty-minute conference. Finally, they signed a release; *Bebe* was free to stay.

But then I made a terrible mistake. I announced that my heifer would be stabled on John Mackie's farm. Then the officials had me. Mackie was a "Labourite." No way could one of Her Majesty's bulls serve Her Loyal Opposition.

Jim Rawe and Bebe *in London.* —Rural History Centre, University of Reading (England)

I left my heifer in England, and as far as I know she died a virgin—never bred by a Charolais or anything else.

But that's not the end of the story. In 1963 I tried again, shipping three rising two-year-old heifers to England by boat. When they came ashore at Birkenhead, the British government condemned them as "unsuitable for breeding."

"Okay," I told the officials, "I'll move 'em to Scotland and take 'em home when they're clear."

You see, you can't ship cattle direct to Canada from England; you must first take them to Scotland, have them tested, and leave them for sixty days. But the British officials were onto me; they knew as soon as my heifers were on Scottish soil I'd round me up some semen and breed them. They wouldn't let 'em leave England.

Once more, Dr. Wells came to my rescue. If the English would certify that my heifers hadn't been in contact with other cattle, he'd give me a permit. So across they came to New Brunswick, where I drove in the dead of winter to haul three very well-traveled, very expensive, very virgin heifers home to Alberta.

I was "zero for two" in the import game.

But that's still not the end of the story. I had purchased some $^{15}/_{16}$ "purebreds" from Mack Braly in Oklahoma. Then, early in '64, I went down to the performance-test station at Tishomingo, Oklahoma, and purchased *Paul*, a bull with a five-pound-per-day gain—a new world record! Soon, I had a letter from Armour & Company, the big American packer; they wanted *Paul* for BCI, their beef cattle improvement center based at the Codding ranch in Oklahoma.[82] They wanted just a half interest at a very nice profit for me, and I began getting inquiries on all my Charolais cattle.

"It's about time," I thought. "I'm gonna make some money."

Ha, ha, ha! Just then the Canadian minister of Agriculture made an announcement: "You been wantin' French cattle, boys. Now you can go get 'em."

So the monster had backfired, eh? Who'd want "domestic" cattle now? Who'd want cattle from Oklahoma, England, or any place else, when we could get 'em direct from France!

TO ME, JIM'S GREAT ADVENTURE *follows the course of government-sanctioned business:*
First, official regulations result in SHORTAGE.
Then, people with business sense smell PROFIT.
Next, elaborate schemes evolve to supply DEMAND.
Now, add a shot of taxpayers' MONEY.
Just before "harvest," regulations CHANGE.
And the entrepreneur reaps a pile . . . of EXPERIENCE.

21　The Wide Atlantic

M ANY ELABORATE SCHEMES *were hatched for importing French Charo-lais, and no one knows how many millions were spent. My old friend Professor Hill was involved in one such scheme—an apparent loser—but one that opened the way for future success.*

DR. HAROLD HILL

One man who was very alert to the opportunities of frozen semen was William Wood Prince, president of Armour & Company, the nation's largest meat packer, and president of the Chicago Union Stockyards. I knew and admired Mr. Prince very much, and for several years enjoyed the prestige of serving him as a consultant. My involvement with his Charolais scheme makes a pretty good story.

He was born William Wood about 1914, and his father was no whizbang, so they say, so his uncle, Frederick Prince, adopted him, gave him his name (making it Wood-Prince to please the father), and taught him the world of commerce.[83]

Old man Prince was kind of a genius who held a lot of Armour stock and left it all to Billy when he died; so, by the early 1950s, Bill Wood-Prince was president of Armour, and he liked to say (it was almost true), "The whole damn thing is mine!" Then he dropped the hyphen.[84]

Now, Mr. Wood Prince, when I knew him, was a man who could do what he pleased, and what pleased him most was messing around with cattle. He owned a plantation on Eleuthera and, sometime after World War Two, he stocked it with black Angus cattle, thinking to supply the Bahamas with beef. Those Angus looked pretty common to me, but Eleuthera was a pretty poor place for cattle—salty forage, hotter than hell, and the wind howling all the time.

This honorary portrait of William Wood Prince hangs in the Saddle and Sirloin Club, Louisville, Kentucky.
—Saddle and Sirloin portrait

Digressing for a moment: You could, in the 1950s, ship American cattle to Britain and bring British cattle back as far as Canada, where they stayed long enough to be "naturalized" before coming on to the States with little trouble. And—remember!—Eleuthera was a British Crown Colony in the fifties.

Now, I don't know how long Mr. Prince had been hatching his plan, but he was ready and waiting on Eleuthera when Dr. Polge announced his frozen semen breakthrough, and he realized it could make his dream come true. If his little Eleutheran Angus cattle could be bred up with French Charolais, well, American breeders would be waiting with open arms.

So Prince built a Stateside partnership whose members were glad to contribute high-percentage "domestic" Charolais females. Bill Sidley and Clint Ferris shipped a few heifers from Wyoming; Buddy Cobb sent some from Montana; even Senator Eastland, of Mississippi, consigned two or three.

Well, I had pregnancy tested a lot of Bill Sidley's cows and fertility tested bulls on his Wyoming ranch, so one day he visited me at Fort Collins: "Doc," he said, "I have a friend who is ready to invest in beef cattle research . . ."

Say no more! Sidley had my interest! And one thing led to another, and before long I was retained by Sidley's friend, Wood Prince, to evaluate bulls at the other end of the pipeline—France—and to work out the freezing and shipping to Eleuthera.

226

Mr. Prince kept a suite at the Hotel George V in Paris, and he might call me any time of the day or night: "Harold, get over here, quick!"

"Mr. Prince, I'm a college professor; I can't just leave . . ."

"Well, when can you be here?"

"Next weekend, maybe."

"Fine. I'm going to Austria; back on Sunday. Be here!" And his secretary would buy me a ticket from Denver and send a car, but it was a damn long haul to France in propeller days.

Sidley would already be over there, lining up bulls for inspection, and when I arrived I'd give them a thorough exam. If I approved, a final offer was made, and Mr. Prince could be a very generous person. I was surprised to hear him tell Bill Sidley, "Just keep everybody happy. If they want two thousand, offer 'em three."

That was back when I still believed Mr. Prince was aiming to make a profit (in which I'd hopefully share), but I once saw him pay 3,000 good American dollars for a bull that could hardly walk. Caught in some wire . . . lacerated fetlock . . . Nobody in France or anywhere else ever heard of a $3,000 bull that couldn't get up. So profits were elusive, and I believe Prince laid the ground-work for the high prices paid by Americans ten years later.

But the lucky bulls were quarantined on the Maurice family farm at Allier, France, for a hundred days.[85] Then, if all went well, with all health tests behind us, I would freeze-test sperm. If the survival rate was good, we'd begin freezing semen in earnest, and we froze "Fort Collins-style," in fire-sealed glass tubes in the familiar dry ice sludge in familiar styrofoam cylinders. That was the last familiar part of the operation.

Bull at Allier, France, controlled with a stick (right). —H. Hill

By then we knew, of course, that the foot-and-mouth virus could be present in body fluids, including semen. We also knew that viruses, like sperm, are preserved at ultra-low temperatures, so all precautions were taken, starting with calf-hood vaccination.

Still, it was conceivable that a virus could be hidden in frozen semen. There was just the remotest chance, but no sense waving red flags. So it was decided to ship our semen, via Air France, to the French-controlled island of Martinique in the Lesser Antilles off Brazil, simply labeled "agricultural product."

At Martinique, if accompanied by a French Herd Book representative (that would be me), the containers could be transferred to Mr. Prince's private Lockheed Lodestar for the 1,200-mile trip to Eleuthera without passing through customs or attracting any attention of any kind. This was considered practical because one of the partners, M. René de Chambrun, was an attorney for Air France and son-in-law of the famous General Pétain.

M. de Chambrun arranged "sleeper" accommodations on one of Air France's twin-finned Constellations, and you can imagine me in the boarding line at Orly, dressed in Levis, western shirt, and boots, carrying a styrofoam cylinder spewing clouds of vapor. You'll appreciate that this was before the days of airport security, bomb threats, and hijackings, but we caused quite a stir at boarding, just the same.

It was a twenty-two hour flight from Paris to Fort-de-France, where, once the passengers deplaned, our pilot was instructed to taxi the lumbering "Connie" to an inconspicuous location on the airport, where I would haul my steaming "seatmate" down a ladder, across a dirt strip, and load it aboard Mr.

Old Crooked-face, *a ⅞ bull on Eleuthera in 1960.* —H. Hill

Dr. Hill with the "dud," Gander. —Dick Goff

Prince's Lockheed Lodestar without ever passing through customs. Then we were off on the 1,200-mile trip to Eleuthera.[86]

I made that trip six times in the 1950s, giving a wide berth to Hispaniola, where Dominican Republic and Haiti were at war. After a flight of six or eight hours, we'd arrive at Rock Sound, Eleuthera, with our dry ice almost exhausted—which, I'm sure, accounted for the less-than-perfect conception rates achieved by my colleague, Chris Christensen, our highly trained technician from CSU.

And now, for the rest of the story: In 1958 a calf was born on Eleuthera to a $^{15}/_{16}$ Colorado cow and sired by a bull called *Gandin*—one of the most prolific semen producers ever collected in France. We named the calf *Gander,* hoping he would proliferate like his father, and in 1962 we shipped him to Denver. He arrived after thirty days quarantine at St. John, New Brunswick, and sixty days at Guelph—for "naturalization" purposes.

Four-year-old, sixth-generation *Gander*—considered "pure"—was perfect for the U.S. market, and I made the first semen collection with leading members of the Pan American Charolais Association looking over my shoulder: Dick Goff, executive secretary; Mexican directors General Alejo Gonzalez and Max Michaelis; Buddy Cobb from Montana; Bob Purdy, Bill Sidley, and Clint Ferris from Wyoming.

Exciting stuff! The climax of almost a decade of planning! And, would you believe? *Gander's* semen contained not a living sperm!

Well, I told Mr. Prince and the rest of the anxious world that a few weeks rest in our fine Colorado climate, mixed with exercise and nutrition, would restore *Gander's* shattered virility. But it was not to be. Not once, during nine anxious months of exercise, rest, nutrition, and the best of care, did *Gander* produce a live sperm. The bull, in short, was a dud!

There were three other bulls in the shipment. One stayed in Canada, producing some live semen. I forgot what happened to the others, but *Gander* went to the butcher in 1963.[87]

Mr. Prince was to have his hide tanned, but I never learned if that occurred or not. It didn't really matter because, just a few months later, Ottawa announced an importation direct from France.

WELL, THE "FUR-HAT" GUYS IN OTTAWA *and the "black hat" guys in Washington were the kind of people who had been driving Mack Braly nuts. Mack had seen Charolais on the fighting fields of France and had tried them on the Oklahoma prairie. He was among the rich and famous—businessmen, bureaucrats, governors, senators, cabinet ministers, and so forth—who had visited Eleuthera and knew what was going on.*

But he wanted to test the system on his own. All the roadblocks he encountered appealed to his entrepreneurial spirit. Mack was never one to just take no for an answer.

MACK BRALY

My first contact with the government was in February 1957. By 1960 I was in touch with the BAI in Washington and Health of Animals, Canada. Everyone was courteous, but whenever I broached the subject I got the same old story: "Too much chance of bringing in foot-and-mouth disease."

I learned of *endemic* areas, where foot-and-mouth is indigenous and controlled by vaccination—meaning France and most of the world—and *epidemic* areas, including England, where continental starlings sometimes drop the disease, at which time steps are taken to wipe it out. I learned of really contaminated areas in other parts of the world, from which zoo animals have been accepted for generations.

I heard that the zero meridian [the degree of longitude at Greenwich, England], or (sometimes) the thirtieth meridian, had been accepted as an arbitrary barrier: No cattle were to cross it.

But, I thought, "If cattle can come to Oklahoma from the British Isles, why shouldn't they come from the Brittany peninsula, no farther east and under quarantine for generations." I concluded that the barrier was more politics than science, and my legal instincts came rushing to the fore.

Weren't our regulators risking criminal penalties if they sanctioned any exceptions to their rules? And, unless such exceptions were based on science, weren't American cattle at risk?

The more I investigated, the more I became convinced that there was some kind of conspiracy in restraint of trade designed to protect some breed associations. I talked with one southern gentleman who had purchased some British Herefords; after a short "naturalization period" in Canada, he had brought 'em to Tennessee with no trouble at all.

"Hmm," I thought, "the boys have got a little cartel goin' here. The Canadians accept British cattle; then the USDA declares them 'Canadian' and welcomes them into the States. Maybe we'll have to declare Charolais as something other than 'French.'"

So I got out my geography book and atlas. Why, France has territories on this side of the ocean. Here's Guadeloupe and Martinique in the Caribbean: French "overseas departments" represented by senators. And way up here, off the coast of Newfoundland, is the little French "overseas territory" of St. Pierre et Miquelon—three little islands, really—ruled by a governor. I found no mention of these islands ever being infected with FMD.

As this sank in, the thought occurred: "Now, these places are beyond the jurisdiction of our USDA. If I can get clean cattle onto one of these islands and keep 'em free of disease, why, they (or their calves) should be acceptable in this country, the same as cattle from Britain." An idea began to hatch.

So, off I went to Washington. And the stonewalling began: "But, we cannot approve cattle from an endemic area," said Dr. L. C. Heemstra, the director of BAI.

"What about Herefords and Angus from *infected* areas, like Britain?"

"There's a distinction; Britain is an *epi*-demic area."

"Your regulations don't make that distinction."

"No, but in this case we are making it."

Excuses, excuses, excuses; I never heard *reasons*. I'd researched my project carefully, studied the regulations; knew what I was doing. I decided: "Full speed ahead!"

In my last visit with Dr. Heemstra, I said, "Doctor, my mind's made up. I intend to bring cattle from France, either to St. Pierre-Miquelon, or to Martinique."

"And we'll fight ya ever step of the way," the director countered.

And then a funny thing happened: One of the bureaucrats said, "But if you must go ahead, Mr. Braly, we would recommend St. Pierre over Martinique."

"Huh? How'zat?"

"Because . . . a virus is not as likely to manifest itself farther north, in a cooler climate."

Whether that was a good enough reason or not, I thanked my bureaucratic friends and came home wondering: "How do I get to St. Pierre?"

"Cattle always graze toward higher prices."

—Jerry Callis

PART FOUR

THE IMPORTATION

Part Four Contents

The Risk Takers

The Risk Takers

"It is not from the benevolence of the butcher, the brewer, or the baker that we expect our dinner, but from their regard to their own interest." So wrote Adam Smith in The Wealth of Nations *and, as we clean up the crumbs of our banquet, it's intriguing to find a butcher and a barrister at plate.*

The straightforward (if not benevolent) efforts of butcher extraordinaire Billy Prince did not go down well with Canadian Charolais breeders. When four Eleutheran bulls appeared in New Brunswick, the directors of the Canadian Charolais Association choked over the word of a "secret" entry.

A special 6 A.M. meeting of CCA was called for June 25, 1962, at Winnipeg, after which director Gerard Lalonde, who lived near Ottawa, was dispatched to meet with CDA officials. At the same time, secretary-manager Rodney James wrote "an eloquent letter of passionate reason" to Agriculture Minister Alvin Hamilton, expressing shock that cattle conceived on Eleuthera by semen from infected France should be on our shores. When a reply was received, it was signed by the minister's young private secretary, Brian Mulroney—future prime minister of Canada.

The department was satisfied, wrote Mulroney, that the Bahamas were "free of . . . serious animal plagues." Semen had come to Eleuthera "under control of the Bahamian government," and "official supervision" had led to acceptance that the island was clean.

Was Mulroney referring to the "official supervision" of Harold Hill, or of the Air France lawyer, or of Billy Prince's pilot? One may well wonder. Anyway, his letter went on to explain that, "while actual ownership of the Eleuthera bulls was not under CDA control," the department had a commitment that one bull, at least, would remain in Canada, producing semen for Canadian farmers "at an equitable, but undetermined, price."[88]

Finally, Mulroney's letter credited his department with "bringing improved breeding lines to Canada without risk to domestic livestock," a morsel the breeders found hard to swallow. Who was bringing cattle in? It wasn't the Department of Agriculture, and it certainly wasn't Canadian breeders who had been applying for permission for years. Lalonde had copies of pleading letters to Hamilton, to which the answer was always "No!"

And there were other aggravations. As we learned in chapter 19, before the Pan American Charolais Association (PACA) was formed in 1960 by Dick Goff, Buddy Cobb, and others, AI was scorned by the beef associations—including AICA, to which most early Canadian breeders belonged. Furthermore, even when available, semen from American bulls was effectively barred from Canada by import restrictions imposed by Health of Animals.

So, rumors were rife of bull sperm riding under automobiles, in luggage, even in "secret places of the body" for the trip across the U.S.-Canadian border. One notorious high-gaining progeny group had—officially—no sire. Not in Canada, at least.

Even some of the "characters" in this book were feuding among themselves. Wayne Malmberg, an officer of CCA (incorporated in 1960), was also a founding member of PACA, which he hoped would win international recognition for Canadian AI cattle. Jim Rawe saw this as an affront to AICA and organized a fight against the Pan American alliance.

So, ulcers were already flaring when the Eleuthera syndicate offered semen drawn in Canada at $250 a shot. Alternatively, breeders could ship high-percentage cows to Eleuthera to be inseminated at $10,000 per conception. In 1962, this was too much for the average rancher to stomach.

Only maverick Jim Rawe smelled the food and went for the feast. If French-bred Charolais bulls could come to Canada from British Eleuthera, then surely a Canadian heifer could visit England and return in-calf to a full-French Charolais bull. A few weeks later, Rawe and his heifer Bebe deplaned at Heathrow airport, where they ran afoul of British—not Canadian—rules.

Now, with these things reviewed and explained, it's back to our banquet with "barrister" Mack Braly.

Saint Pierre: capital city of the French overseas territory St. Pierre et Miquelon, two little islands a few miles off the coast of Newfoundland. This photo, taken in the mid-1960s, shows some of the quarantine barns, just to the left of the airstrip. —National Geographic

And he told of his friend, Morazé, who had worked for Al Capone while he, himself, had worked for another mobster. "We was always fightin' to get our booze out first," Gautier said, "but we never took it serious; Henri Morazé is a lifelong friend. We just had to play the game."

I told Gautier what I wanted. "For sure we can keep your cattle," he says. "Come, get in the car," and we drove past cattle grazin' on some of the prettiest pasture you ever saw—almost as pretty as Pontotoc County Midland [referring to the Bermuda grass Mack spoke of in chapter 6].

"Don't worry, Mock," says Henry (he never could say "Mack," and I always called him "Henry"). "Cattle can survive on St. Pierre; ya just can't leave 'em out in winter or they die."

Then he drove me to the mink barn—six hundred feet long and a hundred wide, open along the sides with a center aisle—built by the French government to encourage mink farming many years before. Like all such projects, it had failed, but there it sat, and Henry says, "Now, Mock, you can't buy that, but I own the land next to it; you can rent it for fifty bucks a month, and we'll build you a barn on that."

The land was nothing but rock, but the price was right.

"Suppose we go ahead," I said; "who'll look after the cattle?"

"Don't worry," says Henry. "I'll supervise."

"What do you know about cattle?"

"Enough, I guess. I been runnin' cattle for forty years, like my daddy before me." And it was true; one of Henry's businesses was fattening Canadian "canners" on the lush St. Pierre grass and making beef for the Russian, German, Spanish, and Portuguese fishing fleets that called in for supplies.

"So, I'm off to buy cattle," I says, thinking St. Pierre and Miquelon couldn't be no worse than Minnesota or Manitoba.

"Not so fast," says Henry. "Stick around. See the governor. Let him show his authority." And it was good advice because the governor and his wife gave me a dinner—beautiful dinner, beautiful service—and I was welcomed by a group of prominent citizens, Gautier included. Obviously, this would be a very big deal for the 4,500 people of St. Pierre.

N OW MEET *a globe-trotting Frenchman—one of the great breed promoters of all time. We'll hear a lot more from him as the discussion progresses.*

LOUIS de NEUVILLE

England invented the "double route": exporting genetics, importing meat. A very good way. Good trade! Good business for everyone! Argentina, Australia, and New Zealand were all colonized with that double route. The old trade companies were extremely strong, and moving cattle was easier.

Then disease woke us up! Foot-and-mouth started somewhere and spread, but it's wrong to say that some countries didn't have it; foot-and-mouth has been everywhere to a more or less degree.

So, the French and English disagreed on how to fight it: Eradication? Vaccination? Quarantine!—which affected all of world trade. The Hundred Years War all over again. Incredible!

MACK BRALY

In the spring of '62 I went to France, where I met M. Emile Maurice, president of the Charolais Herd Book, and M. Georges Gaillion, president of *Le Syndicat pour la Exportation de la Race Bovine Charolais*—we called it "Syndex"; it later became "Cofranimex." Then, with a Syndex guide, I visited farms and met French breeders who treated me royally—while, of course, they were *really* settin' me up. They were sure I would place an order, direct, for five or ten bulls, which *they* would pick and I would pay for in dollars—just like that. But, of course, that wasn't my way of doing business; I told them I hoped to be back buying cattle the next spring, but I made it clear I would pick 'em myself. Then I went to Paris.

"Fine," said the ministry of Agriculture. "But what about *le problem?*" (by which they meant the USDA). The French had been waiting at the gate for years and thought I had the key. Of course, I didn't; I knew it'd be a fight every inch of the way.

BOB ANDERSON, DVM

We were always resisting pressure; I was on the front lines—black hat and all—forever accused of foot-dragging, and I hope you appreciate why. If we had allowed an importation and had a break, cattlemen would have been first with the guilty finger. I can hear 'em now: "Danged bureaucrats; shoulda known better!"

And, of course, we *did* know better; our terrible experience in Mexico in the forties was the foundation of our knowledge. Mexican cattle had moved on foot, for the most part, and we realized how difficult it would be to eradicate a disease like foot-and-mouth in a country with a modern transportation system like ours. Folks like Mulhern and me who witnessed the horrors of the Mexican outbreak were determined that it wouldn't happen here.

MACK BRALY

So, before leaving Europe in 1962, I visited Dr. H. S. Frenkel, the world authority on FMD, in Amsterdam. I spent a wonderful evening at the Frenkel home, picking the doctor's brain while Mrs. Frenkel played beautifully on the grandest grand piano I ever saw. I learned that several top young USDA vets had been students at the institute bearing his name.

And, on the way home, I called for further advice on Dr. R. Willems, at Brussels, and Professor W. I. B. Beveridge, at Cambridge; they agreed with Frenkel: Buy unvaccinated calves at the youngest possible age and move them immediately to an uninfected area (in France, the Brittany peninsula had been protected for years). That was the way to minimize the risk.[90]

A Canadian importer who studied the rules explains:

DOUG BLAIR

The idea was to import calves that *had not* been vaccinated to ensure that later blood tests would be accurate—that is, that their blood wouldn't show a titer from the vaccination itself.

Now, the French (for their own purposes) required that calves be vaccinated for foot-and-mouth before they were six months old, which meant that calves for export must be selected at a very young age. That was one big problem.

MACK BRALY

I had begun attending Charolais meetings at home and had made some interesting friends: fellows like Morris Cohon, a stockbroker with a farm at the edge of Manhattan, where he'd been raising Holstein milkers and—for almost a decade—Charolais. [Remember Cohon from chapter 19? He offered Buddy Cobb a $5,000 chance on an unborn calf in the 1950s.]

Now, people like me and Cohon were "outsiders" to the Texans, so we stuck together. I told him of my import plan, and he said, "Mack, if you need a partner, count me in."

I was glad to hear it; nobody else seemed to have the stomach for it. Soon, Morris brought a friend, John H. "Ben" Phipps, who had been raising Charolais on his Florida plantation, and the three of us agreed to invest in St. Pierre. Ask me how much and I'll tell you: a pitifully small amount compared with the ultimate cost! We didn't know just how to proceed or just how long it would take, but we agreed to do things *my* way, and in the end we were successful. And no one ever had finer partners.

So, in 1963, back I went to France for serious business, and Syndex assigned me a guide, Pierre Dewavrin. Young Pierre spoke good English, and we got along well, but the way the syndicate wanted to show me cattle was to schedule *presentments* in various villages.

When we arrived, the local officials would be waiting in front of an old stone barn; they'd open the door for "Monsieur Braly" to enter and observe. And I'll never forget how they walked, hands clasped behind their backs; I used to walk the very same way—hands behind me, nodding at the rows and rows of tails.

About twice was enough of that! On the third occasion I reared back: "*Merci beaucoup* for the nice presentment," I said. "But I don't buy cattle this way."

"What?"

"I must see the *meres* and *peres*!"

"*Pourquoi, Monsieur Braly?*"

"Because I wanna see how they'll look when they grow up! What did this calf weigh at birth?"

"*Je n'sais pas,*" with a shrug of the hands. But I knew they knew; the French had beautiful records and were performance testing long before we started—France is where I first got sold on performance. "I want to see *le performance*," I said.[91]

"But Monsieur Braly, we've never heard of such a thing! All the records are at the *eleveur's*—the breeder's," and we had two- or three-day arguments, but, "Sorry, gents; I'm just not interested until I see *le performance*. Now, if you have weights . . ."

Finally it was agreed: "We'll go to the farm."

But I remembered what my Oklahoma neighbor Carlton Corbin had told me about cattle and cattlemen—same the world over: "Fine!" I said. "And we'll look at cattle in the pasture!"

So we walked the pastures, and I liked the French very much. I understood they were hiding some of their best so I wouldn't buy 'em, and some of their worst out of pride, but soon I had twelve bulls and eighteen heifers purchased and ready to go to Brest, the quarantine station on the Brittany peninsula.

As an aside, the perceptions of some other honorable men:

DICK GOFF

I traveled with Mack Braly for a time, and my perception was that he never *walked* anywhere; he was always on the run. My recollection is of Mack *running* down a hill, through a farmer's herd, pointing at bull calves, shouting, "I'll take him . . . and him . . . and him!" All the attention to performance must have come later.

LOUIS de NEUVILLE

But Mack knew what he wanted, and price was no object. Once, a few years later when he was buying Limousins for a friend, I was interpreting in the field when Mack saw a tremendous heifer.

We were asking $2,500, but this heifer the breeder did not want to sell; Mack went to $12,000, and the breeder, M. Hillewaëre, was becoming totally frustrated. He said to me in French, "Tell Monsieur Braly that asking to buy this heifer is like asking to buy my wife."

And Mack—superb! not hesitating—drew himself up haughtily and said, "Tell him I have bought many Charolais wives and government wives as well."

And when I interpreted this to Hillewaëre, he looked at Mack kind of funny and would not have sold him that heifer then for all the money in the world. Later, in the car, I said, "Mack, I guess you've had to twist a few arms in your time."

"Yes," he said. "I win; I lose. But I usually get my way."

MACK BRALY

. . . Like the matter of export permits. Lord! By 1963 the French had progressed so far down the road to socialism that you could hardly *feed* your cattle without a permit. Well, we are on that track, ourselves, which doesn't make me happy.

So my cattle were chosen, down payments made, paperwork delivered to breed headquarters at Nevers, everything ready for fall, and I was asleep at my hotel when the phone rang. It was two o'clock in the morning; Pierre Dewavrin was calling.

"Get up, Mack! We must go to Paris immediately!"

"What now?"

The ministry again. So we leave in the dark and arrive in Paris at eight. "Gentlemen, a problem . . . ," as a ministry lawyer hands me a five-page Telegram of Protest from the U.S. State Department.

"We will try to work this out, Monsieur, but we don't know what to do. Your officials want us to hold all cattle bound for North America: a serious problem, n'est-ce pas?" (Hell! You'd have thought the United Nations was collapsing.) "You must remain in Paris, Monsieur Braly; we will call you this afternoon."

Three days later I stamped into the office where this was all goin' on. "Listen!" I says, "Unless I have a permit by six o'clock this evening, I'm takin' the next plane home."

"Just another day, perhaps?"

"Nope. No more delays. All you got to say is, 'Oui.' Don't matter what they want in Washington; the decision's made, and the answer will be no. The question is are *you* ready? I don't have time to mess around anymore." I wasn't bluffing, but, dealing with bureaucrats anywhere, you must never let up the pressure—can't let 'em push you around. So I got on a plane for home and hadn't no more than hit Ada, Oklahoma, but I found a cable waiting: "M. Braly: Return at once. We will release the cattle."

So my calves were moved to quarantine near Quimper in mid-July and shipped to St. Pierre in October. Henri Gautier, meanwhile, had built me a

Calves were housed in deck huts on the banana boat Sougueta.

barn and put in a supply of hay from Newfoundland and Ralston Purina protein cake from Quebec. Ol' Henry didn't miss a trick: he was the local agent
for Purina, and his seventeen-year-old son, Pierre, was home from school in
Canada ready to take charge of the calves.[92]

And I was there with the Gautiers, waiting on the cold rainy November
day when the banana boat *Sougueta* came steamin' into the harbor, deadheadin'
home to Martinique with my Charolais calves on deck. And it's lucky the
crates were strong because *Sougueta* had run through a storm—the worst Captain Persson had seen in the North Atlantic—and I was surprised when Gautier
told me, "Looka here, Mock. You didn't have no insurance."

No insurance, hell! I'm particular about details and was covered by Lloyds
of London. Hell! For a while I thought I *owned* half of Lloyd's of London!

"But you are lucky, Mock," Gautier said. "I read the fine print, and your
insurance didn't apply to on-deck cargo."

"Oh boy, Braly!" I thought. "Have you got a lot to learn!"

But my cattle were safe ashore on St. Pierre.

ACTUALLY, *on November 26, 1963, two consignments of Charolais cattle
went ashore at Saint Pierre.*

*Mack Braly's twelve bulls and eighteen heifers were actually consigned to Franco-
American Charolais, Inc., of Ada, Oklahoma (Mack's company), from the official
French export agency Syndex.*

246

Sougueta's deck huts also housed six bulls and twenty-five heifers belonging to Charolles Saint Pierre, Ltee., a subsidiary of the Eastern Charolles Cattle Company of Paris and consigned by a competing private export agency known as SEPA. These were the so-called Baar-Nason cattle, which will soon be referred to by Gerry Lalonde.

Mack didn't mention any cattle besides his own in his interview with me. They show up, however, on old manifests provided by Pierre Gautier, now a Saint Pierre customs broker.

The Baar-Nason cattle (housed and cared for separately by another local agent) were just as "pure" and just as important as Braly's. In fact, they arrived on the mainland first, and for that reason alone they deserve mention. But it was Mack himself, in my opinion, who forced the gates for "The Importation," and I include the involvement of others only in passing.

DR. JERRY CALLIS

U.S. legislation restricting livestock imports from disease-infected countries came as a rider to the Smoot-Hawley Tariff Act of 1931, which still comes back to haunt us as evidence of a nontrade tariff barrier. In fact, the rider was used to get quick action following the serious FMD outbreak of 1929, and a subsequent agreement between all three North American countries was designed to bar the disease from the entire continent.[93]

The Mexican foot-and-mouth outbreak of 1946 spurred Congress to further action. Public Law 498 of 1947 authorized half a million bucks for planning a research lab, but not a penny for construction. Then came February 1952, with FMD in Canada. The April issue of *Farm Journal* headlined: "We have the plans. We have the need. Now, where's the money?" That got congressional attention, and by May we were looking for an island.

In the spirit of the continental agreements of 1931, Public Law 498 stipulated an island site surrounded by deep, navigable waters. To quell the fears of insular constituents, the island could not be connected to the mainland by bridge or tunnel. So, we checked out islands from Narragansett Bay to Alcatraz in San Francisco harbor before selecting Plum, off the northeast point of Long Island, which fit all specifications: a wide, 190-foot channel with a current of about eight knots; several well-constructed concrete buildings well suited to our needs; no bridge—access only by boat.

247

In the fall of '52, I was just back from studying FMD in Amsterdam [at the State Veterinary Institute where Mack Braly's acquaintance, Dr. Frenkel, was director], and one of my first assignments was to "sell" the research lab scheme to residents within a twenty-five mile radius of Plum Island. Frankly, most people could not have cared less about the island (the contentious issue being whether it belonged to New York, Connecticut, or Rhode Island across the Sound)—until, at nearby Greenport, rumors somehow got started of rotting, infected carcasses polluting beaches, ruining oyster fisheries, destroying the tourist trade—every possible detraction except danger to local cattle, scarce in that truck-farming area by then.

Eventually, most people saw the benefits and approved Plum Island (though never with open arms), and in January '53 I moved to Greenport and helped design a brand new maximum-security facility for the study of infectious disease. Plum Island was never a quarantine station—animals never leave. Nor has any disease escaped from Plum Island.

*T*HE RESULTS *of early Plum Island studies justified the importation of semen, even from "FMD" countries.*

MACK BRALY

The feds had said I could *not* import semen, but in 1966 I collected my bull *Uranium* at St. Pierre, and they let me ship his semen in through Clifton, a minimum-security entry point (for zoo animals) in New Jersey. They adopted special measures for *Uranium*, see. They didn't quarantine semen; they quarantined the *can*! They could make special regulations however they wanted.

But, of course, everything costs money—in this case, mine. I built a special barn with a special lab for freezing. Then I brought in a USDA vet and paid his expenses for thirty days. *Uranium* was in isolation for a total of ninety days; then his semen spent another ninety in the can.

I BELIEVE, *unlike Mack Braly, that great care was taken by the scientists on Plum Island. Consider this:*

JERRY CALLIS

Five highly qualified, super-conservative, nongovernment scientists carefully checked our findings before we released them. When we first presented our conclusion that semen could be safely imported, they didn't all agree; Dr. Roger Herriot of Johns Hopkins, a veteran of Salk polio vaccine studies of the fifties, said, "I think this needs more study; better wait."

Back to the drawing board; much more work; some years later I could point to two million semen doses imported under Plum Island regulations.

"Two million doses? No incidents? Many years?" Dr. Herriot said, "Now, Jerry, I call that a good, safe test!"

Another longtime advisor was Dr. Richard Shope: discoverer of the influenza virus; discoverer of the rabbit epiloma virus [related to cervical cancer]; discoverer, during the Pacific war, of several penicillium molds—a fascinating character! I would sometimes meet Dr. Shope in New York and drive him to our meetings just to spend a couple of hours soaking up the lore—he was my idol. His son is still [in 1987] a Plum Island adviser.

ROBERT SHOPE, MD

My dad, a physician like his father before him, always loved animals; so, after Iowa State, he applied for a job studying animal diseases with the Rockefeller Foundation. Then came World War Two. Dad joined the navy to go to war, and found himself on an isolated island.

On Grosse Ile in the St. Lawrence River he commanded a group of doctors developing a vaccine against rinderpest, known to be under study by the Ger-

Millions of human immigrants were processed at Grosse Ile. Tens of thousands died of typhus and cholera and were hauled to the island's mass graves in horse-drawn hearses like this one. —National Archives of Canada

mans. Rinderpest spreads quickly by the respiratory route, leaving cattle dead by the thousands. Without a suitable vaccine, such a virus could destroy a country's meat supply with all its important by-products. Grosse Ile in the 1940s was a very important outpost of Allied defense.

A ND, TWO DECADES LATER, Grosse Isle was a very important gateway to North America.

In the 1960s and 1970s immigrants of another species were held on Grosse Ile for several months before being lightered ashore in Quebec. —CDA Archives

23   Exotic Breeds

SARAH GARST, DVM

I was at Antioch college—the last bastion of radicalism, I always say—and my economics professor, a Hungarian, asked the class: "What would happen to the price of milk if a combination beef and dairy breed was developed?" Radical question, right?

I spoke up: "There is such a breed," I said; "it's called Simmental," and from that day forward my professor called me his "farmer." Well, I was the only farmer or farmer's kid he knew, and I'd taught him something. That was 1973, when no one in America knew of the Simmental breed.

Nowadays everyone's seen pictures of red and white cows with enormous udders and big bells around their necks high up in the Alps. "Oh, yeah, I've seen those pictures," they say.

"Those are Simmental," I tell 'em.

HANS ULRICH

Simmental is certainly the most numerous breed in the world; in France they're called "Pie Rouge," in Germany and Austria "Fleckvieh," but they're all the same with Simmental. And Brown Swiss is another breed known around the world—very popular as a dairy breed in Mexico; very successfully crossed with Brahma in India.

All Swiss farmers have small herds and their milk checks are very important, so Simmental and Brown Swiss were dual-purpose breeds to begin with; Simmental, especially, was ready-made for this country because it color-crossed so well with the numerous Hereford.

Travers Smith—"Travelin' Smith"—introduced Simmental to America. Smith had a ranch near Cardston [in southern Alberta] and traveled all over the continent talking "performance." He was an early user of the high-perfor-

Swiss Simmental cow with bell. —Karen Morrison

mance Cooper-Holden Hereford bulls from Montana and, by the sixties, had a lot of "growth" in his herd.

But Smith wasn't satisfied, and he knew he could do better when a Brown Swiss milk cow on his ranch raised the biggest calves. So, when he learned of Simmental at the Lacombe experiment station, he went and studied the breed, waited for his chance, and hit the jackpot with *Parisien*—the first Pie Rouge, or Simmental, to arrive in North America in this century.[94]

MARSHALL COPITHORNE

We were always trying to improve the feet and udders on our Herefords, culling the "swing bags" and "banana tits" that "snowburn" so bad [from bright sunshine after a spring snowstorm]. Yet we wanted more milk for heavier calves, so, in 1967—much to my father's horror—I bought a string of American Brown Swiss bulls.

Now, Brown Swiss were imported to the States over a hundred years ago as dairy cattle, and the bulls I bought were ugly-lookin' dairy-types, for sure. Our good old whitefaced cows raised some funny-lookin' calves for the next few years, and the neighbors scoffed and made fun of them at brandings. At the same time, anyone with eyes could see that the udders on our cows were improving.

Then "Travelin' Smith" showed up at [the stockmen's school at] Banff, talkin' *Parisien* and showing slides of Europe, and in 1968 we bought semen, and in 1969 the CL brand went on a few crossbred Simmental calves for the very first time.

And it's a damn good thing they were branded because, although Simmental cattle are gentle enough in Europe, with a shot of hybrid vigor and a summer in the bush—Wahoo! These were the wildest buggers we ever weaned! Now, after ten years of selection for disposition and performance, Simmental genes have become a valuable part of our CL seed-stock herd.

DOUG BLAIR

Twenty-six new breeds in all, I think, arrived from Europe in the 1960s: Charolais came first, contributing size and muscle.[95]

The Simmental group came second, contributing milk and growth. It breaks down into nationalities—Simmental from Switzerland, Pie Rouge from France; Fleckvieh from Germany and Austria. I liked the Austrians best because they were selected primarily for meat; they were redder in color and generally better hind-quartered than the rest of the Simmental family.

Limousin came third. It's probably the only breed in Europe selected solely for meat. The Limousin breed was slower catching on than some of the others because, I think, its "Godfather," Louis de Neuville, kept the price so high. Folks who would pay $1,500 for a Simmental balked at $10,000 for a "Limo."

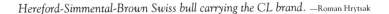

Hereford-Simmental-Brown Swiss bull carrying the CL brand. —Roman Hrytsak

But Louis, by that time, had seen the mark-up with Charolais and figured it wouldn't be long till the bubble burst. He was right, of course, but in the long run his strategy limited the North American base of a very fine breed.

*D*OUG MAKES A GOOD POINT, *but notice that Limousin placed second to Angus in annual U.S. breed registrations in 1994.*[96]

Angus (black)	210,000
Limousin	84,300
Simmental	80,600
Hereford (horned)	71,800
Polled Hereford	61,000
Charolais	56,500
Beefmaster	50,000
Gelbvieh	31,500
Red Angus	27,300
Shorthorn	21,010
Saler	21,000
Chianina	9,500

The North American Limousin Foundation (NALF) was another of Dick Goff's brainstorms, like the Pan American Charolais Association he dreamed up in 1960— the first beef organization to register AI calves.

In 1968, each NALF founding member was entitled to forty ampules of semen from Prince Pompadour, NIM 1 *("NALF Import Male number one"), the first bull ashore of the breed. Dick was first executive vice president. Dr. Jim Scott and I were founding members number five and four.*

In 1969 one of the first ten "Limo" calves in North America dropped on my SN ranch. As I remember, the first was born on the Geesen ranch in Colorado; the second on the LK ranch at Bassano. Such things were very important at the time.[97]

M Y PRIME INTEREST in the Limousin breed was in its potential for adding "carcass value" to my already crossbred herd—on the outside chance (yet unrealized) of being paid for a meatier carcass. In time, I grew to like the overall efficiency that Limousin gave my cow herd, and today no critter looks "right" to me unless it shows at least a trace of Limousin blood.

Interestingly, the breed might have disappeared had it not been for Louis de Neuville. Claire and I heard him tell this classic story on a visit to Combas, his domaine, or "ranch," in France.

Prince Pompadour, *shown here with young consultant Dr. Jim Scott, came ashore at Rimouski, Quebec, in the summer of 1968. Pompadour sired over 60,000 calves in North America.* —Dick Goff

LOUIS DUFOUR de NEUVILLE

The evening of third December 1958 is unforgettable for me: It was Friday; it was raining; a few of us near the little Limousin village of Magnac-Bourg had taken our cattle to market, and the sale had not gone well; we were not happy. Then, like twenty-five or thirty-year-olds anywhere, we went to an inn and over drinks started rebuilding the world.

I spoke of the future of our cattle, and one of our group, Hubert de Blomac, said, "Louis, you are totally wrong; only Charolais will make it." Well, the Charolais breed was certainly in full bloom; only recently our inspector general of Agriculture, Monsieur Quittet, had called our Limousin breed "totally hopeless"; it had no future at all, he said, and should be blended with all the other breeds of southwest France: Garonnaise, Lourdais, Agenais, and the rest. I thought Quittet a fool! He was crushing the fruit of the Limousin region—my home. He became my personal enemy at that instant!

I suppose I could be *Count* Louis, but that is a typical English thing, and I do not want to be taken as an English. The title started with my great-grandfather, who did tremendous things but was a humble man who liked to be called just "Louis." Then, instead of "Count Louis Dufour de Neuville," a pretty long name for our world of speed, I am just "Louis" also.

I did never envisage to be a cattleman. Instead, in high school I took Latin and Greek and philosophical things, but circumstances interfered: When I was fourteen and a half my father was killed in the war; then my brother, who I always thought would manage Domaine de Combas, likewise. Then I knew what I had to do; Combas has been our family home since almost 500 years—the time of Columbus.

Then I changed completely. My studies became mathematics and physics and biology. I took a master's in animal husbandry while my mother managed the estate; then, at age twenty-five, I came home to Combas, which, with 2,000 acres of pasture, woods, and farmland, is about ten times any other farm in the area.

I had much to learn. Soon it became obvious that—even the scale is larger at Combas—growing cattle and sheep is an expensive operation; in the Limousin we compete with more fertile parts of France, where milk is the main production and beef is a by-product only.

Soon I began to see our animals as part of our "animation" or environment. The real vocation of our Limousin province, I began to think, was *tourism*. We have a great "particularity" in our region. Our people are very attractive, but different from other French in appearance (a little of Spain) and customs (archaic) and language (unintelligible to outsiders).

For many years isolated, there is a certain degree of linebreeding in our people, who seem extremely shy and insular and generally less audacious than most French; they don't really dare to adventure, yet they have a certain finesse and are never "boresome." The Limousin countryside, with its balance of hill and valley, forest and meadow, is a pleasant place to live, as it is to visit; not only have we the people speaking the strange Limousin patois, also we have our unique Limousin races of pigs, sheep, horses, and cattle.

Our cattle has always been here, for as long as we can know; we point to the Lascaux Caves, a hundred miles from Limoges, where Magdalenean-era paintings clearly show long, red animals with well-developed rumps, while most other European caves show huge-shouldered bisons. I do not say this is proof of any antiquity, but 17,000 years ago the local people were painting what they saw, and obviously the Limousin aurochs had plenty of meat. So, today, our Limousin cattle are famous for carcass.

The de Neuville home at Domaine de Combas.

Our Limousin version of the European species *Bos taurus* is *dolichocephalic*, meaning "long headed," unlike the Hereford, Simmental, or Charolais, and—interestingly—Limousin bulls *shape* their progeny more and *color stamp* them less than the other breeds. Also, the Limousin breed seems very adaptable to continental climates and may subsist on mineral-deficient grasses, which explain why the breed has done so well in so many parts of the world.

But I didn't know these things on that rainy night in 1958 when I was drinking with my friends and thinking only of "le beau Limousin"—the *country*. That night, in our little tavern, Albert Nicolas, a young veterinarian and perhaps the most intelligent of us all, said, "No, no, no, my friends! I tell you, neither Limousin nor Charolais is going to make it; dairy cattle will soon supply all our beef." And Albert's theory was sound; the heavily subsidized dairy industry was providing 70 percent of our meat already.

A second one, Jean Bonnin, said, "No, you are all wrong; the real future is in sheep." And he was damn right, too; I also had sheep, and they were doing extremely well.

Then—I remember like yesterday—my good, good friend Henri de LaCelle said, "I don't share your confidence at all; I think that French agriculture is no more a proposition. While our land is still worth something, we should sell and move to Canada." There was a big, big trend for Canada at that time.

And so the evening could have gone on forever, but I, unfortunately, am sometimes a little tempered. I got out my nerves and jumped on a little table.

"My friends," I said, "our Limousin cattle has fed our ancestors well. But we don't know much about them; we don't know what they weigh; we give our product for nothing at the market, leaving the dealers, only, to make money; we don't even know what they cost to produce because we don't do any accounting. Now, instead of complaining, we must act and, by acting together, can go altogether quicker and more healthy."

As I talked, I became furious! I loved our Limousin country and our cattle which were part of our environment, but when I talked "environment," nobody understood; all anybody understood was cattle.

So you can see that I am here by accident. I went with cattle first for family reasons; later, for tourism's sake, I thought, "The Limousin region can't be the widow of its farmers." Then, I had to convince those farmers to fight for their lives.

Well, to make a long story short, we organized ourselves into ELPA—*Eleveur Limousin Plein Air*, Open Air Limousin Breeders; up to then, all Limousin farmers had sheltered their cattle in winter. Now, a cow is a factory, a barn is a tool, and in farming there are tools which don't make money. Our preference was the *factory*. In the summer of 1959 we put our cows outside, and they never got inside more—the most commonsense decision we ever made.[98]

258

Meanwhile, ELPA had grown to twenty-six breeders, mostly from the departments [states] of Correze and Haute Vienne, and we turned our eyes to the world. Since 1960 we have exported to almost seventy countries in many climates. But, without that handful of friends who gathered at the inn at Magnac-Bourg that rainy evening in 1958, the Limousin breed would not exist anymore.

*A*NOTHER FRIEND *of my Limousin days is Carlton Noyes, a commercial feeder who finishes high-percentage "Limos" and merchandises a trademarked product in urban markets. Here's the story:*

CARLTON NOYES

In 1969 I was running 3,000 cows on our Nebraska and Idaho ranches when, looking for something different, I went to the very first Limousin sale at Denver. I came home with some heifers bred to *Prairie Pride,* and I also bought some semen. Next spring, when I saw my first *Pride* calves, I wanted more.[99]

On one ranch we were breeding two or three hundred yearling heifers to Angus bulls, hopefully for ease of calving, and it was normal to have a twenty-four-hour crew. Of course, an occasional "Limo" bull jumped the fence, and the second year Tom, my foreman, reported, "No problem calvin' heifers to Limousin bulls." With that, it wasn't long till we were breeding everything Limousin, and the calving crew loved us for it. I was even more pleased with the calves coming into the feedlot.

The first Limo carcasses? Well, the buyers had never seen their likes before; they accused me of shipping *bulls*—great big ribeyes; little, thin rinds of fat. Right then I knew we were doing something right! I've been raising, finishing, and selling Lean Limousin™ "in the box" over twenty years. The breed works great from the pasture to the palate.

*A*ND CARLTON *also likes the crossbreds he gets from Jerry Adamson, in Nebraska, and Tom Schmidt, in North Dakota—top ranchers with top cattle—which brings us to the Chianina breed.*

*J*ACK PHILLIPS, *Ph.D.—"the kind of doc who don't do nobody no good," as one old guy said—the fellow who bantered about "Ol' Red Eye" in chapter 4, was amazed when he saw Chianina! Here's what turned him on.*

Chianina bull in Italy, 1970.

JACK PHILLIPS

On a trip to Alberta in 1969 I met Rik Bronson, an archaeologist by train-ing, who was raising Brown Swiss cattle in the Canadian Rockies.

Rik quizzed me: "What do you look for in a calf?"

I said I was always searching for a longer, meatier animal.

"Well," said Rik, "if it's size you want, you should try Italy. I dug there for years and saw many bulls that would go 4,000 pounds."

"Four thousand pounds! Two tons . . . lotta bull!"

"Yep," said Rik, ". . . big as horses . . . Old-time Romans rode 'em into battle; plenty of Italian cows weigh over a ton. They've been pulling plows for thousands of years and—with twitching muscles, big splayed feet, and small tight udders—are the closest thing you'll find to a cow-horse cross."

That night, gathered around a table, Rik showed me a Chianina pam-phlet. When I saw the bull on the cover I said, "This is the critter I have in mind when I go to sleep at night; this is the muscle and skeletal structure I dream of. I was hoping to find it *tomorrow*; I've found it today." I couldn't believe my eyes—like, six feet tall and 4,000 pounds.

"Too much for me!" I said, "Can I keep this pamphlet?"

"Sure," said Rik, and I sent the pamphlet straight to Jonathan Fox.

NOW, TO DIGRESS *for a moment: Performance Registry International, PRI, convened at Miles City, Montana, in 1959. Representing Alberta were Charlie and Opal and Neil and Lucille McKinnon, Fletcher and Eleanor Bennett, Wally Wells, and Claire and I—along with Doug Baird, Mack Braly, Sally Forbes, Harry Hargrave, Curt and Tommy Hughes, Sid Lore, H. H. Stonaker, and, I'm sure, other characters in this book.*

Ray Woodward, then the U.S. range experiment station director, and his wife, Betty, entertained dozens of delegates at their home.

And, if you think concern for "genetic diversity" is new in the 1980s and 1990s, I recall one 1959 discussion as to whether the "by-the-numbers" selection advocated by PRI would "shove all the breeds down one throat"; that is, result in loss of genetic diversity.

"No problem," opined Oklahoma Angus man Carlton Corbin, the newly elected PRI president; "I never met two cowboys yet who agreed on everything—much less the best kind of cow." And, less than ten years later, the first of dozens of "new" and "exotic" breeds entered upon our shores.

Speaking of diversity!

THAT SAME PRI MEETING *was attended by Rock Prentice of ABS. He and Ray Woodward got to drinking whiskey and talking, and within a year Ray had quit the government and become a genetic consultant to ABS.*

So there he was, perfectly placed to participate in the new genetic diversity of the 1960s.

Captain, *the Piedmontese bull available through ABS, shows the extra muscling that made this breed famous among dairymen (and infamous to ranchers). In 1994 there are 7,500 Piedmontese of record in the United States.* —Doug Johnson

RAY WOODWARD

Twice a year for about ten years, starting in 1966, I went to Europe, picking bulls for ABS and its clients. From the start I was impressed with the use of performance by European Simmental and Pie Rouge breeders; they had surprisingly good data and seemed to use it. Later, when I saw how well the Simmental crossed with American Herefords, I became a "believer."

The Italian breed that most intrigued me was the Piedmontese [Piemontese, in Italian], intentionally bred for "double-muscling" and producing about twice as much lean (while being about half as fertile) as normal cattle.[100]

I wasn't as impressed with the French Charolais or Limousin breeds or with their use of data in selection; and I wasn't enthused with Chianina or the other Italian breeds, although I have to admit that those big white long-legged cattle have made themselves a natural part of the scenery on at least one Montana ranch. By God, ya have to comb 'em out of the 8,000-foot peaks at roundup time each fall.

A NOTHER BREED CONSULTANT who knows his business is Doug Blair, of Western Breeders in Calgary; he once served as president of the Canadian Gelbvieh Association.

DOUG BLAIR

Charolais, Simmental, Limousin, Tarantaise, Blonde D'Aquitaine, Salers, Gelbvieh, Chianina, Marchigiana, Romagnola . . . Twenty-six beef breeds imported in all—some too few to be remembered.

I liked Salers when I saw them in France; they had calving ease and milk and decent legs. Pinzgauer was another good breed that came in very small numbers, leaving its impact small.

One of the most interesting is the German Gelbvieh breed: same color, same hindquarters as the French Limousin, but a lot more milk and better feet and legs. Had Gelbvieh come in sooner, it'd be more important now, but it missed the first big rush of the importation.

Competing with its followers, though, Charolais is a very strong breed. In Canada, at least, the breeders never forgot their roots, although some were deeply involved in, and very excited by, the importation. When the chips were down and the oil money rolled, attention to meat production kept the Charolais breed strong.

Gelbvieh, a good-milking, growthy breed from Germany. —Browarny Photographics

Tarentaise, another popular breed from France. —Browarny Photographics

NOW, HAVING MENTIONED *a few new "exotics," back to Charolais:*

GERRY LALONDE

It was the fall of 1962 and Jim Rawe was at my farm, waiting to get his heifer on a plane for England, when a Frenchman, Jacques Baar-Nason, phoned up all excited. He had heard Jim on the radio, talking about Charolais. I told him, "The Americans are buying in France right now."

"How do you know this?" he asked.

"Well, I *do* know, and it's true. . . ." There seemed to be quite a bit of money involved, and I knew that an Oklahoman, Braly, was talking about St. Pierre.

This French guy was so excited that he said, "Let's do the same." He was selling a property in Paris but couldn't take the currency out of France. So, he was thinking of buying French cattle; then, if he could get them to America . . . Voila!

What he needed was a few Canadian partners. He said, "Do you think you could round up any Canadian money?"

"I'm pretty sure I can round up quite a bit of Canadian money," I told him. And I was right; with a few other breeders, we formed Charolles Canada Ltd., a subsidiary of the Eastern Charolles Company in France.

So I bought, with Baar-Nason, twenty-five French heifers with the idea to calve them on St. Pierre. There, a bunch of nominally French-owned cattle with the right Canadian connections could possibly compete with Braly; it was risky but worth a try. Our cattle arrived with the same shipment as Mack Braly's.

THIS IS WHAT Mack told me (with no mention of other cattle):

MACK BRALY

I went to St. Pierre-Miquelon every three months, and my cattle were getting fat! On my second trip I told Henri Gautier he was feedin' 'em too much.

"They need it, Mock," he said. "In this cold place we must keep the energy up."

And we argued, and he agreed, "Awright, awright . . . ," but he never did cut back. Finally, on my third trip, I asked why on earth he was feeding them so much.

"Because, of course, cattle are supposed to be fat!"

"No," I said, "they are *not!* We don't want 'em fat."

"But what will that Canadian vet say when he comes?"

"I don't give a damn what the vet says; he's not gonna see 'em, anyway."

But Dr. Wells had been nosing around in France, and I knew, with all the speculation, that he certainly might show up on St. Pierre.

Canada's chief veterinarian KENNETH WELLS, DVM

By agreement with the French we had full authority to visit their offshore islands to satisfy ourselves that they were free of foot-and-mouth and to be sure they would remain free, but it wasn't easy for the French to give up power.

Five years later, needing another quarantine station, supplementary to Grosse Ile, I made an inspection of St. Pierre and Miquelon and saw very few cattle of any sort—certainly no Charolais—on the islands. The place wasn't all that big. I don't think I could have missed any big white cattle if they were there.

Veteran French cattle exporter LOUIS de NEUVILLE

As I told René Breton, the head of the French export agency, Cofranimex, "Don't be naive; with all the Canadian interest, you must be organized. You must prepare St. Pierre-Miquelon for an inspection."

There had been no reason for an inspection when Mack Braly and Baar-Nason first went to St. Pierre, but now . . . "Don't worry," René Breton told me, "the people will be advised." And I know the French people: They would have shown Dr. Wells the town and the barns, but, if he was not specifically looking, they may have forgotten completely to mention Charolais. He really may never have seen any Charolais cattle, even though they were there.

Five years later—like, in 1968—when Canada was considering a secondary quarantine station, the status of St. Pierre et Miquelon was changed from a French "overseas territory" to a "department" [like a state]. That was done, diplomatically, to give Canada a feeling of administrative control; in other words, the terminology was changed, but the status was never *really* changed or advertised publicly. Dr. Wells may not have known or did not care.

I know some vets who don't care a bit for genetics or anything else; they just want the title of "healthiest in the world," and so they go exactly by the letter of the law. Dr. Wells was an honorable man who had the *spirit* of the law, and so he was always sorting for the best between animal health and the health and wealth of the people. He wanted the best for the farmers—the center of life.

Canadian Charolais secretary RODNEY JAMES

I attended the inaugural meeting of the World Charolais Federation at Vichy, France, in 1963. Manuel Garza Elizondo was there for Mexico, and many other countries were represented.

As CCA secretary, I was the closest thing to a Canadian official there, and I addressed the meeting on the situation in my country as I saw it. I had just finished telling the boys that Ottawa was going *nowhere* with an importation, when damned if I don't look up and see our brand new Agriculture minister, accompanied by several assistants, listening to my talk.

Harry Hays was that new minister, and it wasn't long, I can tell you, before his assistants got the message, and we were getting vibes out of Ottawa. I don't dispute that Alvin Hamilton was in office when the initial steps were taken; but, by late 1963, his government had fallen, and the Liberals were in power.[101]

So Harry Hays was minister when word got out at Vichy that Mack Braly from Oklahoma was ready to ship his cattle to St. Pierre. I can tell you, that news *really* got everybody's attention!

24   Exotic Imports

MY FRIEND AND NEIGHBOR *Gordon Burton was a Liberal, and not one of the modern "small-l" variety, either. He was a longtime member of the Liberal Party of Canada, but no one to my knowledge ever led a stiffer fight against "big government."*

Rather, Gordon used his training in "human action" and his talent as a speaker to argue for limited government, free enterprise, and free markets—Gordon was an unorthodox *liberal, if ever there was one.*

GORDON BURTON

Harry Hays, our Agriculture minister, regarded me as an *unreliable* Liberal. We'd meet on airplanes and sit and drink whiskey together on the way to Ottawa, and he'd say, "It pays to stick with the team, Gordon; the team has been good to me."

Well, the team was certainly good to Harry—a good, uncritical member of the Liberal Party and a classic *opportunist*; in my opinion, the man's greatest achievement was the "Hays Converter" breed—for which he paid a high price. Widely acclaimed for performance, it would have been even more outstanding (at least, financially, for Harry) without the "exotic" competition he arranged.

Now, the story I always heard was that, in 1963, Hays bought a bull in France, and when Wells, his chief veterinarian, asked, "How do you plan to get him past the health rules, Mr. Minister?" the reply was, "That's your problem, Dr. Wells."

True or not, everyone thought if Canada allowed French cattle in, the Yanks would close the border, as they had with the foot-and-mouth outbreak in 1952. We got away with it, this time, only because of very good work by the many very good people in Hays's department.

Canada's Ag minister Harry Hays. —Ted Pritchett

ROY BERG

In Ottawa they took Harry Hays for a bumpkin. Well, I'll tell you what he was: a very sharp cookie! One of the very few ministers to ever really take hold of a department.

Harry had been in the international Holstein trade and knew his way around. No doubt some other minister would have opened things up, but it would have taken longer. I'm sure many people lobbied, but no way would Harry have buckled under pressure; he understood that a deeper gene pool would serve Canadians well.

But, whatever it was that turned him on, the veterinary complex would have balked: "No way!" And at that point, Hays would have exploded: "It's going to happen! Get it done!"

Harry Hays was a man who got things done.

DR. KENNETH WELLS
veterinary director general of Canada

It's important to understand that the involvement of the government of Canada goes back to the earliest days of confederation; the control of livestock importation was the subject of one of the earliest acts of Parliament.

Laws controlling the importation into the United States go back, at least, to 1905 [as with Shanghai Pierce's Brahmans]; and the absolute prohibition of animal products from infected countries goes back to the 1930s when a congressional act was followed by a tripartite agreement signed by all three countries of North America.

Now, it's certainly my recollection that Alvin Hamilton was the minister who gave the initial order for the European cattle importation of the 1960s, but no permits were issued until the spring of 1965—by which time Harry Hays was minister. It was another year before the cattle were released from quarantine. And by that time Harry Hays was out office.

WHEN MEMBER OF PARLIAMENT for Qu'Appelle-Moose Mountain (Saskatchewan) Alvin Hamilton heard I'd been in Ottawa asking questions about the great importation of the sixties, he wrote me, volunteering his side of the story. He has since retired with the Order of Canada and other honors.

ALVIN HAMILTON

When I took over as minister in 1960, cattlemen were clamoring for imports, and veterinary director general Wells was pressing for a decision. My first responsibility, however, was disposing of the surpluses of the Wheat Board, and I simply didn't have time for a study of animal health.[102]

For over a year I'd been in contact with my European counterparts and considered some of them pretty good friends (you develop good friendships quickly, disposing of surpluses).

We would meet at various conferences, talk on the phone, and so forth, and I like to think I knew what was going on; I knew, for instance, that certain wealthy Americans were paying unheard-of prices for cattle in France, and I knew that the British government had imported French Charolais in an attempt to put more meat on English tables. But I had been turned down cold when I proposed the same for Canada; it was not in European interests to let their bloodstreams get away.

Then, in the spring of '62, four white bulls from Eleuthera appeared at St. John, New Brunswick. During one of my regular morning meetings, I received a message to that effect, and I wanted full details; I wanted control. I asked my secretary to locate Dr. Wells.

Veterinary director general Kenneth Wells, DVM.
—Ted Pritchett

"Dr. Wells," I said, when he joined our meeting, "the policy you've been pushing is now in effect! As chief veterinarian, you will investigate the options. Furthermore—with reference to the bulls now at St. John—semen must be available to our farmers."

As I say, I was busy with the Wheat Board and didn't know the details, but nothing would have pleased me more than to go on the road, myself, distributing this commodity to constituents.

My staff, however, had trouble visualizing a federal minister delivering bull semen door-to-door. Furthermore, legal ownership was in doubt. So, I let my able young assistant, Brian Mulroney, handle the matter, which is how a future prime minister of Canada came to introduce the Charolais bloodstream to America.

University of Alberta geneticist ROY BERG

We received some semen from the Eleutheran bull *Francois IV* at the Kinsella ranch, which surprised me. Our vets had always treated foreign se-

270

men with suspicion, claiming it could possibly carry disease, but in this case it was collected from a bull already in Canada. Still, the circumstances were mysterious; I never knew in detail how it got here.

Chief veterinarian KEN WELLS

We always considered semen to be potentially more dangerous than livestock, the reason being that semen was more difficult to examine and, in early years, impossible to test.

The Americans had a different outlook with their sophisticated Plum Island facility, where, under tight security, they could legally experiment with live material—a luxury we didn't have.

Health of Animals' DR. BERT LEWIS

And, it shouldn't be forgotten that, since the Canadian foot-and-mouth outbreak of 1952, some very significant tests had been developed. Ten years later one could, in fact, test for foot-and-mouth quite easily and quickly.

Specifically, a Danish scientist, Dr. Probang, had established that, if the FMD virus was present, it would likely show in the larynx. Then the Probang test using laryngital scrapings was developed at the Pirbright Virus Research Laboratory, the venerable English equivalent of Plum Island. With that, diagnosis was sure and simple.

ALVIN HAMILTON

So, with such assurances, we were able to supply the needs when Canadian research stations, colleges, and individuals requested semen from the Eleuthera bulls. I didn't know who all the applicants were—there are things a federal minister shouldn't know. But then, I was never one to worry over details; I just directed and let things happen.

Perhaps you'll notice how I got things done in the early sixties!

S. B. "SYD" WILLIAMS
served as deputy to four Canadian Ag ministers over twenty years.

It was the statute prohibiting cattle from any country with FMD that kept the Americans from going it on their own. No importation—period! Although they were certainly anxious to have one.

Harry Hays was my minister from 1963 to 1965, and he had many years of experience as an exporter; he knew the strategies, risks, and opportunities, and he had been in Europe many times and thought it would be a great idea to bring in cattle from France—just France, to start with, mind you.

So, the minute he took office he asked me to arrange a meeting with U.S. secretary of Agriculture Freeman. That meeting was held in the New Zealand Room of the Parliament buildings in Ottawa; Ken Wells was there from Health of Animals, and I was there as assistant deputy minister.

At that meeting we put forth a proposal. We proposed to import cattle under *maximum security* conditions and to include USDA in our considerations. We were prepared to accept the consequences when and if foot-and-mouth was found. We understood the risks! We had encountered FMD a decade earlier and eradicated it completely. Our confidence was high, our credibility good; all we asked was *not* to be declared "infected" *unless and until* an actual infection was found.

After listening to our proposal, Secretary Freeman said in essence, "Politically, this sounds good. Send your technicians to Washington; have them talk with our technical people. Unless they find some holes, this has my blessing!"

Simultaneously, we were working things out with the French. Harry and I met with Edgar Pisani, his counterpart in Paris. First, we asked for permission to send our own veterinarians onto French farms—that took a lot of diplomacy. Then we asked for control of the French export station at Brest, and—believe me—that took *real* diplomacy! Finally, of course, they agreed because they saw a buck in it for France—and rightly so.

Harry Hays was a trader! Earlier, he arranged through Edgar Pisani for a herd of Canadian milking Holsteins to be displayed at fairs throughout France; if enough people saw our cattle, he knew, they'd pressure their own politicians to bring them in.

Of course, he was right; in effect he established trade as a two-way street, smoothing a way for beef cattle out of France.

From then on, our biggest fight was with our own department of Trade and Commerce, which saw all this as their business, not ours.

*H*ARRY HAYS *(who died in 1982) comes across as a canny fellow with a good combination of political, business, and cow sense, which is more than I will say for Orville Freeman.*

Freeman, long-retired secretary of Agriculture under Presidents Kennedy and Johnson, was in Great Falls on a speaking tour in 1986 or 1987, and I—equipped with my tape recorder—volunteered to drive him to the airport. And he wouldn't talk! I had introduced myself as a rancher—big mistake! Freeman had had political differences with ranchers. No talk!

*F*ORTUNATELY, *I had only the greatest cooperation from retired government veterinarians on both sides of the border. Drs. Callis, Lewis, Mulhern, and Wells could not have been more helpful; Dr. Bob Anderson and his gracious wife, Eloise, put Claire and me up at Poverty Ridge, their farm near Marshall, Texas, and spent hours filling in details of the aftosa campaign and other events leading up to "The Importation." Even with my normal rancher bias, I tried to record their recollections accurately and use them fairly in my story.*

DR. FRANK MULHERN—USDA

With Eleutheran cattle on their shores and rumors of various schemes in the North Atlantic, the Canadians came to Washington and told us they were yielding to import pressures; they invited us to monitor the situation.

Our position was: "If you have to do it, we'll help." There had always been a free exchange of ideas between our departments, and in this case nothing was done without our consent—of that I'm sure.

DR. KEN WELLS—CDA

USDA sent a committee of veterinarians and livestock people to Ottawa to study the project with us. We met for a couple of days, and I laid out all my plans. We discussed them fully, and it was obvious that under our proposed conditions there would be no problems with Washington.

The committee went home and recommended, "For."

DR. JERRY CALLIS—USDA

I attended those meetings as director of Plum Island, and I had the distinct impression that Dr. Wells's mind was made up: He was going to bring in cattle; he just wanted to tell us how.

Ken Wells had guts! He *hoped* we'd approve of his plan; if we didn't, he'd go ahead, anyway. And Ken Wells was also a diplomat! He left it to me and Dr. John Brooksby, an observer from the Pirbright lab in England, to write the official protocol. We were glad to do so, and we did.

DR. BERT LEWIS—CDA

The chairman of the U.S. committee was a very sound, rational person: a senior retired USDA veterinarian with a forward-looking view; one who understood that nothing ever stands still. If science indicated that cattle could move safely, he saw no reason to stop them. He could have been a person who just said "No!"

*D*R. LEWIS *thinks the name of that sensible person may very well have been Anderson, and "our" Dr. Robert Anderson was definitely there.*

DR. BOB ANDERSON—USDA

We never said the Canadian plan was *safe*, but we took this position: If they applied all the tests and quarantines and inspections as proposed, we wouldn't automatically classify Canada as "infected." We wouldn't approve, but we'd go that far: We wouldn't automatically close the border.

Instead, we assigned USDA veterinarians to oversee inspections. The material—swabs and blood—would go to Pirbright for disposal. Finally, we approved Grosse Ile as the official Canadian maximum security quarantine station.

*G*ROSSE ILE *was the "Ellis Island" of Canada since the early 1800s; it is a graveyard for thousands of cholera and typhus victims.*

No longer needed for immigration in the 1930s, the facility became a laboratory for anti-biological warfare studies during World War Two. The "enemy agent": rinderpest. The department of Agriculture was the agency in charge of investigations. For cattle quarantine purposes in the 1960s, security was already well established. It would only be necessary to enlarge the barns.

But demand remained the unknown quantity.

ROD JAMES

I don't suppose the good Lord himself could have satisfied demand after word got out on *Appollon*.

It's the fall of 1965, and I'm in France lining up shipping. The smallest Cunard cattle boat holds 600 head—too large and too expensive. I find a wine boat that will take our calves on deck; my Alberta cowboys work as carpenters building deck huts.

A day at Lloyds. We insure for purchase price plus costs: $2,000 for heifers, $10,000 for bulls. No one knows their worth this side of the water. Then in January word gets out.

Appollon is owned by Lloyd Wilder of Fairmont and Winston Wolfendon of Brisco, British Columbia. While Winston is in France overseeing selection,

Appollon, *the bull that established the market for* "*exotics.*"—Browarny Photographics

Lloyd contacts a group of Charolais breeders at Caldwell, Idaho; eighty-four of them want in on the action.

Lloyd pitches them a deal: A quarter interest in *Appollon* with so many ampules of semen—$84,000!

Suddenly, cost is a minor factor. There's semen to be collected! Thousands of cows to be bred! Every bull on Grosse Ile is suddenly worth a third of a million bucks!

KEN WELLS
Veterinary director general of Canada

We soon found out that demand exceeded capacity; our first quarantine barn on Grosse Ile held 120 head, and we exceeded that with Charolais alone. The next year we doubled the space, but demand kept rising. In 1969 we met the demand by taking over the mink barn on St. Pierre.[103]

Permit applications were turned over to a committee of two research geneticists, two Charolais breed representatives, and two provincial civil servants. Then our Dr. Walter Moynihan assigned each applicant a coded serial number (I remember that so clearly) keeping his or her identity unknown. And we tried to see that each province got permits; it didn't seem fair that Alberta and Ontario should have them all.

There were allegations—but never official knowledge—of buying and selling permits. What we *did* know was that cattle went to the farm of the legal importer for the appropriate period of time—our district veterinarians saw to that. And quarantine costs were paid by the permittee.

There were rumors, but I can't recall canceling a single permit because of illegitimate activities. I was never under any pressure, never experienced interference, never received a political "recommendation," and I would be quite prepared to swear this under oath. In fact, in thirty years in Ottawa, under eight ministers of Agriculture, never once did anyone interfere with my decisions. Animal health is difficult to compromise.

NOW WE COME *to an area where some of our characters are still—after thirty years—"a little bit tempered." But controversy is history.*

BERT LEWIS—CDA

We in the Health of Animals branch had practically nothing to do with it, but my impression is that permits were never allocated under pressure. Having said that, it's also fair to say that many applicants invested heavily in developing and expressing breeding plans—no problem with that. Others, of course, may have counted on political influence; many folks do.

But, our department bow to political pressure? No, no, no! That just did not—could not—happen under the system we devised.

Importer DOUG BLAIR

Whether our civil servants knew it or not, there was plenty going on behind the scenes. In Saskatchewan, they say, a rancher's *horse* got a permit. On Prince Edward Island most permits were in the hands of Sandy Best.

Alexander "Sandy" Best was an entrepreneur with what you might call "close political connections." The son of a famous doctor—the discoverer of insulin—he'd had a term as member of Parliament and knew his way around. Sandy would talk a Maritime farmer into applying for a permit; he would line up the bulk of the money and end up "owning" fifty or sixty animals on each importation. He controlled and sold more Simmental, Limousin, Chianina, and Maine Anjou than any single person I ever heard of.

The problem was that Sandy's cattle, each worth $10,000 or $20,000, were imported in so many different names and never got properly registered—which made it tough to take care of little details, like transfer of legal ownership after sales. As it turned out, Sandy's business skills weren't quite up to his imagination; he died quite young and *not* a wealthy man.

Rancher GORDON BURTON

The application form was nonsense and treated as such: "Who are you? Where do you live? What do you plan to do to benefit Canada?" And there was inherent socialist bias: Help the little guy . . . in the Maritimes . . . knowing full well that the "little guy" would probably sell his permit to Sandy Best. Sandy learned to work the angles for all they were worth.

With his "associate," Howard Webster, one of the richest men in the world, Best went whole hog—maneuvering permits, collecting Charolais, Simmental, Limousin, Maine Anjou, and other breeds at Webster's Dundas Farm on Prince Edward Island. Hell! Webster owned the whole east end of Prince Edward Island; I attended his first "dispersal sale," which grossed $800,000.

But there were alleged "internal problems." Land and cattle were bought on Webster's account with titles in Sandy's name. Now, Howard Webster may have known bugger all about cattle, but he was an all-out whiz at balance sheets and deeds! It was only a matter of time until high living and fancy footwork caught up with Best.

MARSHALL COPITHORNE
first president of the Canadian Chianina Association

Permits! The shoddiest business that ever was! Shady, crooked, manipulatin' deals! As a Chianina officer, I was responsible for unscrambling many early Italian imports, so I know! We found owners of record [permittees] who had been dead for many years when the permits were issued.

One of my problems involved some Quebec farmers who had purchased hundreds of ampules of Chianina semen. They were sittin' on a fortune—*if and when* their calves could be recorded[104]

But, first, the sires had to be recorded. And, when bulls were found to have been imported in fictitious names, registrations could not be transferred. Somebody was making a fortune in semen while leaving their customers (our members) holding the bag.

Inquiring on behalf of the Chianina association, I was directed to a government office where I met an assistant deputy in charge of production [whose name is not mentioned in this book]. So this guy sat me down in his office and said, "If I were you, in the best interest of my health and that of my family, I'd forget all about this deal; I'd get right back to Alberta with my nose clean." I can still see the face; I can still hear the voice. There's a hell of a lot to forget in "official" Ottawa.

GERRY LALONDE

And, of course, there were the Bronfmans—the Seagrams whiskey people . . . with the Nova Scotia feedlot, where good Ontario whiskey-slush was fed to Quebecois cattle. Bronfman permit applications would surely include dozens of good things they would do for Canada.

Could that explain why they got two or three import permits every time they applied? [Gerry laughs.]

ROD JAMES

As Charolais association secretary in 1967, I was in Ken Wells's office with a group of Charolais breeders protesting the Bronfman imports going straight to Texas. This was common practice in 1966, but it was contrary to the newest regulations, and we presented Ken Wells with the facts.

"I don't believe there's a word of truth in this," says Ken, "but, tell you what: I'll phone Sam Bronfman right now." And he picks up the phone—doesn't even look up the number—and, as I remember, [his end of] the conversation went like this:

"Sam? Ken Wells here. There's some cowboys in my office who claim you're fronting for Texans . . ."

". . . How's that, Sam? No, I'm sure you don't need the money. If you wanta import cattle, you'll import 'em for yourself . . ."

"Sure, Sam. Thanks! Sorry to trouble ya."

Then he turns back to us, "See, boys? Not a word of truth in your story. Sam Bronfman says so himself."

We had some hot discussions in the Charolais association on the subject of selling permits. We had worked very hard to get cattle in; now there was quite a market just in permits.

Most of us were pretty naive: "Oh, no! We'd never sell permits!" But then there were the realists like Wayne Malmberg. "Boys," said Wayne, "my wife and kids are the only things I got that ain't for sale. Everything has a price—just a matter of how much."

"I don't know," said Wayne, "just how much is 'much.' Might be ten, might be fifty, might be a hundred thousand bucks. But, somewhere along the line,

278

*Charolais pioneer Wayne
Malmberg.* —Ted Pritchett

one of these chunks of paper might be enough to lift a mortgage . . . save a
ranch. So let's not point the finger at those who would sell their permits."
(And it should be added that Wayne was not among them.)

GERARD LALONDE

You remember Baar-Nason, the Frenchman? As soon as he learned about
Mack, he went right home and formed a company and sold half the shares to
Canadians and started buying cattle, which arrived at St. Pierre-Miquelon
with Mack's, two years before the official importation.

But then this Frenchman got a little bit hard to deal with; he was the manager, and in a French company the manager has control. So, when he offered to buy us out, we were glad to sell and import on our own. But, somehow, Baar-Nason got permission to bring a bull and two cows into Canada from St. Pierre as soon as Grosse Ile opened. Mack didn't get a permit; Baar-Nason did. How did that happen? Just "one of those things," I guess. Anyway, the [older] Baar-Nason cattle arrived in Canada with ours.

ROD JAMES

By the middle of March, the imports were ready to come ashore, but the river was still frozen except for shipping lanes. How about bringing them off with a helicopter? A couple of companies were bidding for our business.

"Ever haul a live animal under a chopper?" I asked a pilot.

"No problem," was the answer.

"We'll pack 'em tight in their crates," I said, "but they'll be swinging. Will the swinging create any danger?"

"No danger at all," said the pilot; "I got a button right on the stick. All I have to do is push, and the load will drop in the river. No danger at all."

"Maybe not for you," I thought, "but my clients will certainly kill me," and that ended any thought of a helicopter.

Next I found an old steel hulk made for breaking into icebound harbors early in spring; she was made to order, and we fitted her out with stalls. It was an overnight voyage downriver to Grosse Ile, and I settled down in a bunk near the engine room and tried to sleep with the engines pounding in my ears. Next morning when the boat pulled up to the wharf, the loading went smoothly; the crane operator would pick up a crated animal and drop it into the hold, where it would be uncrated and tied in a stall for the twenty-four-hour voyage back upriver.

There were hundreds of people waiting on the dock when the cattle arrived at Quebec City, and the press was with them—*Appollon* had seen to that. With the media in attendance, everyone's talking French, and one of the boat crew tells us that the stevedores won't let anyone touch an animal.

What would it cost to have *them* do it?

Four hundred fifty dollars an hour. And we're about to have a war. But just before the cowboys and stevedores tangle, the cops come along and say the stevedores are right: It's their dock; nobody touches a hair without their say-so. Then the fun begins.

Baar-Nason's two-year-old heifers have to be reloaded into crates to be swung ashore. They have horns, and they look dangerous! The longshoremen try to untie them with a stick.

The bigger Baar-Nason cattle were crated down in the hold.

Next they attempt to shoo them into their crates: "Shoo! Shoo! Shoo!" at $450 an hour. At last, we pay 'em to stay the hell out of the way, and we get the cattle ashore.

GERRY LALONDE

And once ashore, you can sell a yearling heifer for $10,000 and upwards over the phone. All a Texan wants to know is: "How many ya got? How soon can ya ship 'em? What bank d'ya deal with?" And the money is always waiting at the bank.

ROD JAMES

As CCA secretary, I'm the only "civilian" authorized on Grosse Ile, but when I board the boat the second year, here's Bert Wheeler: not a veterinarian, not a technician, just a liquor store owner from Texas dressed like a rancher, big hat and all.

"What in hell you doin' here, Bert?" I asked.

"Oh, I got a letter . . ." Bert was a good supporter of Senator Connally of Texas, who had pressured Washington to pressure Ottawa to approve a pass for Bert. That way, he gets to see the imports before they are seen by their owners or anyone else; then, back in his hotel room, he's on the phone makin' deals before the owners even know what they got.

That's politics! Not much Dr. Wells could do about that.

ROD JAMES

Once ashore, the imports were quarantined at home for ninety days, and a like number of native cattle with them; a government vet was to periodically visually inspect them all for brucellosis and TB. One day an official car drove into the Malmbergs' yard: "We're here to test your cattle."

"Fine," said Wayne.

"If you'll show us where they are, we'll get started."

"They're right out there in the pasture."

"How about runnin' 'em in where we can see 'em?"

"I'm busy," said Wayne. "You can see the cattle right out there in that field just as healthy as can be," and quite an argument ensued before the cattle were properly tested.

The next year Wayne didn't bother to apply for a permit, but he gets a call from Wells: "We're going over applications, and I don't see one from you."

"You can stick 'em up your ass," said Wayne—which was vintage Malmberg.

And he got a permit, anyway—which was the way things were.

AND THIS is also the way things were:

DR. BERT LEWIS—CDA

The Malmberg brothers had been keenly interested in getting Charolais cattle from France; they had been forceful in exploring all possibilities but weren't particularly known for cooperation.

I especially remember Wayne. I condemned his first imported bull to slaughter when he tested positive for TB!

DR. BOB ANDERSON—USDA

Canadian breeders very rightly pressured their government: "These new genes are a national asset; they shouldn't be exported! They should be used to build Canadian herds."

GERRY LALONDE—*Ontario cattleman*

My imports came to my farm to stay, but the first year many went across the line [to the States] as soon as they came off quarantine.

But the second year, if you were exporting anything French—even the full-French offspring of an import—you had to have a Trade & Commerce permit. That was horseshit—filling out all those forms, which you couldn't even get for a couple months, anyway.

JONATHAN FOX—*Saskatchewan breeder*

But, after all the trouble gettin' 'em here, making 'em stay for a couple of months—even a couple of years—was a very good thing. Made it easier for the breeders. Kept the profiteers out—well, slowed 'em down a bit; we needed the profiteers, but we also needed the breeders—the sincere ones, anyway.

MACK BRALY—*Oklahoma importer*

That Canadian export embargo caught me off guard—set me back when I had it made. Damn bureaucrats and politicians!

I don't include Dr. Wells; it was that boss of his, that deputy. We were sittin' in his office just at sundown and could see way out to the west. What a pretty sight it was! How good I felt! I should have known he might betray me.

He was sittin' there—typical stiff-necked civil servant: "Gentlemen, we have determined that you can bring your St. Pierre cattle through Grosse Ile. Matures will stay in Canada for awhile, but calves born on St. Pierre can go direct to the States after the normal three-month, on-farm quarantine."

As a result, about twenty St. Pierre-born bulls were sitting on a farm just outside Ottawa. Six months, eight months, up to two-year-olds, they were, and folks from Ohio, Oklahoma, and Texas were there to buy them. They all had price tags on 'em, and the buyers had papers and pencils and were makin' selections; we had agreed on prices and everything right there in that farm-yard. Everybody was happy. Feelin' good!

Then, just as we finished our business it started to rain. We got in the cars and motored back to the hotel and were just gettin' in the elevator when a newspaper headline hit me:

Including calves! They had changed the rules and killed my deal! Even Canadian-borns had to stay. I rushed to Ottawa: "How can you all break your word like this?"

"Sorry, Mr. Braly. Parliament has determined that cattle coming through quarantine are a national resource. Blame Parliament, not us," said the deputy minister.

But politicians do what bureaucrats tell 'em! Remember: *You must never let up the pressure on bureaucrats, ever!*

Once Canadian breeders were into production, I went to Dr. Wells: "How about some of these old cows goin' to Oklahoma, if I promise to bring 'em right back? Just to let people see."

"Well," Ken said, "might be all right."

Then, exploring possibilities: "How about, when these cows are ready to calve—how about calvin' 'em in Oklahoma, weanin' early, leavin' the calves, and bringin' the dams on back?"

"I'll see about it," said Wells, and he called back later: "You can plan on it, Mr. Braly. Go ahead!" And he just kept extending the time until finally: "You can take all your females down, and you don't need to bring 'em back."

And, right then, Dr. Wells won my fullest respect as an administrator and gentleman. Soon, even my original imports were at home on my Charolais ranch in Pontotoc County.

Eventually, four or five of our shipments came in direct to the States—bang, bang!—like that. It was my young son, George, done that; just a jug-eared, green Oklahoma boy, who went to Washington and learned to handle the bureaucrats! He was great!

Our last imports came in 1975: over fifteen years after my first Charolais bull, "Seguter"; almost twenty after beginning my investigations; more than thirty after seeing those big white cows laying belly-up on the fields of France. Come to think, a tremendous lot had happened.

And, come to think, it was mostly because of a fella named Charlie Bates. If it hadn'ta been for Charlie and his little screwball piddlin' sprigs of Midland Bermuda grass, just a heck of a lotta things would never have happened!

Here's to ya, Brother Charlie!

25   Exotic Buying

TOM GILCHRIST

In 1968 we imported *Carnival*; bought him in partnership with American Breeders Service and the Campbells in Arizona, who had introduced us to Charolais in the first place. Quite a commotion about importing a bull with American partners, I can tell you! So we didn't talk much about it. *Carnival* was lodged with ABS at Calgary, and we used him heavily on Charolais cows whose calves could go to the States as "domestic fullbloods."

RAY WOODWARD

I picked *Carnival* and many others for Canadian and American owners, and, with little objective data at such a young age, all we could do was pick calves from mothers that showed good udders, feet, and legs—"structurally sound," we said. What we didn't consider was whether those bulls would cross on Angus or Hereford—the basic determinant of a good European import. How in hell could we figure that, with nothing to go on?

So we arrived in France to make our selections, and the first trouble spots we encountered were the agencies—Syndex, Cofranimex, and so on; their agents were on commission and fought like tigers for our business.

GERARD LALONDE

Pierre Boudry was the head of Cofranimex, and he had a partner who stayed in Nevers [the Charolais center] to catch the buyers near the farms and do the export. Pierre, acting as guide, stayed in between.

All the buyers were staying at the same hotel and often the western lads would tell me, "Heads up, Gerry! These French buggers are trying to put one over." Being completely bilingual, I kept the playing field level; for instance, we thought they were trying to cheat us on performance. The first year we asked for records, and they were vague; the third year they had details for twenty years back. That was a joke!

And they tested our ability to drink: Every time we looked at a bull there was another bottle of wine. They were very, very good hosts; we could have feasted every day. But finally I told Boudry, "Enough! Enough!" I had orders for thirty head; I wanted to buy cattle; I had to be right!

But Boudry would say, "If a breeder invites you in for champagne, Gerry, you must go in!" and he was serious. "Maybe in your country, if you're busy, you can refuse. But here in France, you cannot! Things are different in France."

The French breeders, they would assess you, not becoming friends right away; then, if they liked you, they were sincere, and I liked them, too. So, over I'd go and make my pick at the required very young age and come home happy. Then, as my calf grew, if they didn't want to let go, how very easy to vaccinate it for foot-and-mouth and disqualify it for Canada.

"But, surely, you don't think we would do a thing like that?" . . . and with a big smile, you know.

No, no, no! I didn't think it—ah, they were sincere. It was not their fault. I could understand. Such things just happened.

DOUG BLAIR

Doug Baird and I were buying in France with Albert Massier, our guide. (If you ever drove with Albert, you'd remember him forever.) So everyone wanted to be the perfect host and offered a bottle of wine, and, visiting at least eight farms a day, we could hardly *see* the cattle. Finally we called a halt.

"But, we will insult the breeders, non?" said Albert.

"Perhaps," I said. "But from now on it's a bottle of wine in the morning, a bottle in the afternoon, and you figure out who to insult and who to drink with. And another thing, Albert, no more two-hour lunches!" But we always had two-hour lunches. Albert was sure that anything less would be inhospitable, and in retrospect he was right. *We* were the crazies; we should have taken more time for the wine, the people, the history. But we were young Canadians in a hurry to make money.

286

HANS ULRICH

I was visiting home in 1966, when I learned that "Travelin' Smith" had been in Switzerland, asking questions, looking at calves. He had finally found an unvaccinated Pie Rouge in France—luckily, a good one, because that was *Parisien*: good enough to give the whole Simmental breed a running start in America.

At home in Alberta I looked up Smith, and he (being short of cash) invited me in on *Parisien*: The best investment I ever made! So I never imported an animal myself; instead, I became a shareholder of Simmental Breeders of Cardston, Ltd. (SBL, for short), which sent me to Europe on company business once a year, at least, for the next five years.

Alberta rancher WES ALM

I had never been to Europe until the importation; then I made three trips in as many years. The Swiss were great hosts, but I was just too busy with cattle to do much partying—all day, every day, looking at cattle.

The hard part was assessing what we saw. At a sales station, we didn't know where the calves had come from, how they'd been raised, under what conditions. If they appeared to be growing fast, had they been half-starved before weaning? Were calves from good milking cows now standing still? Picking bulls at such a young age made the chances of getting a "powerhouse" pretty slim, but those were the rules of the game, laid out in the name of health and safety.

HANS ULRICH

I'm kind of proud of the role I played in selecting the Swiss cattle; with so much family in Switzerland I had an advantage.

Swiss calves are often pail fed (which many people didn't know), and so, when you looked at a "pail bunter," it was hard to tell the genetics. We realized pretty quick that we had to do something different; then Father started gathering good prospects and testing them on my brother-in-law's farm for a hundred days. That was the key to our success in importing Simmentals.

*I*N 1966, I WAS OFFERED *a share in* Parisien *for something like $2,500. I declined. It was one of the best investments I ever missed!*

Travers Smith with presentation portrait of Parisien, *the first imported Simmental.*
—Ted Pritchett

SUDDENLY WAKING UP in 1969, I applied for a Limousin permit and asked
Louis de Neuville to pick me a heifer. Never having seen a pure Limousin of any
sex at the time, and never having been to Europe, it seemed like a good idea to visit
France.

Late winter of 1970. School break. Calving not due to start for several weeks.
Our whole family flew to Amsterdam, drove to Paris, had a look at the Arc de
Triomphe, the Tour d'Eiffel, the Louvre, and then hit for Limousin country: capital
city Limoges, the center of famous pottery; Domaine de Pompadour, a fortified
"farmhouse" built by a king for his mistress; the homelike Limousin hill country,
good pasture for sheep and cattle; Domaine de Combas, the estate of friend Louis de
Neuville; the ELPA test station, early performance center; M. DesChamps's farm,
birthplace of our heifer. Everywhere, red, well-muscled cattle—walking stores of
power and meat (and cash) for Limousin farmers.

After a long morning's drive in the hills of Correze, we were invited to dinner at
the Bourbon family farm. Seated at a long, wooden table in an old stone farmhouse
with M. Bourbon at one end and Louis de Neuville at the other, we enjoyed a ten-
course meal, one course at a time, served by Mme. Bourbon and her mother-in-law,
an old lady dressed in black.

First, an anise aperitif; then soup; then wine; then rabbit; then wine; then peas;
then wine; then beef, potatoes, ham, and so on, each with a different wine, ending

I liked this well-muscled calf and the typically well-shaped udder on this Limousin cow in France.

the meal with anisette—a powerful cordial. This was a memorable "lunch" for our teenagers, while I, myself, feared for the honor of Canada (famous the world over for 5 percent beer) until I noticed our host diluting his grape with water—a "barbaric" Gallic custom noted in Roman times.

Educational! Unforgettable! Great merchandising!—as we staggered out to inspect M. Bourbon's stable.

After a very good dinner, the hospitable M. Bourbon showed us his young herd prospects.
—Claire Ewing

Pinzgauer, a growthy Austrian breed that probably didn't arrive early enough or in enough numbers to achieve its full potential. About 1,500 animals are registered annually in the United States in the 1990s. —Browarny Photographics

Blonde D'Aquitaine, a composite breed from southern France, was another late arrival. One hundred fifty breeders registered about 1,200 animals in 1994. —Browarny Photographics

DOUG BLAIR

"First-in-itis," it was called, and it was catching. You came down with it when you realized what the very first bull of the latest breed was worth. You could presell $50,000 or $100,000 worth of semen from such a bull, whether bull or breed had any merit or not.

Meuse-Rhine-Yssel? Belgian Blue? (Breeds hardly ever heard of again.) The first bull in . . . Worth a fortune! Simple as that!

INFECTED WITH "first-in-itis" and hearing of bigger cattle over the Alps, we left the range of the Limousin and drove to Italy to meet Vittorio Rizzo, our summer-of-'63 ranch hand who conducted us on a tour of the hill country near Sienna, home of Chianina cattle and Chianti wine.

I thought of my pal Jim Gray as we watched a hitch of white cows cultivating a field, and I'll never forget a herd of Chianina heifers galloping into the high-walled cobbled yard of the Forteguerri farm like so many unbroke fillies. They'd been living on poplar trees, Sr. Forteguerri said—quite a promoter, he. They would be breeding and browsing "combines" on foothills ranches.

That was our first look at the Chianina breed, and we were impressed but too-late smart. First-in-itis vanished as we learned how well the Italians knew the market: Forteguerri kept an apartment in New York; "the contessa" was even then in Ottawa drumming up trade. We returned to the Porcupine Hills, aware of the competition. Jonathan Fox had been there first!

JONATHAN FOX

Chianina: Greatest cattle I ever dealt with. Only one thing wrong—disposition! Too much "cow" for the average cowman. Gotta be a horseman to get along with Chianina.

It was different in Italy. When Molly and I first went there, we saw kids and calves sleeping together in the stalls; teenagers leadin' 'em, playin' with 'em; old women putting them in the mower, cutting hay. We never expected they'd get such a wild reputation. They earned it, though, in Canada! [He laughs.]

MARY GARST: We call them "Kees" or "Ki-a-ninnies" in Iowa.

BUDDY COBB: It's "*Kick*-aninnies," in Montana.

JACK PHILLIPS

One day my phone rang in Missouri, and it was Jonathan Fox; he and Molly were back in Canada from Italy: "Git your bag packed, Jack. I got two permits, and you're my partner. You got just seven days to get over and pick 'em out."

"Hell," I says, "I never been out of the country; I don't even have a passport! I *cain't* get a passport and all in just seven days."

"Well, one of us must go," said Jonathan. "What'll I pick?"

"The only way we'll make money is with semen," I said, "so what we need is a semen-producing bull. So, look for the biggest-nutted herd sire you can find. Then buy the biggest-nutted calf. He'll make us money."

"You gotta be kiddin'!" Jonathan had never heard such a thing before; it sounded like an old wives' tale to him.

But I wasn't kidding; this went a long ways back beyond research. So Jonathan went to Italy and came home laughing: "I found a bull named *Bando* with the biggest nuts I ever saw in my life. I bought a son with the biggest nuts and, wait till you hear his name! It's *Friggio*, the way the Italians say it, but we're gonna call him "Frig-io." And I hope to hell ya know what you are doin'."

So we made a deal with Blair at Western Breeders where *Friggio* produced 4,000 straws a month for a solid year.[105] "Fertile Frig-io!" He went in the books for the most first-service conceptions ever recorded. So I did know what I was doing. There was truth in the old wives' tale.

MARSHALL COPITHORNE

Jonathan bought *Faro, Fonto,* and *Friggio* in 1970, and he and his American partners and Doug Blair at Western Breeders were makin' nothin' but money with "Frig-io" semen. In 1973 Jonathan went back with a pocket full of permits for himself and other ranchers, and I went with him. We traveled with agent Lucio Salone of the export agency, Cemex, and a guide who showed us Italy at 120 miles an hour.

TERESA COSTANZI—*Cemex driver/interpreter*

Well, I want to make two things clear. I never got caught speeding, and I never heard Salone cheat or mistreat anyone—neither customer nor producer. He was as honest as he could be. And I should know! I translated everything he said.

And a wonderful job it was! We guided dozens of Canadian and American ranchers through Chianina, Marchigiana, and Romagnola country; we made side trips to see the "double-muscled" Piedmontese breed; we saw the Maremmana cattle in their swampy area near Rome—they are the same as Chianina only smoky-colored and smaller, with great huge horns. Oh, it was a wonderful job, showing those cowboys the cattle and the country.

MARSHALL COPITHORNE

We traveled the back roads and found the rural Italians to be the friendliest people on earth. I remember watching a team of cows pulling a chunk of steel attached to a wooden stick. Some kind of plow that was! And, my goodness! First thing ya know, the farmer is taking *our* pictures plowing his field.

Next he invites us to visit his farm a quarter mile away. The guy goes runnin' ahead, calling his wife, waving his arms; then he digs out some wine from a room in his barn and glasses from under four or five inches of dust. But that's not good enough for company, so over to the well—a real old, stone-cribbed well, with chickens roostin' on the windlass, poopin' into the water—and up comes a bucket. He shines up the glasses and pours, and it's really good wine! I've tasted it all and know the good stuff by now.

There was lots of good wine, but not many idle moments, traveling with Jonathan. He and I alone, I think, brought 250 Italian cattle into Canada over the next three years.

Back in Ottawa, deputy minister of Agriculture

S. B. "SYD" WILLIAMS

There had been all kinds of pressure for an Italian importation, and all kinds of people coming to Ottawa. I remember one old duchess—what was her name? She hounded us to let Italian cattle in. Apparently, she had an "in" with External Affairs—something about helping prisoners-of-war during World War Two.

TERESA COSTANZI

That was "the old contessa"—Contessa Marinetta di Frassineto—who owned a famous Chianina herd and must have been eighty years old (and not a youthful eighty, either). She was tall and must have been good-looking in her youth—used utterly *pounds* of makeup, *tons* of jewelry, and had been through at least four husbands in her time.

The contessa didn't like me. I was "that interpreter for the agency," and I was probably out to cheat her. She was belligerent as heck. Of course, I didn't take it personal—*everybody* was cheating the old contessa. I remember her crying that "they" were taking advantage of her age—nobody cared, nobody was looking after her affairs . . .

The contessa traveled the world, speaking excellent English with four diamond rings on her fingers and a legendary wartime record, helping Allied prisoners escape. *Nobody* took advantage of the old contessa.

And she was hell-bent on sellin' calves to Jonathan Fox. The rest of the boys were *peasants*—Fox's foot soldiers, we called them.

—Ball Studios

294

JONATHAN FOX

I had to get rough with the old contessa once. We were negotiatin' a bull sale, and she wanted out, claiming government interference. "Welsh on this deal," I said, "and I'll call Dr. Wells in Ottawa; that'll end your exports forever."

There was lots of Italians around, and I couldn't speak the language. "I better put this in motion!" I thought, so I started bangin' the table—bangin' my fist till the goddam wine jugs jumped right off the boards.

Then Forteguerri taps me on the shoulder: "Be calm, Jonathan," he says. "I'll look after the matter." And he did—a hell of a fine gent, was Forteguerri. But the old contessa, findin' she couldn't pull the racket she was tryin', started to cry; "You are *toro*, Jonathan. Big, fat *toro*!" [Jonathan laughs.] Later she says, "That was a compliment, Seenyor Fox. You are big, strong bull!"

As I used to say in the show ring: "The real is never obvious, and the obvious never real." And that sure as hell held true dealin' with the Italians.

TERESA COSTANZI

The Italian idea of cowboys was unreal. I remember a night when Salone and I were showing the boys the town: Sienna, a very quiet, reserved, Italian hill town.

Well, Jonathan showed up in the palazzo in Indian moccasins, green western pants, a bright, bright blue shirt, a red velvet jacket with black satin lapels, a cowboy hat, a bolo tie, Hereford cuff links, and the ever-present cigar. Half the town was following, laughing, in stitches tugging at his elbow trying to figure him out.

I had never seen anyone dressed like that myself, never before nor since; nor has anyone else. But Jonathan saw nothing funny about it; he had done himself up quite nicely for a quiet night on the town. For the locals, it was a taste of "spaghetti western."

Full-French Limousin calf Louise was born to the imported Esmeralda in the Porcupine Hills.

*J*UST A SAMPLE *of ranching activities in the seventies—an era unlikely to be repeated on The Ranch.*

Our imported Limousin heifer, Esmeralda, grew into a gentle cow who took to the Alberta hills like a native and adapted well to scavenging the range. We bred her to Dandin C, *a bull imported by the Brandon (Manitoba) research station, and we named their calf* Louise, *in honor of Louis de Neuville, who was visiting at the time.*

Right after weaning that fall, the American auctioneer Jim Baldridge bought Louise for $20,000. Esmeralda was what Jack Phillips would call a mighty efficient cow!

26   Big Bucks

DOUG BLAIR

I remember the Pie Rouge [Simmental] bull *Parisien* coming off the boat looking very much like a Guernsey. I thought, "Nobody's gonna breed to a bull like that!" That was 1967.

I thought differently a year or so later, when word spread through the industry that Travelin' Smith had fleeced a doctor of $500 a head for half-blood calves! A couple of years later we were selling tons of semen, and our customers were getting tremendous premiums.

This is how it worked on the Bar 15:

WES ALM

Dr. Ken Graham, the local vet, had twenty-three ampules of *Parisien* semen: "Better take 'em home and try 'em," he said.

They were fifteen bucks an ampule—an unheard-of price at the time—but curiosity kills the cat, you know, so I stuck 'em into some cows, and next fall the neighbors were joking about "Alm's Dairy."

Then a guy drove into my yard—a doctor: Would I sell my *Parisien* heifer calves?

I guessed I would. I set a price of $500 a head. With good Hereford heifers going for a hundred bucks in those days, he wouldn't bite, I was sure. But hadn't some doc paid Travers Smith $500 for crossbred calves just a few months before?

"It's a deal," the fellow said, and before I could change my mind he had contracted a hundred Bar 15 cows to be bred the next spring to *Bismark*, a new Simmental bull just imported by ABS. I soon found out that Dr. Dixon knew what he was doing.[106]

297

SID LORE

Alan Dixon was a highly qualified MD and an excellent businessman. I was the livestock fieldman for the province, and he often called for advice, so I got to know him well.

Dixon owned the Bar 11, a small ranch west of Nanton, and he was upset because he couldn't write off expenses. He needed a profit. "If I can clear a single dollar," he said, "I can declare it as taxable income and prove my point to Revenue Canada: Bar 11 is a *business*, not a hobby!"

"You're unlikely to see that dollar," I thought, "with the wages you pay and only seventy cows."

But, then I thought: "Maybe with purebreds . . . Perhaps with exotics . . ." I suggested Limousin, Charolais, Simmental. And with Alan's wife, Hermie, being of Swiss descent, Simmental it was, and before long the Dixons were applying for permits.

Now, after the first couple of years, Dr. Wells was screening out doctors and lawyers, and most permits were going to legitimate, full-time cattlemen—with exceptions, of course.

Alan Dixon, first president, Canadian Simmental Association. —Browarny Photographics

Dr. Dixon was an exception, and he phoned me one day: "Got some permits! Goin' to Switzerland! What do I look for?"

"The first thing to look for is Hans Ulrich!" I said.

"I know; I know. I've already contacted Hans," Alan said, "but I'm gonna be there, too, and whaddaya think I should look for?"

"You'll be shown 'pail bunters,'" I said, "and you won't have a clue on performance. So ask to see the parents. Look to the sires for muscling, length, feet, legs, and structural soundness. What you want in a cow is fertility and mothering ability, so look to the dams for plenty of bone and good udders."

"What's a 'good' udder?" Alan wanted to know.

"You're an MD," I said. "You know what a good *human* udder is, so just imagine four of 'em in a cluster."

And I guess my advice was good, because Alan exceeded his goal for taxable income, and before he died, a few years later and much too young, he had sold one calf for $100,000!

DOUG BLAIR

June 1968: My partners and I decided to bite the bullet and go into business for ourselves. Our staff as we started construction consisted of Gordy DeLair as lab-man; Joy, my bacteriologist wife, as lab assistant; and Gordy's wife, Pat, as secretary. A few months later, Western Breeders Service, Ltd., opened its doors with fourteen Charolais bulls and a pen of Holstein "teasers." And our timing was right on the money! In just a few years our annual sales hit $5 million. You see, the rule that had stumped Mack Braly by keeping imports in the country, was a big, big advantage for Canadians. Unbeknownst to the general public, many imported bulls were placed at our stud for management, collection, and sales. A golden opportunity for a young company!

In 1969 I applied for and got four "open" permits, meaning we could bring in any breeds we wanted. I chose one Limousin bull, *Eros*; one Maine Anjou, *Capone*; and a Simmental, whose name doesn't matter because, a few weeks later, Werner Wyss from the Swiss Federation phoned me early one morning: "Bad news, Doug; your Simmental calf went down on test. But the good news is your second choice is okay. Do you want him at $756?"

Disappointment? Sure! Beginners luck? You bet! My second choice was *Extra*, and the price was certainly right. I knew very little about picking bulls at the time; in later years I would learn just enough to be dangerous and was never so lucky again.

Western Breeders, our young company, had been managing bulls for Simmental Breeders of Cardston, and when Travers learned of *Extra* he saw conflict: We might start pushing our bulls and holding back theirs. "Perhaps SBL should *lease* your bull," said Travers; "I've checked with our lawyer and, within regulations, we could 'lease' him from you now at his true market value and 'buy' him for a dollar three years down the road. Whaddaya say?"

Well, *Extra* was still in quarantine, but based on bulls like *Appollon*, he had to be worth at least thirty-five grand the minute he stepped ashore. That was lots of cash for youngsters on a shoestring.

DeLair and I had each put in $10,000; Rod James had kicked in $7,500, and his brother, Earl, the land; we were already into the bank for $30,000, and the slightest bump would leave us dead in the water. This plan gave us room to breathe, so we signed the lease, and SBL was the actual owner of *Extra* when he came ashore—which was not announced, of course.

A couple years later the SBL boys began building a stud of their own, which meant they might move *Extra*, which begged the question: "Wouldn't it be embarrassing if we appeared to be 'trafficking' in imports?" Travers thought all our names could stand protection, so he agreed to sell *Extra* back for $70,000—plus $10,000 in royalties on semen in the tank.

We closed the deal, and three years later, when results of the Canadian Beef Sires progeny test were in, *Extra* was one of the great bulls in his breed! In the next few months we would sell over a million dollars worth of semen.

Extra. —Browarny Photographics

300

COMMERCIAL ranchers and feeders were quick to get on board.

EION CHISHOLM

It was our oldest daughter, Donna, who got us into "exotics." Having seen what happened with Charolais, she begged me to go for a permit; I applied for a Simmental, and the heifer we purchased cost us $4,000 off the boat.

That was a pile! "I'm outta my tree," I thought, "no matter how good she is."

My son-in-law, Don, had it right: "All we need is 400 bucks a calf, and in just ten years we'll have our money back without any interest. That is, if the cow don't die!" he said.

But her first calf, sired by *Florian*, sold for $16,500 at four-and-a-half months of age, and thereafter things got better. A couple sales later, a solid red heifer came through the ring and, liking everything about her, I just shelled out $10,000 and brought her home and bred her—didn't even bother Thelma or the kids.

Well, before she even calved, Donna phoned from the ranch: "Dad, there's a fella here lookin' at *Julia*. What'll ya take?"

"She's a pretty damn good heifer," I said, "and I'm not very fussy about sellin' her. But, if the guy's got fifty grand . . ."

"He's only got forty-seven thousand five-hundred . . ."

"We can't afford to own her . . ." [And Eion laughs.]

On the Bar 15, WES ALM

We plowed all that first easy money back into the ranch. I built a quonset barn for our first big sale in 1973, and everyone thought I was nuts. That sale averaged $4,000 a head, and nobody could believe it.

Then things really went crazy. I think of the "ballroom sale" in Denver, where Owen Rogers from Frenchman's Butte sold a mighty Simmental heifer; several Albertans—to promote the breed—formed a partnership to buy her.

I could have gone it alone. Jim Hadley, the Bank of Commerce manager in Claresholm, told me just before I left, "Anything looks good, Wes—just buy it!" That was the craziness of it; I could have wrote a check for $150,000. The bankers were generous, generous—got lots of people in trouble!

I got off easy that time! I was to go to $35,000. The auctioneer started at $25,000 and was soon at $47,500. I bid forty-eight; someone else forty-eight and a half, and they stopped the sale. Then the sale manager, Casey Anderson, made a speech about the breeder and the Simmental breed in general, and when the sale got goin' again you could hear a pin drop.

Then one of my partners, Ward Robinson, slipped in beside me and whispered, "You're on your own now, Wes. No bull's worth $50,000." And I'm sure as hell glad he did, because the bull went to Oklahoma for $51,000, and neither he nor his buyers were ever heard of again. Fantasyland, while it lasted!

And on the T Bar, ROL AND CAROL MOSHER

ROL: Travelin' Smith came by talkin' Simmental, sellin' semen. We bought some *Parisien* semen, and his calves weighed 700 pounds at weaning—we'd never seen the likes! Along towards fall you couldn't tell the calves from their mothers beside them.

CAROL: A couple of years later we had seventy *Parisien* daughters bred to drop three-quarter calves, when along came this Texan . . .

ROL: . . . Albert West, insurance man, Rio Vista Farms. Wanted in when the breed was just gettin' hot. Talked us into selling three-quarter blood Simmental heifers and calvin' 'em here on the ranch. And how we sweated them out! Lucky to lose just one calf and cripple just two heifers. Pullin' too fast, I guess.

CAROL: Sweatin' them out, I guess! At $3,250 a pair!

And at Coon Rapids, Iowa, STEVE GARST

Marv Staten, selling for Curtis [Breeding Service], said, "Buy our exotic semen and I'll get you an extra fifty bucks for your calves."

Well, we already had an AI program using Brown Swiss for milk, so switching to the new breeds looked like a cinch to me. Word of the early contracts got us so excited that we used, I'm gonna say, 20 percent of all the available Simmental and Limousin semen in the country before we were done.

A couple years later we attended the first big Simmental bash in Denver; that's when we knew we were going to hold our own sale. Daughter Sarah worked like crazy organizing, and she was very successful, too—with lots of help from Albert West and the Joneses.

Buster and Irene Jones—what a couple they were! Buster had red and white Simmentals; Irene, white Charolais (so they could tell 'em apart, they said). They'd sit up front in the sale barn and make a production of bidding—well, they made a production of everything they did, but their bidding was *strategic*: Bluffing other buyers; acting like they were prepared to go on forever.

Albert West had a different approach; he'd sneak in the back and flick just a finger—just enough for a ring man to see. At our 1970 sale, the Joneses sat up front and hogged all the Limos while Albert skulked in back and took home $56,000 worth of Simmentals. Hell of a sale!

*N*OW, THERE WERE PLENTY *of honest, aggressive, able cattle auctioneers in the country (Ken Hurlburt at Fort Macleod, Tony Perlich at Lethbridge, Pat Goggins at Billings have done great work for me) but, back in the 1970s, with so much "exotic" money around, specialists were called in to tie it down. Curt Rodgers and Jim Baldridge were among those who made it their business to know the strengths and eccentricities of all the big spenders.*

CURT RODGERS

My firm was blessed to hold the first of many new breed sales—Gelbvieh, Maine-Anjou, Tarantaise, Chianina were some of my "firsts"—and before the rush was over we'd managed hundreds of sales from Prince Edward Island to California. Well, we sold over 60,000 head of breeding cattle in the 1976-1986 decade, and that was after the rush. Not bad at all.

The high point, though, would have been l973, when we managed eighty sales, sometimes calling six a week, everyone looking for something different, wanting to be on the edge. Wes Alm's sale broke all records with thirty bulls grossing over a million dollars. That was the fewest cattle I ever sold for a million dollars. Big money changing hands!

Auctioneer Curt Rodgers calls a Chianina sale, while Nebraska cattleman Jerry Adamson (rear) and breed association manager Bob Vantrease look on.

303

The late auctioneer JIM BALDRIDGE *remembers*:

What'd I give for *Louise* out of *Esmeralda* by *Dandin C*? $20,000? The most you ever got for a heifer calf, I bet!

But a few months later, I sold her on the lawn of the Denver Regency Hotel for $39,500! [Jim laughs, as well he might.] Doubled my money in about eight months—those were exciting times! But the event I remember best was the Calgary sale where I knocked down *Dandin C* for $176,000—a record price for a beef bull at the time.[107]

I'm third generation in the business. Grandfather Hugh in Missouri sold more Shorthorns than anyone in the world; and there were auctioneers before him: old-timers who traveled by buggy and sold "bare-handed"—no electricity, no bullhorn. It took a very strong voice to call a sale in those days.

Me, I think of myself as a psychologist and try to establish a mind-set for the bidders. Early on, I get their attention, like: "How many think the Denver Broncos will win the Superbowl?" Then I loosen 'em up, gettin' 'em in the right mood. I start a bull at $1,000 just to give the crowd a positive feeling; then, once I get things snappin', I do everything I can to build momentum.

But buyers have strategies, too. One guy comes on strong, as if he doesn't give a damn if I go twice as fast or ten times as high. Another moves his thumb or blinks an eye and bids as slow as he can to cut my momentum. So, I have to know my buyers—what they like, what they want, how they buy. I keep it light and pleasant. I like people!

But, to be honest, I'm their antagonist; my job is to make people think I'm their friend and counselor while extracting more than they think they want to give. Of course, they *really* do want to buy, so I'm just helpin' 'em out! That's the auctioneer's game. And—oh!—it was really fun in the 1970s.

ON THE LK RANCH *at Bassano, Alberta, the 1969 breeding season came to an end with one exotic ampule in the tank. "Just stick it in the milk cow," Neil McKinnon told technician Bobby Hale.*

One year later at the LK ranch's "Agrobeef" sale, a distinctively marked Holstein-Maine Anjou went to a Kentucky buyer at $500. "Imagine! . . . for a milk cow's calf!" said Neil.

A year later still, at "Exotic Week" in Denver, "I know that heifer!" said Neil. And sure enough: the milk cow's calf, bred back to a Maine Anjou, went for $5,000. All bred-back "Maines" sold for $5,000 that day, and most of them went to Kentucky. "Playin' games with the bank," said Neil McKinnon.

DICK GOFF

I've seen big spending in my time, but nothing like those sales of the early seventies.

Here comes a guy with a million bucks to spend on exotic cattle. Then you hear of him no more; he fades away. How come?

'Cause, what can you do with a quarter-million-dollar bull? When the excitement's over, turn him out with the cows at a hundred times over market value. The only market left is back at the ranch.

MEANWHILE, back at the Cobb ranch: reality.

BUDDY COBB *of the Lazy AC*

Joe Gilchrist and Charlie McKinnon drove into my yard one day in 1960: "We hear you got Charolais," they said. "Can we see 'em?" Thereafter, Charlie came back every year for a lot of years.

Nine years later, one Sunday soon after we came off test, three cars drove into the yard within fifteen minutes; Charlie and Joe were in one, four guys in the others. Well, I'm not much of a salesman and don't really like to be bothered on Sunday afternoon, so I handed the record book over: "If ya see a bull ya like, I'll be up at the house drinkin' coffee."

Of course, three of 'em picked the same bull, so I got 'em together. "Would you mind," I asked, "if next year we held an auction?"

"No auction!" said Charlie McKinnon. "Too many bulls at auction sales sell to the 'Flying Rafter.'"

"Now, what do you mean by that?" I asked.

"Why, bids are pulled from the rafters; ya don't know who you're biddin' against. I won't go for an auction sale at all."

"Well," I said, "would you mind a *silent* auction, where we don't allow no yelling, and the bidder must raise his hand?" I'd heard of a recent sale like that at Fort Robinson, Nebraska.

No, they didn't think they'd like it. They didn't know if they'd be coming or not. But I said I was going to try, and they came and bought and have been buying ever since. But, aah, I never attend my own sales. I'd rather be in the office, drinkin' coffee.

D R. LAVON SUMPTION, USDA *geneticist of Fort Robinson, Nebraska, gave Cobb the "quiet sale" idea and was his first "silent" auctioneer. But Lavon overdid it, Buddy says. He* whispered *the bids. He was so low key that the buyers couldn't hear him.*[108]

Since 1974 Buddy's sales have been "announced" by Bruce Cornell of Augusta. The cadence is loud but slow; the cattle are sold on performance; and you may be sure no bulls are sold to the "rafters."

S̲O, THE EXCITEMENT *that began with Appollon grew through the 1960s. A decade later we would import few "exotic" cattle at any price.*

But, as rancher WES ALM *says:*

The importation was the greatest thing ever. For a while, people saw only glitter; for a while, all they touched turned to gold, but anybody could see it wouldn't last. Meanwhile, it brought new blood and outside dollars into the business.

And it lasted long enough to bring competition. That's what was needed—competition. That was the thing! Now we're breeding *cattle* again, and good ones.

If we don't breed good ones—Boom! We're out of business.

On the CL ranch,

MARSHALL AND TERESA COSTANZI COPITHORNE

MARSHALL: Well, the "exotic" business changed my life forever, that's for sure. My dad's calves used to weigh 350 pounds; now we're unhappy with weaning weights under 600 pounds and yearlings under 1,100 pounds. Partly management, I'd say, but mostly an incredible supply of genes.

It was an incredible era, really! But for "exotics," I'd never have left the ranch . . . probably never got to Italy. . .

TERESA: Surely never got an Italian wife!

MARSHALL: Probably would have been cheaper. . .

TERESA: That's undoubtedly right! There's an old Italian saying: "Exotic wives, like exotic cows, are adaptable—but expensive!"

27 Designer Genes

A RANCH IS A CLASSIC FACTORY, *where a businessman (the rancher) applies capital, labor, and "tools" (in this case, cattle) to raw material (grass) to produce a useful product (meat and offal). When profitable, the product is more valuable than the ingredients, but the process takes time—it takes a thousand days, at least, to turn range grass into roast beef.*

Now, some would call such a slow-moving business dull, but there is always the unexpected: The "tools" have minds of their own and stray into trouble; weather forecasts, critical to the rancher, are often wrong; technology breaks through (and sometimes up); long-range breeding plans turn out better—or worse—than projected. Such things keep ranch life exciting.

So far you have read of the age of growth and some of its new technologies; you've read of the development of homegrown breeds, the Beefmaster and Red Angus; you know how other "exotic" breeds made their way to this continent, adding adventure—and new genes—to the business. I guess it has been the genetic opportunities that made ranching so fascinating to me and my family and friends.

B UT LET'S GO BACK *a minute. Remember Jim Bailey, the Montana veterinarian? He spoke of mustangs in* The Range *and of dwarfism earlier in this book. He's still excited.*

DR. JIM BAILEY

Forty years ago a rancher rode in from his calving field one morning shouting, "Call the vet! We got a *dwarf*!" Then the same damn fool brought "exotics" across the water, and one of these days it'll be, "We got a *giant*!"

And the vet will find a nine-foot-tall, fourteen-foot-long, 3,000-pound "monster" chomping away at the grass, and we'll have to get rid of it, too! On The Ranch we still sell pounds, you see, but they better be efficient; and, for that, it's hard to beat an 1,100-pound black baldy cow that brings in a 550-pound calf every year of her life.

*S*O THE ARGUMENT *about cattle size goes on. Cattle feeder W. D. "Bill" Farr, of Greeley, Colorado, was an industry leader for fifty years. This is what he said one day in 1987.*

BILL FARR

Exotics? Sure, they're impressive. I've seen 'em in Europe; seen 'em here; fed thousands in my feedlot. But they're too darn big! If they're used at all in the future, it'll be in a "terminal cross" because 1,200 pounds is maximum slaughter weight; there's just no place for anything bigger than that.

Like it or not, those who survive the next thirty years will be forced to be more efficient. Here's a scenario for an ideally structured industry: A rancher on a sparsely settled range—say, eastern Montana—will raise the finest cross-bred heifers possible; he'll winter 'em at home and ship 'em to me as yearlings, ready for breeding on my eastern Colorado ranch. I'll pay him a premium price to cover the freight.

Now, I'll use terminal bulls because all my calves—steers and heifers—will be going to slaughter. My ranch is just twenty miles from Farr Feedlots, which is just down the road from Monfort's, one of the largest packing houses in the world. I'll stop the freight on heavier cattle by producing the ultimate meat-type close to the plant.

Shipping cattle all over the country, up and down, back and forth, as we do today is extravagant! We have the infrastructure; let's use it efficiently. Otherwise, a few years down the line, instead of a hundred million cows, we'll have fifty million, maybe.

Cattle numbers (in millions of head) as of 1 January 1993:

	United States[109]	Canada[110]	Mexico[111]
Total cattle	100.9	11.7	30.2
Beef cows	34.0	3.8	—

Beef cows in North American
beef-producing states and provinces in 1993:

Texas	5,570,000
Missouri	2,070,000
Oklahoma	1,895,000
Nevada	1,783,000
Alberta (Can)	1,620,000
South Dakota	1,542,000
Chihuahua (Mex)	1,500,000
Montana	1,460,000
Kansas	1,350,000
Kentucky	1,115,000

H H. "Stony" STONAKER *was a professor of animal science at Colorado State University for decades. A few years ago I visited him in retirement at his farm near Fort Collins.*

STONY STONAKER

With all the new tools at our disposal, I suspect the time has come for breeding programs designed to fit our resources. Maybe, as in corn breeding, we'll have one hybrid suited to short, dry Colorado summers, and another for long, wet Iowa winters—that sort of thing. Whether or not we become as sophisticated with cattle as with corn, surely we'll optimize by using what we've got more efficiently.

And BOB de BACA in Iowa:

Every geneticist wants to develop a breed for a given environment, and most ranchers, if they get the chance, will try to develop a breed. Sometimes I wonder if there's not too much fervor for developing new breeds. Just part of the ego thing, I guess.

W E ALREADY KNOW *of a couple of ranchers who established new breeds to suit their own environments and ideas:*

•*Red Angus, fixed for color and performance by Sally Forbes*

•*Beefmaster, fixed for Tom Lasater's "six essentials"*

Impressive accomplishments! Impressive egos! Breed development goes on.

There's the Hays Converter, an official breed developed in Alberta by Canada's former agriculture minister Harry Hays. The Converter was bred up from daughters of the Holstein bull Fond Hope, *whose ancestry traced back, no doubt, to Parmalee Prentice's Mount Hope Farm and the research that inspired Parmalee's son, Rock, the founder of ABS.*

Fond Hope daughters were bred to sons of the Hereford bull Silver Prince 7P, *whose performance was proven at the ABCPA test station at Bassano; granddaughters were bred to grandsons of the Brown Swiss* Jane of Vernon, *then considered the best-uddered cow in the world. Finally, from such unorthodox combinations, Harry Hays and his advisers (to soothe their egos) selected* Tom, Dick, *and* Harry, *progenitors of the Hays Converter breed.*[112]

And there are "composites," considered by proponents to be "breeds" complete with registries and shows. But some are designed, specifically, for commercial beef production. Jerry Adamson, a Nebraska rancher, uses three combinations of the large and lean Chianina breed: Chi-Simmental, Chi-Maine (Anjous), and Chi-Angus.

Modern Hays Converter bull, carrying the Hays ranch Quarter Circle 57, left-rib brand.

Jerry Adamson Chi-Angus composite pair.

A ND THERE ARE MANY *other combinations that could become breeds but probably won't (though not for lack of ambition). They may be bred specifically for research, as with Roy Berg's Kinsella hybrids, or for the seed stock of an individual herd, as with Neil Harvie's Glenbow strain. Or, as with the Burton family's Hereford-Red Angus-Simmental cross, designed for efficient production on their Burke Creek ranch in the Porcupine Hills.*

Burke Creek pair wearing the UL brand.

Whitemud bulls, branded VI right hip, on the Gilchrist ranch in southwestern Saskatchewan.

OR, AS WITH the "Whitemud" strain in the Cypress Hills:

BILL GILCHRIST

I haven't used a purebred bull since Ray Woodward [of Miles City] told me thirty years ago, "Bill, with a couple hundred cows, no need to worry about inbred depression. You can use your own bulls safely. Go ahead."

Since then, I've been letting Hereford, Angus, Shorthorn, and Brahma genes (the latter from Santa Gertrudis bulls) combine with no record keeping at all. I keep it simple: Keep the best and sell every cow that's dry; leave the details to Mother Nature.

As Tom Lasater says, Nature is seldom wrong . . . works like a damn!

*A*T THIS POINT, *all the history, tools, and breeds discussed so far come together in one word: Beefbooster. Fair enough, then, and appropriate, I think, to conclude with the Beefbooster story that has been so important to me and my family. The ego thing, again . . .*

I wrote in part two about my SN ranch Hytester strain, to which no bull was "born"—each had to be "proven." And so it is with Beefbooster, in which no calf is elite by birth alone; I think of it as a "panning" process, sluicing off lightweight genes and leaving only nuggets in the pan. Perhaps inappropriately—but interestingly, I hope—I begin with a three-generation pedigree of the character behind the Beefbooster system.

*O*N AN EMIGRANT SHIP *bound for Cape Town a century ago, a baby was born to a Scottish couple, the Smiths. They named their son Jack Saunders.*

Jack Saunders Smith became a famous scout and hunter who explored the veld before settling in Kenya with three sons of his own: Stewart, Seymour, and Grant, who—to avoid confusion—hyphenated their names before starting "lines" of their own.

Thus, Stewart-Smith married Christina, a pioneer girl of hardheaded Voer-trekker stock, and the couple trekked on to Tanganyika, where they produced a son named John.

John fell in love with a Greek girl, Avgi Fieros, whose parents farmed the fertile upland slopes near Kilimanjaro; after World War Two they married, grew cattle and coffee, hunted lions and leopards, and lived at peace with their cattle-raising Masai and Warusha neighbors while producing Jennifer, Ken, and Bruce.

So much for pedigree. John's future would ever be tied to performance.

AVGI STEWART-SMITH *remembers:*

Tanganyika was a wonderful place for farming and a wonderful place to live until we joined with Zanzibar and got independence from Britain.

John was for it; I was not. We had had no say as colonials; we would have none as white Tanzanians. I saw us as second-class citizens with first-class taxes and zero political power. Thinking of our children, then, I had my reservations about staying in Africa.

JOHN STEWART-SMITH

But Tanganyika was a fantastic grass country—a second Argentina—that's why all the game and the millions of livestock. Much grazing was held in common by clans and tribes, most cultivation controlled by African women, some with customary title, some with formal, written deed. We Europeans owned less than one-half of one percent of the country but, on that small land base, produced 90 percent of the foreign exchange. Tanganyika was a food-*exporting* country in the 1950s!

Then came independence and, under the new regime, racial, marketing, labor, and hunger problems. With totalitarian socialism, Tanzania would soon become one of the poorest countries in the world by UN standards—you can look it up. What a pity!

Of course, I soon fell out of favor with the government and saw that Avgi was right; it was good we left when we did, although it meant abandoning everything my family had built in three generations in Africa. We could take less than $15,000 with us—little enough for a start in middle age.

In Ontario, in 1967, I found a job with a marketing board collecting a checkoff on old chickens. There, I noticed that modern broilers and eggs were produced by nondescript white birds, while the flashy, well-known breeds could only be found at poultry shows and fairs. I found that modern poultry breeders rarely, if ever, go back to traditional breeds, even in crossing. I learned about *synthetic* hybrid strains.

While learning from my chickens, I encountered by chance a group of western cattlemen—ranchers. They seemed free-enterprising chaps, and we hit it off quite well; soon, one of them phoned from Calgary: "John, would you think of coming west as manager of our new Alberta Cattle Commission?"

Would I . . . ? And I hadn't been long in Alberta before one of my new directors offered a chance to become a working partner in a cow herd. Opportunity! Avgi and I invested our little equity with three like-minded partners: Marshall Copithorne, Tom Gilchrist, and Neil Harvie. Soon, we had moved to the Horse Creek ranch, west of Calgary.

My new friends were aware of Roy Berg's work at Kinsella; I made it my business to engage in a careful study of all the research—Kinsella, Lacombe, Manyberries, Miles City, and MARC [Meat Animal Research Center in Nebraska]. The upshot was, we combined our bovine resources into three synthetic strains ("synthetic" meaning, roughly, that component breed percentages aren't fixed), and selected each strain for important economic characteristics.

313

That was back in 1973. Rockets were headed for space and the news was full of "boosters." At a brainstorming session Robin Harvie came up with "Beefbooster"; the name seemed appropriate and stuck.

I WANT TO EMPHASIZE *here that the trademark "Beefbooster" defines a system of synthetic strains, while "Beefmaster" is the name of a well-known beef breed first delineated by Tom Lasater. Any similarity in names is coincidental.*

On the other hand, I hope the reader will notice how much the Beefbooster system owes to the Beefmaster philosophy. A tip of the hat to Tom. Imitation is the sincerest form of flattery.

Neil Harvie's performance-proven Glenbow herd became Beefbooster M1, a synthetic maternal strain to which Welsh Black, Galloway, Tarantaise, and Saler could be added in any amount at any time. M1 bulls would be selected from among their peers, first, on weight at weaning, then adaptability, fertility and soundness at a year of age. —Roman Hrytsak

Marshall Copithorne's Hereford-Simmental-Brown Swiss herd became the Beefbooster M2 strain. Again, M2 bulls would be selected on weight at weaning, adaptability, fertility, and soundness at a year of age. —Roman Hrytsak

The SN ranch, with its long performance history and recent infusion of Limousin, Beefmaster, and Gelbvieh genes, provided the all-purpose M4 strain. Selection would be on weight, fertility, and soundness at a year of age. Charlie Ewing became the M4 founder-breeder. —Roman Hrytsak

A "terminal" strain, ideal for use on older cows no longer needed for replacement heifer production, was based on Horse Creek Charolais cows topped off with Holstein, Maine-Anjou, and Chianina. "Tx" bulls would be selected on feedlot gain, fertility, and soundness, with minor negative pressure on birth weight. John Stewart-Smith was the Tx founder-breeder. —Roman Hrytsak

M3 pair selected on yearling weight, with birth weight restricted. Longhorn and Red Angus were used in developing this strain, but Jersey, a dairy breed with a fine reputation for meat, proved the best initial supplier of calving ease. —Roman Hrytsak

JOHN STEWART-SMITH *continues*:

One of my partners, Tom Gilchrist, contributed Charolais to our Horse Creek herd, and I soon found out that some of our Charolais heifers needed help at calving, especially when bred to larger breeds. So here was another challenge: birth weights!

I begged the fellows to start another strain and, before they could say "No," I swapped a Charolais heifer for a little Jersey bull and put him out with twenty of my smallest cows. Everyone thought I was crazy, but that was the start of our easy-calving M3 strain, developed by ranchers Alvin Kumlin and Jim Burns into the most popular strain of the lot.

It wasn't long before most seed stock for all the strains would be drawn from within. As new breeders joined our group, cow populations climbed into the thousands.

So that was basic Beefbooster, a system originally devised to supply the needs of our partners for performance and hybrid vigor. In 1977 Dan McKinnon, another performance pioneer and commercial feeder, signed on. We were beginning to think of selling bulls, and Dan was willing to commit time, expertise and the use of his 3 Cross feedlot as a test center.

Not much later, we hired Roman Hrytsak as salesman and retained Jim Scott as theriogenologist; Jim introduced us to the study of breeding soundness, basic to our selection ever since.

The 3 Cross test station near Calgary, where hundreds of Beefbooster bulls are sold each spring. With only the top 10–15 percent even offered for sale, price can be set in advance, and allocation to clients is by lottery.

316

NOW THE BEEFBOOSTER FRAMEWORK was complete: five diverse strains, each under the committed eye of an experienced owner-breeder, each bull selected under practical ranch conditions, then feed tested and evaluated for efficiency.

Meanwhile, the Stewart-Smith family learned about snow and winter and chinooks at the ranch on Horse Creek. And Avgi learned computers and established an office in her basement, where she processed performance records for the group. And John learned more about ranches and cows and hay from Tom and Marshall and Neil and became an authority on selection. But his special genius was in putting it all—ranchers and capital and genetics—together, and in designing breeding plans for Beefbooster clients.

At the *Deer Creek ranch*, TOM GILCHRIST

After forty years in the business, Dad thought the fifties-style Hereford as out of date as the Model A Ford, and his scales showed our yearling whitefaces growing lighter every year. Performance-tested Herefords were still a dream of the future, so Dad bought some black Angus heifers, supposedly bred to a high-powered Angus bull. They started calving three weeks early and all dropped whitefaced calves! I remember it well! That was 1959: the turning point; the beginning of our modern, crossbred herd.

A few years later, when I took over the ranch, *maintaining* hybrid vigor became my problem. There were Charolais bulls from Arizona and Montana and even Brangus on the ranch, but I packed myself off to Graham School to learn AI for access to any breed.

So, by the early sixties, the Deer Creek herd had blondes and white-faced blacks and smoky grays and skunk-striped reds. (We owned our cattle to slaughter so color was unimportant.) And, by 1967—having tried all else—we were ready for the "exotics."

LOIS GILCHRIST

And the "exotic" years were exciting years at Deer Creek! Our imported Charolais, *Carnival*, selected by Ray Woodward, paid many ranch bills in the sixties, and I think of AI'ing to several new breeds and anxiously awaiting results—some good, some bad.

I think of the "upstart" breed associations with all their hype and hoopla! The travel, the deals, the hedging; the big sales, high-rolling buyers, and flamboyant auctioneers.

317

I think of *Loio*, our gentle Chianina giant, who roared up and down the creek all summer—but you could throw a rope on him in the pasture and lead him into a stock trailer with ease.

I remember the flashy sale at the Calgary Inn where the Groenevald boys, having bought *Loio*, rode him into the hotel ballroom. Later, in the lobby, in the wee hours of the morning, a drunk was discovered sleeping in *Loio's* pen, snoring peacefully with his head on the big bull's neck.

So many exotic things happened, and they made life exciting on the Deer Creek ranch in the 1970s. Then Beefbooster, with its practical plans, made them all obsolete.

THERE'S AN EXCEPTION to every rule, and Tom Gilchrist is the exception: a rancher who doesn't want to develop a breed. And not from lack of ego or ability, either. Tom is a practical cowman, internationally recognized for commitment and skill with grass. With his experience, Tom would have made an ideal Beefbooster breeder; instead, he became a client, taking advantage of the best breeding plan that John Stewart-Smith could devise.

TOM GILCHRIST

In 1974 the market fell. No longer would it pay to import exotics; no longer could we justify AI. We had all the genes we needed; now we had to use them to advantage. We were ready for a practical strategy.

Now, John Stewart-Smith loves acronyms, and a rancher looking for diversity soon had the choice of a Beefbooster "COBBETY" plan (standing for Change Of Bull Battery Every Three Years).

There are variations. At Deer Creek we run our first-calving heifers on good, clean range and ride through 'em once a day. We don't want trouble, so they're bred to M3 bulls selected first on birth weight. And it works! We may help one heifer out of twenty. And, since M3 bulls are also selected for growth, their calves work well as yearlings and right through the feedlot.

If we wanted to get fancy, we would sort off our oldest cows to be bred "Tx" with no saw-off at all for "maternal" production, while younger cows would be bred M1, M2, M4 on a three-year rotation. That should maintain, with little fuss or expense (so say our genetics consultants), 80 percent of all possible hybrid vigor.

In practice, I run all my mature cows together using a mix of "maternal" and "terminal" bulls. John Stewart-Smith doesn't like it, but I think I get optimum production; terminal-type heifers are easy to spot by eye and are fed for slaughter, while maternal types remain in the breeding herd.

So that's a "COBBETY" plan adapted to Deer Creek conditions—not perfect, maybe, but practical. And Beefbooster is a practical proposition!

Result of a COBBETY plan, and a Beefbooster Tx bull. —Roman Hrytsak

JOHN STEWART-SMITH

And Beefbooster expanded beyond my dreams of the 1970s. In the '90s, with over thirty seed-stock herds in Canada and the USA, only one bull calf out of eight earns our "tag of approval"—I'm proud of that! Only 12 percent of production qualifies as seed stock; the rest go to slaughter as low-fat, virgin bulls. Is that consistent with "population genetics" or what?

One reason for my success is that I came with an open mind: I had never been in a show ring but had seen, with poultry, what modern breeding could do. Genetics fully applied!

In the end, I was lucky enough to fall in with practical ranchers who were selecting functional cattle for the market. Purebredism: ready for replacement. Beefbooster: an idea who's time had come. Coordination: needed! That's where I came in.

28   Terminal Strain

Geneticist H. H. "STONY" STONAKER

What does the future hold? Terribly hard to predict! In 1947 one nutrition philosopher told our students at CSU, "Boys, in twenty years we won't be feeding beef cattle a mouthful of grain; they'll be on roughage, 100 percent." He couldn't have been more wrong.

And in 1967 Secretary of Agriculture Orville Freeman spoke to a meeting of college deans, saying, "Gentlemen, in twenty years, Americans will be starving to death—fighting it out for food!"

And here we are, swamped with food . . . giving it away . . . don't know what to do with all we produce. The advances made in the last forty years are staggering! We can hardly imagine what the future holds for agriculture.

But scientist JERRY CALLIS *said in 1987:*

The revolution is embryonic! And I hope our research people are paying attention because the embryo is where it will happen.

Embryos! Within a decade we'll be removing and inserting genes. The wave of the future. [It's happening now!] In my opinion, this is a development that will make us all—plant, animal, human—genetically more resistant to disease.

At Cambridge, England, the "father" of Frosty the First,
DR. CHRISTOPHER POLGE

In 1890, a century ago, Walter Heape, a Cambridge don, ran a little experiment. He collected fertile eggs—living embryos—from a rabbit; then he planted them in a rabbit of a different color and was able to prove by the markings that the offspring of the surrogate had originated in the donor. Nobody took much notice, of course, but that was the first recorded embryo transfer in mammals. It was considered just an "observation."

Many decades later, I was involved in one of the first transplantations to be taken seriously, and it happened like this: We were learning to keep embryos alive outside the body, and a lot of techniques were tried without much success. Finally, somebody observed that an oviduct provided quite a good (and economical) incubator; one could actually pop a sheep embryo into a rabbit oviduct and keep it alive for four or five days. The first international transfers were collected from ewes here at Cambridge and carried in rabbit oviducts out to South Africa, where—fortunately for the rabbits—the embryos were transplanted into native sheep.

It was late in the 1960s, many years after sperm freezing was established, that we began to exploit the genetic potential of females. Embryos are much bigger conglomerations than ova or sperm and have to be dehydrated slowly before being frozen; that way, intracellular crystallization is avoided. The first calf from a frozen embryo was born at our ABC research station in 1973.[113]

Now, since nonsurgical techniques have been established, a new commercial industry is born. We had working with us at Cambridge for about twelve years a Dr. S. M. Willadsen, who developed techniques for splitting embryos, creating identical twins, quadruplets, and so forth. He's gone to Canada now and is working with Alberta Livestock Transplants [later Alta Genetics, Inc.] and the University of Calgary, where his specialty is cloning by nuclear transplantation.[114]

Seemingly farther out: It's been known for some time that you could mix cells from two different embryos and get them to combine in a composite in which both genetic entities are represented. Usually this is only done *within* species. When accomplished *between* species, the offspring is a chimera—not too successful a beast, in general. An exception is the sheep-goat, or *geep*, which has worked quite well using two such closely related species. If you transplant a goat egg into a sheep, or vice versa, it will develop but not go to term. If you *combine* embryonic cells, however, they collaborate and help each other along. You can cause a ewe to give birth to a goat simply by creating a chimeric embryo where the fetus comes from the goat and the placental compartment from the sheep. When this is transferred to a sheep, a pure goat is born.

What's the point of all this, you ask? The technology has a place in saving endangered species where recipients are scarce—you may call it "chimeric rescue." In this way we have had pure zebra, donkey, and Przewalski's horse foals born to Welsh Cob mares at our Animal Research Station at Cambridge.

French cattle breeder, entrepreneur, exporter, and philosopher
LOUIS de NEUVILLE

We already know that embryos are filtering viruses, which means that embryos from infected cows can be very clean.

This is tremendous! It means that viruses (which can be transported in semen) go not so easily in embryos which have shells—*pellucid* shells—that act as filters. Some, like the IBR-IPV virus, seem to stick to the shell like a tick to the skin, and this is why you have to *wash* the embryo.

Now, that such a thing as "washing" an embryo is possible is not widely known, but I, personally, am ready to go this route both for health and economic reasons (it's cheaper to quarantine and transport an embryo than a cow), and I am planning a bank of embryos for sale to Third World countries—a fantastic door for international trade.[115]

Canadian DOUG BLAIR *of Western Breeders and* Extra *fame*

Travelers may not know that the plane carrying them in comfort over the ocean could be transporting hundreds of thousands of dollars worth of "livestock" in its belly, but so it could. Our new company, Alta Genetics, ships thousands of embryos (which may live in their frozen state who knows how long?), each worth $500 to $2,000. Our sales of cattle, semen, and embryos from high-performance donors hit $19 million in 1993—the embryos destined for transplant into "host" cows in forty-four countries around the world. Our business has come a long way since "hosting" bulls like *Extra* for Travelin' Travers Smith in the 1970s.[116]

Geneticist ROY BERG

So far, the embryo transplant technology has been useful in multiplying and merchandising cattle pedigrees with all the usual hype—that's what it's been about, it seems to me. Yet, the technology paves the way for further genetic engineering in many species. We can only guess the uses it will serve.

There's a new understanding—a new age of growth; as a geneticist, my interest has always been in *growth*. We know that whitetail deer on the northern plains are bigger than those in Texas; we assume that northern ranges provide more food. But what makes a deer on any range a certain size? Why is a mouse a certain size? We find that the size of any organism is controlled by supply of hormone—*growth hormone*. Further, we find that growth-hormone supply is very precisely controlled by a growth-hormone *gene* in concert with other genes and their products. And we know that growth-hormone genes respond to *cellular environment*—simple as that! We only need to understand the mechanics.

The research can be more cheaply and conveniently done with mice. For example: Jack Newman at Lacombe [CDA Research] has selected high-gaining mice through seventy generations. His selected line is 50 percent bigger than his control. What's more, his high-gaining mice are different: They grow faster and are leaner at any point in the growth curve.

Keith Salmon and his cohorts at the University of Alberta have examined the Lacombe high-gaining mice, genetically, and have found a unique growth-hormone gene: smaller in area, shorter in length, behaviorally different, and more potent than the "norm." How more potent? By having a smaller *control area*. The control area of a gene is as important as the gene itself, you see: It tells it when to produce; it responds to chemicals in the surrounding tissue which signal, "We need more insulin or prostaglandin or thyroxin. So get busy! Start producing!" The control surface turns on the pumps in response to chemical signals—chemicals that change with the environment.

So, in the high-gaining Lacombe mouse, the area that regulates growth-hormone supply became shorter (and thereby weaker), with a resultant loss of production. Now, it's more difficult to turn production off, and more growth hormone is pumped into the mouse—not the *kind* of hormone, you see, but control of how much is produced. The Lacombe mouse became bigger and leaner as it received more growth hormone, and here's the important thing: It pumps its *own* growth hormone; nothing needs to be added; a bigger appetite is secondary.

Now the question arises: Is it possible to take the high-gaining gene from a mouse and transfer it to a cow? Think of that gene as a musical instrument introduced into an orchestra: Perhaps, with time and practice, it will become a symphonic part. Perhaps not. The truth is, we won't know until we try. Up to now, the only tool for bringing genetic variation into cattle has been cross-breeding. Gene transfer could be another tool, but the genes may take generations to adapt.

Now, this sort of thing has fantastic implications for human genetics. Take diseases that result from so-called inborn errors in metabolism: Geneticists have spent years in the ongoing search for genes involved in Huntington's chorea, muscular dystrophy, and other genetic diseases. It's now possible to find a gene by trial and error, sequence it, identify its DNA code, know exactly what it produces.

Hence, it should be possible to troubleshoot the product and, knowing what's missing, replace it (as with insulin), thereby treating or preventing the disease.

Farther out, it should be possible to replace aberrant genes, allowing systems to control themselves. That, I think, will be the prime concern of medical geneticists over the next ten years.

At that point the payoff will be tremendous!

And geneticist CHRISTOPHER POLGE *concludes:*

Does all of this scare you? Well, when we discovered how to freeze sperm, people reckoned it fearful—the first step in selecting males for a super race, that sort of horrifying thing. In life, I think, the main thing we have to fear is man—not the technology, but the way man *uses* the technology.

Hopefully, civilization will be responsible enough to make use of good opportunities when they come, and one of the great opportunities today would seem to be in genetic engineering. There's sort of a major biological revolution under way—actually moving the material of inheritance around by natural mating. This is powerful stuff with terrific applications in the diagnosis and cure of disease, as well as in the making of new vaccines.

Please observe how often knowledge gained from the humble cow or ewe has brought our opportunities to fruition.

EPILOGUE

The Roundup

I NO LONGER CONSIDER MYSELF *a rancher—a rancher should live on the land. I live at the edge of town, while my friends and family are out on the ranch with their cattle. I am proud, however, to have been a rancher once.*

Good ranchers bank on renewable resources. With the sun and rain and the pruning and fertilization that come with grazing, a good rancher plans for better grass next spring and, with better grass, a better calf or lamb crop—and, with that, a better living for the family. This is "next-year country." Life goes on, and a well-run ranch is a very effective conservancy.

The land is where basic wealth is created—from which it spreads by a sort of capillary action through a nation's veins. And the faces of those who transform that wealth through livestock are ever-changing: trading up, moving on, marrying in, dying out—time takes care of that. (Joe Gilchrist, whose story began this book, died recently at 92, after 75 years of ranching; his son, nephew, and grandnephew carry on.)

But, fortunes are seldom made in basic production—pure competition, bad weather, and taxes take care of that.

So, those whose lives are invested in ranch production have traditionally traded material wealth for freedom—the freedom to enjoy their property as they wish. And, increasingly, government regulation takes care of that.

Now, this is hard to believe: Just when central planning has proved such a dismal failure around the world, and while homegrown preservationists castigate dam builders, foresters, and all bureaucratic agents—the greatest challenge to the next generation of ranchers is a threat to the enjoyment and management of private property. I believe this to be the case, and I think it is shameful. It seems of such obvious importance to society, as a whole, that control of the land be vested in future production. That is how we have fed ourselves so very well so far; that is how we will feed ourselves in the future. And that is how the private sector stays in better shape than its public counterpart—generally speaking.

I thought, when I went ranching in 1950, that I was born fifty years too late, but the next thirty years offered many amazing surprises: One surprise was steadily

329

rising land prices that drew credit into the business; an even bigger surprise was "The Importation" that attracted new cash. The fast-buck boys came and went—often without their shirts. Some ranchers who wanted to stay were felled by taxes, others by overborrowing, a few by overgrazing. But many prudent, private producers remain on the land—an endangered species. They are my environmental heroes.

At branding time on the Bar 15, Karli and Katie Alm will be old enough, soon, to "wrassle" the calves that Grampa Wes and his well-mounted children and neighbors "heel" and drag to the fire. Like ranch kids anywhere they will learn to ride and rope, and they will also feed and care for those calves and treat them humanely and kindly, and they will understand at an early age how the country's wealth is created.

On the T Bar, Karlee and Ross Mosher will soon be out cutting hay and riding through the AI pasture, "picking up" cows for Kent and Donna—preparing another crop for next spring's calving. They will know, without being told, where wealth is produced.

On Rancho La Rosita, south of the Rio Grande, Mirthala, Manuel III, and Marcella will be learning beef cattle husbandry from their grandfather, Manuel Garza Elizondo. Let's hope these good ranch families, and others like them, can retain their property and traditions for another century, at least. That would be good for the land. The foot of the owner fertilizes the field.

In France, the young de Neuvilles—Martin, Odile, Cristine, and Anne—will put much of Domaine de Combas into trees. This is a common strategy in many countries to lower taxes—and more's the pity, since grass is a better soil builder than trees. Meanwhile, the Combas Limousin herd, made famous by father Louis, will progress under the eye of a new part-owner–breeder. New blood. New ideas. The same old marks and brands.

In cattle country everywhere look for the marks and brands and remember that each landmark has a tale: Domaine de Pompadour—home to a royal mistress, birthplace of a prince; Eagle Pass—port of entry north for a new breed of white cattle; Missouri badlands—source of a phony "race" of midget cattle; Stove Coulee—refuge for stolen horses . . . and the SN brand.

So life goes on: This spring I met my Canadian friend Jim Rawe at Buddy Cobb's twenty-third "silent auction." Jim was bringing Alberta heifers to be "flushed" at the Montana Embryo Transplant Center in Bozeman. His choice of "frozen" sires: Paul, bred by Oklahoma rancher Mack Braly in 1959, and Cometa Antonio 909, a bull tracing back to Perez Treviño's Iroquois—an "invader" of the 1930s.

Which just about brings us around, full circle.

I'm surprised, as I write in the 1990s, to find a big, black breed out in front by several lengths in popularity. In my youth I would have considered the use of old-style Aberdeen Angus as "negative breeding." Well, while I wasn't looking, that collection of belt-high "potbellies" stretched and grew and took new shape . . . and the lead among beef breeds in registrations. At the same time, the ubiquitous black-baldy cow (along with black Simmentals, black Chianinas—black phenotypes, indeed, of almost every breed) became living, grazing proof of hybrid vigor—and of the current "black is beautiful" fad in cattle breeding.

As the century ends, and beef breeds reach the opposite extreme in size from the "dinks" of the 1950s, I see a need for caution. But twenty-first century ranch managers will still be drawing for their decisions on Miles City research, Age-of-Growth methods, and the genes of The Importation, as well as the newest (as yet undreamed-of) information.

And I'm optimistic that demand will continue strong for the many good things that come from domestic livestock. So, next I intend to call upon the customers of The Ranch—the butchers, the tanners, the pharmacists, the chemists, the artists and artisans of every trade. There are livestock by-products everywhere we turn.

Just the other day Pierre Gautier, Henri's son, faxed me from Saint Pierre. He's still in the import-export business and wants me to say the barn Mack Braly built is empty now, but in good repair. The grass is greening up on Miquelon, and the St. Pierrais are waiting . . . waiting for another Importation.

Whether or not that opportunity reappears, new generations of ranchers will be looking to create new wealth from the fat of the land by the sweat of their brows. To those who live on the land and love it, I dedicate this book. May they enjoy the life as I have.

Register of Characters

WESLEY A. ALM (b. 1925), his wife "DIX," and children Anne, Dixie, Glen, and Julie of the Bar 15 ranch were early users of AI and Simmental cattle in Alberta. Wes has been director of the Canadian Simmental Association and president of the Alberta Simmental Association.

ROBERT J. ANDERSON, DVM (b. 1910), was co-director of the Mexico–U.S. Commission for Eradication of FMD, assistant chief of BAI in 1950, and retired as associate administrator of ARS in 1970. He continues to raise crossbred cattle on his ranch at Poverty Ridge near Marshall, Texas.

JAMES H. BAILEY, DVM (b. 1933), was raised on eastern Montana ranch and graduated from Colorado State University in 1957. He has been a general practitioner at Great Falls, Montana, since 1980. Horses have always been Doc Bailey's special interest.

J. DOUGLAS BAIRD (b. 1922), of Ottawa, worked on FMD eradication in Canada in 1952 and served as chief of the livestock branch's production section for Canada Department of Agriculture from 1958 to 1970. Later he became president of Hy-cross Beef Breeders, Ltd., in Ottawa.

JIM BALDRIDGE (1935–1994) was a livestock auctioneer at North Platte, Nebraska, and a breeder of registered Angus, Limousin, and Gelbvieh cattle. During the exotic boom he organized National Livestock Brokers, Inc., a well-known sales-management firm.

DAVID BARTLETT, DVM (b. 1917), conducted research on venereal diseases of cattle at the USDA National Research Center in Beltsville, Maryland. He taught at the University of Minnesota Veterinary Clinic and served as vice president for veterinary affairs at American Breeders Service for twenty-six years.

ROY T. BERG, Ph.D. (b. 1927), was dean of the ag faculty at the University of Alberta, Edmonton, where he taught and researched growth characteristics of cattle for thirty-five years. He developed the Kinsella synthetic strains at the university ranch.

BILL BIG SPRING (1919–1990) and his wife, Kathleen, ranched near Glacier National Park, Montana, for forty years. Bill served on the Blackfeet Tribal Council, Glacier County Commission, and Republican National Committee. The Smithsonian purchased some of the art Bill painted.

DOUGLAS G. BLAIR (b. 1942) led Western Breeders Service, the artificial insemination company near Calgary for twenty-five years. In 1993 WBS merged with the embryo transplant pioneer Alta Genetics, Inc.; Doug is president and CEO.

MACK M. BRALY (1911–1989), an oilman-attorney-rancher of Ada, Oklahoma, played key role in opening United States to European breeds. He was active in the American International Charolais Association, Performance Registry International, and served on the board of regents at the University of Oklahoma.

C. GORDON BURCHER (b. 1939), of Mount Crosby, Queensland, worked on ranches in the Northern Territory of Australia and Alberta, Canada. A cattle trader, breeder, and land developer, he introduced the Charolais breed to Australia.

GORDON L. BURTON, Ph.D. (1916–1991), and his wife, Jean, took over the Burke Creek ranch in Alberta's Porcupine Hills in 1950, after Gordon finished school at Iowa State. He served as president of Western Stock Growers' Association. Their sons, Jay and Rick, and daughter-in-law, Susan, now run ranch.

JERRY CALLIS, DVM (b. 1926), of Southold, New York, worked at the USDA food-animal disease research facility at Plum Island, in Long Island Sound, from its inception until his retirement as its director in 1988.

EION CHISHOLM (b. 1920), of Okotoks, Alberta, founded and managed Western Feedlots, Ltd., Alberta's first custom feedlot. He also served as manager, director, and president of the Western Stock Growers Association, executive secretary of the Council of Beef Producers, and director of the Canadian Cattlemen's Association.

JAMES H. CLARK (b. 1924), of DeForest, Wisconsin, joined American Breeders Service in 1960 and became the regional sales manager for several western states and western Canada. He served as general manager of ABS Canada from 1974 to 1976 and retired as manager of its public relations.

A. B. "BUDDY" COBB Jr. (b. 1920) and his wife, Cecile, brought the first Charolais cattle to Montana. They pioneered the use of "silent" auctions for performance-tested breeding stock and the use of virgin bulls for beef. Their sons John and Mike are on ranch.

MARSHALL COPITHORNE (b. 1937) raised a large family on the CL ranch on Jumping Pound Creek, Alberta. A founder-breeder of the Beefbooster system, Marshall has been vice president of the Calgary Stampede. His daughter, Cherie, now plays an active role in CL ranch management.

MARIA TERESA COSTANZI (b. 1949) is a native of Rome, Italy, and served as an interpreter and guide for the Italian cattle export agency Cemex in 1960s. She married Marshall and came to the CL ranch in 1977, and they have two daughters, Jennifer and Erin.

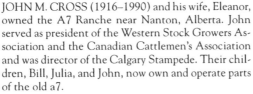

JOHN M. CROSS (1916–1990) and his wife, Eleanor, owned the A7 Ranche near Nanton, Alberta. John served as president of the Western Stock Growers Association and the Canadian Cattlemen's Association and was director of the Calgary Stampede. Their children, Bill, Julia, and John, now own and operate parts of the old a7.

ROBERT C. de BACA, Ph.D. (b. 1930), of Huxley, Iowa, was extension beef cattle specialist and professor of animal science at Iowa State University, editor of the "Ideal Beef Memo" (circulation 25,000), and consultant to cattle producers throughout the Americas.

LOUIS DUFOUR de NEUVILLE (b. 1930) and his wife, Marcia, own Domaine de Combas, a French country estate in the family for 450 years. Louis is a member of the French Academy of Agriculture, president of the Federation of French Herd Books, and chairman of the International Limousin Council.

W. D. "BILL" FARR (b. 1910), of Farr Feeders, Greeley, Colorado, is past president of the American National Cattlemen's Association and the 1986 recipient of the Golden Spur Award for lifetime service to the livestock and ranching industry. His son, Dick, and grandson, Rick, continue the business.

SARAH P. "SAL" FORBES (b. 1920) and her husband, Waldo, of Beckton Stock Farm, Sheridan, Wyoming, founded the performance-based Red Angus breed. In 1993 she received the Breeder of the Year award from Colorado State University. Their sons, Cam and Spike, now run Beckton.

JONATHAN FOX III (b. 1920), a breeder of Hereford cattle and Percheron horses, has judged most of the world's great livestock shows (usually from horseback). He and his wife, Molly, still raise Morgan horses in British Columbia. Their son, Lyle, runs Justamere Farms in Saskatchewan.

HOWARD FREDEEN, Ph.D. (b. 1921), was a CDA geneticist at the Lacombe research station in Alberta for thirty-seven years. Trained in animal breeding, genetics, and statistics at the University of Alberta and Iowa State, he is respected for his ability to communicate scientific information to ranchers.

MARY GARST (b. 1928) manages the Garst cattle operation at Coon Rapids, Iowa. She has been a professional director of major banks and corporations and served as director of the American Simmental Association.

SARAH GARST, DVM (b. 1959), worked with cattle many summers on the family farm and majored in agricultural economics at Antioch, "a school that had no agriculture," then got her DVM at Iowa State University. She now runs her own clinic at Des Moines.

STEVE GARST (b. 1924), a businessman, farmer, and cattle and seed-corn producer at Coon Rapids, serves on many Iowa commissions and was the director of the North American Limosin Foundation. In 1977 he and his wife, Mary, received the distinction of North American Breeder of Year from the Beef Improvement Federation.

MANUEL GARZA ELIZONDO (b. 1922) and his son, Manuel Jr., raise purebred Charolais on their ranch, La Rosita, in Tamaulipas, Mexico. He helped organize first Charolais World Congress at Nuevo Laredo in 1962 and was president of the Charolais Herd Book International in 1963–64.

BILL GILCHRIST (b. 1928) and his wife, HELEN, raise crossbred cattle for breeding and as feeders on the ranch Bill's family homesteaded south of Maple Creek, Saskatchewan, in 1902 and now called the Cypress Cattle Company. Their son, Joe II, and his wife, Brenda, help run the ranch and have a fifth-generation Gilchrist "on the ground."

JOE GILCHRIST (1900–1992) and his wife, MURIEL (HARGRAVE), were partners in the Gilchrist Brothers ranching company from 1914 to 1945. They moved to a ranch on Deer Creek near Milk River in 1939, and ran it with their son, Tom, until retiring in the 1980s.

LOIS SMITH GILCHRIST (b. 1938) was raised in Milk River, Alberta, and earned a degree in nursing at the University of Saskatchewan in 1960, then she married Tom and moved to the Deer Creek ranch, where they raised four children.

TOM GILCHRIST (b. 1934) graduated in ag-engineering from the University of Saskatchewan. After a stint with the Prairie Farm Rehabilitation Administration, he returned to Deer Creek and specialized in grass and commercial cattle. He is past president Western Stock Growers Association and a Beefbooster founder.

RICHARD "DICK" GOFF (b. 1914), editor, writer, and ranch historian of Grand Junction, Colorado, was promotion director for the Pan-American Charolais Association and the American International Charolais Association. In 1967 he founded North American Limousin Foundation (NALF).

MARTÍN H. GONZALEZ, Ph.D. (b. 1930), of El Paso, Texas, was born in Coahuila and grew up in Nuevo León. He directed La Compana range research station in Chihuahua for many years and was president of the international Society for Range Management in 1973–74.

WILLIAM S. "BILL" GRAHAM (b. 1917), of Garnett, Kansas, is a horseman, cattleman, teacher, and president of the Graham School, founded by his father. His son, Frank, and grandson, Bill, guide the family business through its tenth decade.

JIM GRAY (1919–1991) and his wife, OLENE, raised six children on their ranch in the Porcupine Hills of Alberta, where Jim was born and lived his entire life—except for a stint in the Canadian army in the 1940s. Their son, Syd, and his wife, Sheila, continue to raise commercial Simmental cattle.

ALVIN HAMILTON (b. 1912) was Member of Parliament for Qu'Appelle-Moose Mountain (Saskatchewan) from 1957 to 1992. As Canadian minister of Agriculture from 1960 to 1963, he gave the initial order for Grosse Ile quarantine station. Alvin retired with the prestigious Order of Canada.

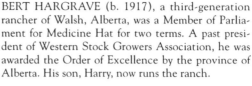

BERT HARGRAVE (b. 1917), a third-generation rancher of Walsh, Alberta, was a Member of Parliament for Medicine Hat for two terms. A past president of Western Stock Growers Association, he was awarded the Order of Excellence by the province of Alberta. His son, Harry, now runs the ranch.

NEIL HARVIE (b. 1929) and his wife, ROBIN, of the Glenbow ranch near Cochrane, Alberta, co-founded the Beefbooster system and pioneered using virgin bulls for beef. Neil was president of the Western Stock Growers Association, director of the Canadian Charolais Assoication, and president of Western Feedlots. Their daughter, Katie (Norman), now runs the Glenbow herd.

HAROLD J. HILL, DVM (b. 1921), of Imperial Beach, California, pioneered the science of theriogenology at Colorado A&M (now CSU) at Fort Collins, where he was assistant professor of surgery and clinics from 1946 to 1962. Later he became a large-animal veterinary consultant to the San Diego Zoo.

GERALD HUGHES (b. 1903), of Stanford, Montana, served several terms in the Montana state legislature and was active in Montana woolgrowers and stockgrowers. With other members of his family, Gerald has ranched in the Judith Basin country all his life.

LIANE "NONNIE" HUGHES (b. 1947) grew up on the family ranch in the Judith Basin country of Montana with sisters Betty, Kathy, and Bev, all of whom had much to do with ranch operations. She is now a school principal in Bozeman.

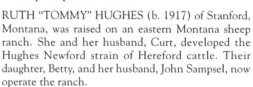

RUTH "TOMMY" HUGHES (b. 1917) of Stanford, Montana, was raised on an eastern Montana sheep ranch. She and her husband, Curt, developed the Hughes Newford strain of Hereford cattle. Their daughter, Betty, and her husband, John Sampsel, now operate the ranch.

KEN HURLBURT (b. 1928) of Fort Macleod, Alberta, is a rancher and livestock market operator. An auctioneer since the early 1950s, Ken was president Alberta Auction Market Association, mayor of historic Fort Macleod, and a Member of Parliament from 1972 to 1979.

RODNEY JAMES (b. 1932) is an early Charolais breeder and pioneer in the European importation. He has served as executive secretary of the Canadian Charolais Association, and he founded and published the *Charolais Banner*. He is now CEO of Transcon Livestock, a sales-management company in Okotoks, Alberta.

RICHARD F. LaFRANCE, DVM (b. 1922), has been in general veterinary practice since 1951. He and his wife, ESTHER, live in Hardin, Montana, and remain active in the horse and cattle business in that area.

GERARD LALONDE (b. 1925) and his wife, Maureen, run a livestock farm in the Ottawa Valley near Fournier, Ontario. Gerard served as president of the Canadian Charolais Association in 1963 and vice president of the World Federation of Charolais Breeders from 1966 to 1968.

LAURENCE M. "LAURIE" LASATER (b. 1941) and his wife, ANNETTE, of San Angelo, Texas, have ranched in Mexico and Texas. They promote Beefmaster cattle through their Isa Cattle Company, and they consult and manage ranches from Florida to Australia.

TOM LASATER (b. 1911) and his wife, Mary, established the Beefmaster breed and the Lasater ranch at Matheson, Colorado. A native of south Texas, Tom has been widely regarded as a livestock philosopher and working geneticist. Their son, Dale, now runs the Lasater ranch.

A. E. "BERT" LEWIS (b. 1918) was CDA veterinarian for Alberta from 1960 to 1966 and kept the imported cattle from Europe healthy during that time. He later became the director of the contagious diseases division at the Ottawa branch of Health of Animals.

J. S. "SID" LORE (b. 1928), of Edmonton, was the livestock supervisor in charge of performance testing for the Alberta Department of Agriculture from 1959 to 1973. He was director of the animal industry division from 1978 to 1986.

HERB LYTTLE (b. 1921), of Kerman, California, learned the feeding business in 1940, then managed the Noble Cattle Company feed yard near Fresno from 1956 to 1975. He is now a ranch management consultant.

M. G. "MAXIMO" MICHAELIS III (b. 1938) and his wife, Sharon, are third-generation Charolais breeders at Kyle, Texas. Maximo's grandfather, Max Sr., was perhaps first Charolais breeder in the United States, and his father, Max Jr., propagated original "Pugibet" Charolais cattle in Mexico.

CHRIS MILLS (b. 1934), of Okotoks, Alberta, has been contributing intellectual power to the commonsense instincts of the North American cattle industry since 1960. He has played key roles in the Western Stock Growers Association, the Canadian Cattlemen's Association, and the Alberta Cattle Commission.

CAROL and ROL MOSHER (b. 1931), of Augusta, Montana, were early supporters of artificial insemination, performance testing, and crossbreeding in commercial cattle production on their Tee Bar ranch. One of their three ranching children, Kent, and his wife, Donna, run the ranch today.

FRANK MULHERN, DVM (b. 1919), was assistant to director for U.S.–Mexico FMD eradication from 1947 to 1952. He retired in 1980 as administrator of the Animal and Plant Health Inspection Service, ARS. Later, he directed the Inter-American Institute for Cooperation on Agriculture.

CARLTON NOYES (b. 1926) and his wife, GENE, operate several feedlots and a ranch in Nebraska as well as a ranch in Idaho. Their Lean Limousin Beef Company merchandises finished beef. Carlton was president of the North American Limousin Foundation from 1976 to 1978.

JACK PHILLIPS, Ph.D. (1927–1990), was professor of animal science at the University of Pennsylvania for many years. Best known as a breeder and a judge of registered beef and dairy cattle, he served as the first president and executive secretary of the American Chianina Association.

E. J. CHRISTOPHER POLGE, F.R.S. (b. 1926), of Cambridge, England, is a world authority on molecular embryology and cryopreservation. He produced the first mammal conceived from frozen semen and the first lambs and calves born from frozen embryos.

JAMES V. RAWE (b. 1929), of Strome, Alberta, was one of the first Canadians to see the advantages of the Charolais breed. In 1962-63 he risked transporting heifers to England for breeding to French bulls. He is still breeding Charolais cattle in the 1990s.

CURT RODGERS (b. 1939), of Platte City, Missouri, was raised on an Angus farm in Iowa. He has been a fieldman for the Aberdeen Angus Association, publisher of *Better Beef Business*, and a livestock auctioneer since 1963. He has sold over 100,000 purebred breeding cattle since 1976.

340

ALYS JANE "AJ" (b. 1921) and LLOYD SCHMITT (b. 1918), of Stanford, Montana, have run ranches, feedlots, and performance-test stations. With their son, Lee, they made a successful business of merchandising frozen beef "packs" to family customers within a 200-mile radius of Stanford.

JAMES A. SCOTT, DVM (b. 1934), taught reproductive physiology at Colorado State University in 1960s, was a founder of American Society of Theriogenologists, had a practice in Great Falls, Montana, for many years that specialized in food animals.

LILLAMAY SCOTT (b. 1937) was raised on a ranch in Oregon. After marrying Jim in 1962, she supervised their Bar 2 outfit near Great Falls while raising their two children, Daphne and Jimmy, along with three quarter horses, fifteen longhorn cows, and innumerable cats and dogs.

ROBERT E. SHOPE, MD (b. 1929), is director of the Arbovirus Research Center at the Yale School of Medicine. His father, Dr. Richard E. Shope, worked with rinderpest at Grosse Ile, Quebec, during the Second World War and was first ever to identify the influenza virus.

AVGI STEWART-SMITH (b. 1933) was raised on a farm in Tanzania and came to Canada with her husband, John, and their three children in 1967. She adapted well to ranch life in Alberta and pioneered the use of computers as ranch tools.

JOHN STEWART-SMITH (b. 1931) immigrated to Canada from Tanzania in 1967. He organized the Beefbooster cattle breeding group and served as president and CEO of its core company for more than twenty years. His and Avgi's daughter, Jennifer, is Beefbooster manager in 1990s.

H. H. STONAKER, Ph.D. (b. 1917), of Fort Collins, Colorado, was professor of animal science at Colorado A&M (now CSU) for decades and dean of agriculture in 1966–67. "Stony's" career spanned important developments in fertility, heritability, and performance.

HANS ULRICH (b. 1930) raises registered Herefords near Claresholm, Alberta, with his wife, Annette, and their son and son-in-law. Hans was a pioneer of beef cattle performance and received the Alberta Performance Award in 1987.

JOE J. URICK (b. 1920), of Miles City, Montana, was assistant animal husbandman of the North Montana Experiment Station at Havre from 1948 to 1960. From 1961 until retirement, he was in charge of animal breeding at the U.S. Range Experiment Station, Miles City.

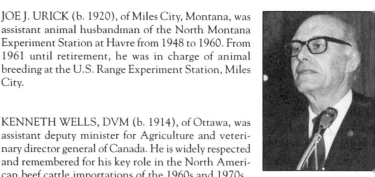

KENNETH WELLS, DVM (b. 1914), of Ottawa, was assistant deputy minister for Agriculture and veterinary director general of Canada. He is widely respected and remembered for his key role in the North American beef cattle importations of the 1960s and 1970s.

S. B. "SYD" WILLIAMS (b. 1912), of Ottawa, was assistant deputy minister and later deputy (top civil servant) to four Canadian ministers of Agriculture, most notably, Harry Hays. Syd played a key role in opening the importation of new breeds into North America.

CLAIR WILLITS (b. 1922), of Great Falls, Montana, worked for American Breeders Service in the 1940s and 1950s. Later, he ran his own AI business, Montana Proved Sire Service, before making a career with the Great Falls Production Credit Association.

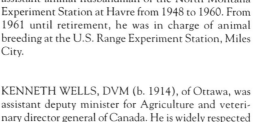

RAY WOODWARD, Ph.D. (b. 1916), directed beef cattle research at the Miles City Range Experiment Station from 1948 to 1960. He selected many European imports for American Breeders Service in the 1960s and 1970s. He won the Portrait Award from the Saddle & Sirloin Club in 1991, and many other honors.

Glossary

ABCPA—Alberta Beef Cattle Performance Association

ABS—American Breeders Service

Aftosa (Spanish)—foot-and-mouth disease

AI—artificial insemination

AICA—American International Charolais Association

Allele—alternate characteristic of a gene or trait

APHIS—Animal and Plant Health Inspection Service (USDA)

ARS—Agricultural Research Service (USDA)

AV—artificial vagina

BAI—Bureau of Animal Industry (Canadian, now defunct)

"Banger"—cow that has tested "positive" for Bang's disease

Bang's disease—*see Brucellosis*

Blackleg—fatal livestock disease caused by clostridial bacteria

BML—Beefbooster Management Ltd.

"Brockleface"—whitefaced, with colored patches ("badger-faced" in Britain)

Brucellosis—contagious abortion in cattle caused by bacteria

Cattalo—low percentage bison-cattle hybrid developed by CDA at Manyberries range experiment station in the 1950s

Cattle liner (Canadian)—truck semitrailer designed to carry livestock

CCA—Canadian Charolais Association

CDA—Canada Department of Agriculture (now Agriculture Canada)

Cemex—Italian syndicated export agency

CHBI—Charolais Herd Book International (formed in Mexico)

COBBETY—(change of bull battery every three years) a cattle breeding system or plan used by Beefbooster

Cofranimex—French export company formerly known as Syndex

Commercial cattle—produced for meat only; unregistered in any breed

Composite strain—cattle composed of breeds in known percentages

Corriente (Spanish)—nondescript cattle of central Mexico, often bred from dairy stock

Criollo—native Latin American cattle descended from Spanish importations

CSU—Colorado State University (Colorado A&M until the 1950s)

"Domestic" cattle—those common in North America before the Importation of the 1960s and later

DVM—doctor of veterinary medicine

ELPA—(*Eleveur Limousin Plein Air*, or Open Air Limosin Breeders) a private French Limousin performance test station

"Exotic" cattle—breeds new to North America before the Importation of the 1960s

FMD—"officialese" for foot-and-mouth disease

FRS—Fellow, Royal Society

Full-blood—an animal with a five-generation pedigree in a specific breed

"Geep"—Goat-sheep chimeric cross

"Gummer"—an old critter with worn or missing teeth

Heritabilities—expected inheritance of measurable traits

Heterosis—"luxuriance of growth" associated with crossbreeding

Heterozygous—having different alleles of a genetic trait

Homozygous—having the same alleles of a genetic trait

Hybrid—a cross between strains, lines, breeds, or species

IBR—infectious bovine rhinotrachyitis

"Importation"—the introduction of cattle breeds to North America after 1965

Inbred depression—reverse of hybrid vigor

M1, M2, M3, M4—Beefbooster synthetic maternal strains

MBPA—Montana Beef Performance Association

MP—Member of Parliament

MSGA—Montana Stockgrowers Association

NAAB—National Association of Animal Breeders

NALF—North American Limousin Foundation

PACA—Pan American Charolais Association

PCA—Production Credit Association, a U.S. agricultural bank

PEI—Prince Edward Island, Canadian maritime province

"Possum-belly"—underslung, double-decked livestock semitrailer

PRI—Performance Registry International

Purebred—registered or enrolled in a breed

Rib eye—cross section of beef cattle loin

ROP—Record of Performance (Canadian government program)

"Six-weight"—cattle weighing 600 to 699 pounds

SBL—Simmental Breeders Ltd of Cardston, Alberta

SEPA—private French cattle export agency

"She-stuff"—female cattle

"Syndex"—French syndicated agency to export Charolais cattle (later called Cofranimex)

Synthetic strain—where percentage of breeds is not a factor

Tx—Beefbooster terminal strain (all progeny go to slaughter)

Theriogenology—The study of reproduction in domestic animals, especially as it applies to breeding soundness

USDA—United States Department of Agriculture

VES—vesicular exanthema (disease of swine)

Vibrio, or Vibriosis—a venereal disease common among sheep and cattle that causes abortion

WSGA—Western Stock Growers Association (Alberta)

Notes

Prologue

1. Alex Johnston, range scientist and historian, in Ewing, *The Range* (Missoula: Mountain Press Publishing Co., 1990), p. 12.

1   A Place to Start

2. "Preconditioned" refers to calves having their immunizations established well before the stress of weaning and shipping.

3. See Goff and McCaffrey, *Century in the Saddle* (Denver: the author and the Colorado Cattlemen's Association, 1967).

4. Warren Cooper, born in 1902, began his career at age fifteen when an arena boss handed him a megaphone: "Stay on your horse and tell the folks what's happening," he said. "Coop" was the voice of the Calgary Stampede from 1939 through the 1970s.

5. Gordon was masterful in debate, especially in defending the Canadian cattle industry against government-imposed marketing boards and other forms of 1960s socialism.

6. "Havre" refers to the North Montana Experiment Station, formerly Fort Assiniboine. The Manyberries range experiment station is headquartered at the One-Four (Township 1, Range 4) post office in Alberta.

2   Miles City—1935

7. See Knapp, et al., "Estimates of Heritability" USDA, Miles City, 1947.

8. USDA geneticists W. H. Black and E. W. Sheets deserve special mention, as do H. C. McPhee and Sewall Wright (see additional information on Wright at note 28), prominent contributors to the Miles City work.

9. Curt Hughes, who died in 1985, was also a prominent breeder of Targhee sheep.

10. Vibriosis is a serious venereal disease of cattle that led many ranchers in the 1950s to experiment with artificial insemination. Well-known Saskatchewan rancher John Minor was killed in a tragic accident circa 1960.

3 Going for Small

11. *Life* magazine, October 31, 1949, p. 71.

4 Niceties and Necessities

12. B. *Beau Truemode 3rd* was bred by D. R. Nelson of Plains, Montana; his sire was *Bonny Truemode 38th*, of Kamloops, B.C.

13. As a further indication of the international nature of the bull trade, *Predominant 25U* was bred by Bill Beck, of Duchess, Alberta; according to Jonathan Fox, Beck used Spidell's Montana seed stock heavily.

5 The Fat of the Matter

14. See Berg and Butterfield, *New Concepts of Cattle Growth* (Sydney, Australia: Sydney University Press, 1976), p. 202.

15. In 1972 Canada updated its meat grading system with codes that indicate leanness and youth (with tenderness in mind). More recently, the United States augmented its grades (Prime, Choice, Standard, etc.) with "yield" numbers that indicate the lean-to-fat ratio.

6 Two Ranches

16. Carleton Corbin was elected president of Performance Registry International (PRI) at its 1959 general meeting in Miles City. A number of Alberta ranchers attended with their families, including Claire and me and our three small children, and it was there that we first met many of the characters in this book such as Ray Woodward, Harold Hill, and Lloyd Schmitt, among others. Murray State College is at Tishomingo, Oklahoma.

17. Rouse, in volume 3 of *World Cattle* (Norman: University of Oklahoma Press, 1970-73), pp. 363-64, is not sure the longhorn can be called a breed. He thinks it may best be considered "a kind of cattle," and that description applies to the longhorns mentioned in this book. However, since Rouse wrote his book, two Texas Longhorn breed registries have emerged: the International Texas Longhorn Association, in Colorado; and the Texas Longhorn Breeders Association, in Fort Worth.

18. See King, *The Great White Cattle* (Chicago: Wolf & Krautter, 1967); two discusses the influx of Shorthorn blood into the Charolais breed in France in the 1850s, and five discusses the Pugibet importations and subsequent early Mexican breeding.

7 Two Breeders

19. Forrest Bassford, now of Encinitas, California, has been called "dean of western journalists" by the California Beef Cattle Improvement Association. His writings about the cattle industry have earned him numerous honors and awards from a variety of organizations.

20. Tom Lasater's original ideas are discussed at length in Laurence M. Lasater, *The Lasater Philosophy of Cattle Raising* (El Paso: Texas Western Press, 1992).

8 Of Tools and Men

21. After decades of experimentation in Europe and Great Britain, a practical combination grain-cutting and gathering machine was developed by Cyrus H. McCormick in the United States in 1831, when farm labor was scarce. Sheaves or bundles were bound by hand until 1880, when John F. Appleby invented a successful knotting machine. Such binders remained a popular way of gathering grain crops for threshing or forage through the 1950s, when "swathing" (simply cutting and gathering into windrows) gained in favor. "Hay-bine" is the trade name for the Ford-New Holland reaper, which combines cutting, raking, and conditioning into one operation. Generic hay swathers may be either pulled behind a tractor or self-propelled.

22. Warren Monfort founded one of the world's largest meat packing companies, Monfort's of Colorado; in the 1990s it is a division of ConAgra, Inc.

9 Know-how

23. Dr. M. E. Ensminger started his famous stockmen's short course while teaching at Washington State College in Pullman in the 1950s. In 1963 it became the Ensminger Agri-Services Foundation International Stockmen's School, which continues to draw students from many countries.

    The Western Stock Growers Association of Calgary, many members of which attended Ensminger's original school, founded a week-long course at Banff that flourished through the 1960s and 1970s.

24. Confusingly, but convincingly, the Graham School preserves a testimonial dated August 1914 from a satisfied alumnus named Christopher Graham, MD. This unrelated Dr. Graham is said to have been a prominent surgeon at the Mayo Clinic and an early proponent of sanitation in surgery.

10 Good Medicine

25. In calving cases, veterinarians often inject procaine (a basic ester of para-aminobenzoic acid) or some other alcohol derivative into the cerebrospinal fluid between two lumbar vertebrae as a spinal block to prevent pain sensors from reaching the central nervous system. Evidently, scotch whiskey may be substituted.

26. The science of theriogenology has won international recognition and acceptance since 1971. *Stedman's Illustrated Medical Dictionary* defines it as "the study of reproduction in animals, especially domestic animals . . . [including] physiology, obstetrics, and genital diseases in male and females."

    Pioneer theriogenologists Harold Hill, Lloyd Faulkner, and James Scott of CSU joined with Dr. Steve Roberts of Cornell and Dr. Dave Bartlett of ABS to form the Rocky Mountain Society for the Study of the Breeding Soundness of Bulls; by 1974 it had evolved into the Society for Theriogenology.

11 Genetics

27. Curt Stern (1902-1981) taught at UC, Berkeley, where his lectures on genetics drew students from all disciplines in the 1940s and 1950s. Stern had earlier been

employed in Columbia University's famous "fly room," where chromosomal behavior was investigated using *drosophila* (fruit flies).

28. W. E. Castle (1867-1962) became a leader in the study of mammalian genetics soon after Mendel's work was rediscovered in 1909. Castle's open-mindedness and common sense have been credited with carrying the young science through early years of skepticism and doubt.

By experimenting with color-pattern selection in hooded rats, Castle extended to mammals the mendelian theories developed with insects and plants. In applying genetic terms to natural selection, he established relationships between Mendelian and Darwinian theory. Beginning in 1912 at Bussey Institute at Harvard, he trained many leading geneticists, including Sewall Wright.

Sewall Wright (1889-?) began his long and illustrious career at Bussey Institute in 1912. After a decade of studying inbred guinea pigs at Beltsville, he spent 29 years in teaching and research at Chicago and another 33 years at Wisconsin, where he inspired many important genetic thinkers, including Jay L. Lush.

Jay L. Lush (1896-1982) was elected to the National Academy of Sciences in 1967 and became an honorary fellow of the Royal Society of Edinburgh in 1972. In addition to producing more than 200 scientific papers, Lush wrote *Animal Breeding Plans* (Iowa State University Press, 1945), which was translated into many languages. An officer of the American Society of Animal Production, he received its Morrison Award in 1946.

29. When Howard Fredeen arrived in 1950, the research station at Lacombe, Alberta, was simply called the "experimental farm." In the late 1950s, when CDA's Experimental Farm Service became the Research Branch, the facilities at Lacombe, Lethbridge, and other places became known as "research stations."

Well-known Canadian geneticist Jack Stothard, the last superintendent of the Lacombe's experimental farm and the first director of its research station, was perhaps the first geneticist anywhere to put Lush's principles of population genetics into practice. Stothard retired in 1976.

30. The wonderful phrase "luxuriance of growth," used to describe the effects of hybrid vigor, is attributed to Theodosis Dobzhansky, who, according to Howard Fredeen, "performed some elegant research" on the mechanics of inheritance using *drosophila* from 1942 to 1947.

31. Laurence Merriam Winters was born at Lake City, Minnesota, in 1891. After retiring from the University of Minnesota in 1956, he served as an agricultural advisor to the government of Iraq; he died in Baghdad. He was a member of the Genetics Society of America and the American Society of Animal Production, which honored his outstanding contribution to animal husbandry in 1948 with its Morrison Award.

32. Andrew Moss was the first animal husbandman at the University of Minnesota.

12   Performance

33. A headline in the September 1, 1992, issue of the *Wall Street Journal* reads: "Bum steer. With stakes high, exhibitors cheat. Never trust a well-groomed steer. He may be wearing a wig."

The article describes the antics of professional steer jocks caught using false hair and spray paint at the Houston Livestock Show. With show animals bringing prices as high as $200,000 for promotion rather than beef, the temptation to use chicanery (implanting, dying, switching) is high and sets an especially bad example when the nominal owner happens to be a 4-H kid. The article concludes:

Behind every bum steer is usually an intermediary, a "steer-jock" who makes a living creating champions. But steer jockeys charge top dollar, sometimes $20,000. So that, alone, keeps most young farmers honest, raising their own animals as the competitions intends them to do."

34. Dr. Ralph "Bull" Durham is described by one of his students (now a professor) as a "colorful, unconventional academic." In the 1930s, the controversial Durham organized an eye-opening, ultimately very successful performance test project in swine at Iowa State. Later he served as head of the Animal Science department at Texas Tech in Lubbock. A fascinating teacher, he was much in demand as guest lecturer at colleges and courses throughout the country.

35. Professor John I. Miller (1911–1983) taught animal science to about 6,000 students at Cornell for more than forty years. He is remembered as a fine teacher and student advisor.

36. I won't swear to the exact forward-contracting price in August 1954, but there was certainly an agreed upon, much lower price or "slide" for overweights. In 1954 the actual price dropped so far before delivery that some contractors slid out of their deals altogether. Nelson honored his bargain with my employer   to the pound.

37. The seventy cows Neil Harvie bred by artificial insemination in 1970 constituted about 10 percent of the Glenbow breeding herd   enough to be genetically significant.

38. Packinghouse managers were cooperative. They were aware that bull carcasses during a 1962 University of Alberta trial had been accepted as "fairly good" to "excellent" by an impartial consumer group; see Berg et al., "Feeders' Day Report" (University of Alberta, Edmonton, June 1963). Seventeen mixed Glenbow ranch carcasses, initially graded Choice by Canadian government graders, were dropped to Good and Standard simply on the assumption that they were bulls. With his excellent identification system, Neil was able to establish that some of the 17 were actually steers, casting visual standards into doubt for evermore.

39. Bob de Baca reports that Farrington Carpenter (1886–1980) had already been selecting cattle for length and fertility for forty years by 1952, when Dr. R. T. "Scotty" Clark (by then USDA director of Beef Cattle Research headquartered in Denver) sent him two Line One bulls from Miles City for use on his ranch at Hayden, Colorado. Ferry Carpenter became a major spokesman for performance through the next two decades.

Although not a "founder" of PRI, Carpenter was certainly an early member of the American Beef Cattle Performance Registry Association, founded at Amarillo, Texas, in 1955; he was instrumental in changing its name to Performance Registry International (PRI) in 1958 and in its subsequent move to Denver, where he served as executive secretary for a while.

Exasperated with the foot-dragging of the beef cattle registry associations in performance selection and the resultant slow growth of PRI, Ferry Carpenter in 1966–68 led the formation of the Beef Improvement Federation (BIF), which he hoped would be a new and dynamic alternative to registration by breed. BIF established the guidelines for most performance programs over the next quarter century.

351

40. Also in attendance at the founding meeting of ABCPA in 1959 were ranchers Bert Hargrave and Wally Wells, of Scandia, and Jon Eaton, of Claresholm. Encouragement and support came from E. Paul Orcutt of the young Montana Beef Performance Association.

41. Montana Hereford breeders Jack Cooper and Les Holden (half brother and brother-in-law to Dr. Ray Woodward) were among the earliest users of Line One bulls from Miles City and were founding members of the Montana Beef Performance Association when it organized in 1957. Although they operate separately, they have regularly exchanged herd bulls, and their performance selection practices have been so closely allied that the Beef Improvement Federation named them, jointly, Seedstock Breeders of the Year in 1975.

   The Red Angus bull *Beckton Larkabeau* (pictured on page 68) became famous when purchased by American Breeders Service on the basis of his high performance potential.

13   Hybrid Vigor

42. Ashfork, Arizona, must have been a center for Charolais pioneers; the oft-mentioned Campbell family had a ranch there.

43. For some fresh ideas on financing and managing beef cattle operations, see Lasater and Kingsbery, *Welcome to the New Cattle Industry* (Woodinville, Wash.: Kingsbery Communication, 1987).

44. Calgary newsman and politician Roy Farran used this term in his well-known weekly, *Foothills News*.

45. The white colored Danish Landrace pig is widely distributed in Denmark, Norway, Sweden, Germany, and the Netherlands. Between 1946 and 1956 eight swine breeds were established at state and federal stations in the United States, each based on a cross of two or more breeds. While differing in color, all but one derived from the Danish Landrace.

46. The Canadian Department of Agriculture carried out the "Cattalo" project at the Manyberries range experiment station under the direction of geneticist Hobart Peters from 1949 to 1964.

   Starting with 39 "hybrid" (more than 25 percent bison) and 85 "cattalo" (12 to 25 percent bison) cows, the herd was evaluated for fifteen years for thriftiness, hardiness, and reproductive capability compared with Herefords under normal range conditions.

   The earlier high-percentage bison crosses were called "catfalo" and failed to produce any live offspring for the first eight years. A limitation was the severe dystochia in domestic cows bred to bison bulls. Eventually, fertile hybrids were produced from bison cows and domestic (Hereford, Shorthorn, Angus, and Holstein) bulls, and a low-percentage bison, or "cattalo," herd was developed.

47. "Hytester" is a trade name first registered by me with the U.S. Patent office and used as an ear tattoo for cattle on the SN ranch. Said to be the first trademark issued for cattle, the mark is now owned by the Beefbooster organization.

48. The practice of artificial insemination began with Lazzaro Spallanzani, an eighteenth-century Italian physiologist who placed semen into the vaginas of experimental animals by "artificial" means, thereby firmly establishing the male contribution to reproduction for the very first time.

    There are accounts of nineteenth-century Arabs inseminating mares with "fresh" semen collected "by hand," in a way similar to that described in this by Jonathan Fox. Dairy and beef cattle may have been artificially bred in Russia before 1917. U.S. ag-extension agent E. J. Perry learned scientific AI techniques in Denmark and introduced them to Hunterdon County, New Jersey, in 1938. Jim Clark thinks Jim Bowman, county agent at Neepawa, Manitoba, may have introduced modern AI to Canada a year or so earlier using three Shorthorn bulls.

49. Corporate lawyer Parmalee Prentice had a consuming interest in livestock and genetics, to the study of which he committed his Mount Hope Farm near Williamstown, Massachusetts. Prentice wrote a number of books on the subject, including *Breeding Profitable Beef Cattle: A Source of New Wealth* (Boston and New York: Houghton Mifflin Company, 1935). The "Hope" name carries on in Holstein pedigrees to this day.

50. According to Snyder, *Fifty Years of Artificial Insemination in Canada, 1934–1984* (Toronto: Canadian Association of Animal Breeders, 1982), p. 221, as late as 1973 the Manitoba government attempted to legislate sole distribution rights to the Manitoba Semen Distribution Centre   a government-inspired co-op. All other AI organizations were directed to take their trucks off the road. ABS Canada refused compliance on the grounds that the government had no right to monopolize the industry. The courts found in its favor in 1974, but by then the bloom was off and interest in beef AI had begun to fade.

51. ABS Canada conducted its first AI rancher-training school at Taber, Alberta, in March 1966; other organizations followed suit. See Snyder, *Fifty Years*, p. 221.

52. Including the famous Line One, thirteen lines were selected on performance at the Miles City station.

53. "Gomer" (after Gomer Pyle, the TV character of the 1960s) is slang for a bull that has been vasectomized to prevent conception, and, since such bulls can still pass a venereal disease such as vibriosis, they were sometimes fitted with a canvas apron to prevent penetration. "Sidewinders" were surgically "diverted" to prevent copulation. Both were useful in "detecting" cows in heat.

54. Roy Berg credits veterinarian Eugene Jansen, of the University of Saskatchewan, with originating the term "low-tech cow."

The Scouts

55. Early North America Charolais associations used a variety of spellings: American *Charolaise* Breeders Association (1945); International *Charollaise* Cattle Raisers Association (1951); American International *Charolais* Association (1957); and the Paris-based Eastern *Charolles* Cattle Company, in which some Canadian breeders participated during the 1960s.

According to Henwood and Carruthers, *White Gold: The Story of Charolais in Canada* (Calgary: Canadian Charolais Association, 1986), p. 27, Canadian breeders accepted the "Charolais" spelling during a much-discussed motion by Wayne Malmberg at their organizational meeting in January 1959.

16   Dripping with Germs

56. This is how Tom Lasater remembers the story as told by his father, who knew Shanghai Pierce and his nephew well. In fact, Ed Lasater's original Brahman cattle (see chapter 7) were bought from the A. H. Pierce estate in 1908.

    Tom also says the "slaughter at Ellis Island" led to the discovery that Brahman cattle have a higher temperature than the British breeds.

57. See Emmett, *Shanghai Pierce* (Norman: University of Oklahoma Press, 1953), pp. 301–9.

58. Surra, or *Trypanosomas*, also causes African sleeping sickness, transmitted by the tsetse fly.

59. For more information on Ed McKinnon (b. 1911), see Ewing, *The Range*, pp. 88–91, in which he discusses exporting Canadian cattle to Britain.

60. Bluetongue is a viral disease disastrous to sheep and the cause of numerous non-tariff barriers to modern world trade. According to Dr. Robert Shope, the bluetongue viruses present in North America are the types commonly found in South Africa, which suggests the disease was imported early in our history with food animals and the slave trade.

61. According to Dr. Robert Anderson, ranchers in Canada and the United States deal with severe outbreaks of vesicular stomatitis almost every year. In the United States there are two common types "New Jersey" and "Indiana" that may occur in mid to late summer. The mosquito is probably the primary carrier.

62. The "Quarantine" was a ten-section pasture maintained by the Canadian government just north of the Coutts-Sweetgrass port of entry; in earlier years cattle were held in there while awaiting veterinary inspection before moving north. The land was allotted to war veterans for farming in the early 1950s, and the sod was first broken at that time.

63. For more on this, see Barlaugh et al., "The Marine Calcivirus Story," *Compendium on Continuing Education for the Practicing Veterinarian* 8, Nos. 9 and 10 (Sept. and Oct. 1986).

64. This was observed in the late 1700s by the English physician Edward Jenner. Working with a boy who had no symptoms of pox, he scraped the child's skin and applied infected matter. The boy caught a light case of cowpox but did not later succumb when inoculated with smallpox secretions.

65. Security at the Arbovirus Research Center is tight! Since 1970 scientists and technicians have worked under laminar flow hoods that shield their faces from viruses by a curtain of filtered air; HEPA (High Efficiency Particular Air) filters were especially designed for the purpose. The same filter is used at places like Plum Island to contain the foot-and-mouth virus and prevent it escaping into the atmosphere from the barns and sheds.

17   The *Aftosa!*

66. Two German scientists, Friedrich Löffler and P. Frosch, discovered the associated virus in the late 1800s. It is very small, perhaps 10,000 times smaller than the smallpox virus.

67. The outbreak of foot-and-mouth occurred in Stanislaus National Forest, near Sacramento, in July 1924. According to A. Starker Leopold, et al., "The Jawbone Deer Herd," *Game Bulletin No. 4* (California Department of Natural Resources, Museum of Vertebrate Zoology, Berkeley, 1951), the disease entered the Bay area aboard a U.S. Navy vessel and by fall had infected Tuolumne deer in the high country. The U.S. Bureau of Animal Industry organized an eradication campaign that resulted in the slaughter of more than 22,000 deer between the fall of 1924 and the spring of 1926.
   To my knowledge, there have been no cases of FMD reported in the United States since 1928 or 1929, and none on the North American continent since 1952. Perhaps the virus has been eradicated, but, remembering Dr. Mulhern's sea lions and Dr. Shope's earthworms, I wouldn't bet on it.

68. As documented by Dr. Alan Heflin of BAI (see "Campaign in Mexico Against Foot-and-Mouth Disease, 1947-1952," unpublished report of the Agricultural Research Service, 1954): Symptoms in one herd were first noticed in two cows; within five days the entire herd of 243 animals had the disease. Twelve calves died suddenly. Older animals went down because they couldn't stand on their infected feet. Unable to eat because of sore mouths, they showed rapid loss of condition. Fifteen cows, five heifers, and two bulls died. Milk production dropped from 1,300 to 400 hundred liters a day. In six weeks, twelve cows had aborted and forty went to slaughter. The owner suffered an actual loss of 29.6 percent of his herd, as well as two-thirds of his milk production.

18   The Pugibet Herd

69. Manuel Garza Elizondo says some of the Louisiana impounds were taken to Ajuchitlán, a town southwest of Mexico City; but Maximo Michaelis seems to infer, later, that his father and partners bought all of the cattle in question and took them to Querétaro, a town north of the capital, before returning them to El Fortín. Apparently there is either some confusion over the exact town in central Mexico, or this herd of genuine Pugibet cattle was split, with one group staying south. Even though Maximo was there at the time, his information does not corroborate a splitting of the herd.

70. According to Maximo, Henderson Coquat struck oil on his ranch south of San Antonio, near Three Rivers, Texas, and the cash helped finance the purchase of the Pugibet herd. After he died, Kimball and Michaelis bought his interest.

19   The Rio Grande

71. The Oak Bar ranch was later purchased by the movie actor Stewart Granger, who became a prominent Charolais breeder.

72. Brucellosis, or Bang's disease, causes contagious abortion in cattle and is a serious ailment. The bacterium responsible, *Brucella abortus*, also affects horses, mules, sheep, swine, and causes undulant (Malta) fever in humans.

The brucella is named for David Bruce, who identified its presence in goats on the island of Malta in 1887. Bang's disease is named for Danish Dr. Bernard Bang, who identified it as the causative agent in cattle abortions in 1897.

Brucellosis differs from most other cattle diseases in that it can be transmitted to the public through the milk supply, therefore requiring supervision by the government and vaccination by licensed veterinarians, rather than cattlemen. With modern attention to sanitation, undulant fever has become very rare; occasionally veterinarians in farm practice contract it by accidentally jabbing themselves with a syringe while administering the "live" vaccine. Many states require official proof of calfhood vaccination before allowing cattle from elsewhere to enter.

73. "Certified Meat Sire" was a status conferred by Performance Registry International on beef bulls with at least ten progeny that met CMS requirements for carcass weight per day of age, retail fat trim, adjusted rib eye area, fat thickness over rib eye, cutability, yield grade, and marbling. CMS status was in its heyday in sixties and early seventies, before the impact of the Importation.

74. According to Maximo Michaelis, the form of record for AICA's three-generation pedigrees use the words "This animal is recorded . . ." Splitting hairs, the USDA held that you don't record *animals*, you record *pedigrees*, therefore they would accept neither the wording nor the degree.

75. Other performance-minded founders of PACA included Bill Sidley, of Encampment, Wyoming; John Ewing (no relation to the author), of Fort Collins, Colorado; and Bob Purdy, of Buffalo, Wyoming.

76. Some of the Canadian imports of the 1960s did get to Mexico; Max Michaelis imported some before he passed away.

20 The Forty-ninth Parallel

77. Henwood and Carruthers, *White Gold*, pp. 14, 15.

78. *Sir Alto* was purchased by Roy Snyder for the Waterloo (Ontario) Cattle Breeding Association, an AI co-op. Bred up from a Brahma foundation by the Askew Ranch in Texas, *Sir Alto* was $^{63}/_{64}$ Charolais one generation more than required for registration. See Snyder, *Fifty Years*, p. 103.

79. *Miss Julie* was the first purebred Charolais in western Canada. She was preceded in the East by several purebreds brought to Ontario from Texas by a man named Abernathy who sold them to longtime Ontario breeder Murray Little.

80. Thirty purebred Charolais bulls were imported into Britain from France in November 1961; sixteen were allocated to the Milk Marketing Board, according to Joe Edwards, an official of the board who wrote about it in King, *The Great White Cattle*, pp. 40–42.

81. The English Importation Order of 1933 was passed to facilitate the movement of Canadian slaughter cattle to Britain after the Smoot-Hawley Tariff restricted traditional markets in the United States. See Ewing, *The Range*, pp. 88–91.

21   The Wide Atlantic

82. This is the same Codding ranch that raised the performance-tested "wineglass" bulls referred to in 12. The very sophisticated Armour BCI program was organized with the help of Dr. Harold Hill. It was too far ahead of its time.

83. Frederick H. Prince (1859-1953), financier, was born in Winchester, Massachusetts, and built a fortune buying and selling railroads. He financed the rebuilding of the Chicago stock yards and environs after the disastrous fire of 1934. He was chairman of the board of both Chicago Union Stock Yards and Transit Company and of Armour & Company, the packing-industry giant. His portrait is among 327 in the Saddle and Sirloin Club gallery honoring livestock and meat industry leaders. The collection, the largest in existence devoted to a single industry, has been housed since 1977 in the West Hall of the Kentucky Fair and Exposition Center, Louisville. Geneticist Ray Woodward was honored with a portrait in 1991.

84. As president of both Armour & Company and Chicago Union Stock Yards, William H. Wood Prince was certainly a livestock industry leader. His travels as an infantry captain during the Second World War may have introduced him to the Charolais breed.

It is worth mentioning that Armour & Company, under the leadership of "Billy" Prince, inaugurated the Armour Beef Cattle Improvement program (BCI) in the 1960s; through it, hundreds of bulls of all the beef breeds were purchased and placed on test to determine their comparative value. The grandiose BCI scheme was exciting but short-lived; several veterans believe that Armour was unable to re-educate its buyers to pay for "cut out" rather than the traditional "dressing percentage."

85. Emile Maurice was president of the French Herd Book Charolais in the late fifties. His son, Dr. François Maurice, is a veterinarian of great assistance in Prince's scheme plan.

86. Dr. Hill remembers Oris Russell, of the Bahamian department of Agriculture, as the most influential and helpful official on Eleuthera; other assorted and cosmopolitan investors included a U.S. attorney general, an attorney for Air France, a former dean from Iowa State College, the governor general of the Bahamas, a customs chief for the island of Guadeloupe, and an official of the USDA.

87. In all, four Eleuthera-born Charolais bulls were shipped to St. John by air in 1962. *Gander* went to Fort Collins; *Francois IV* (see 24) stayed in Canada for collection and was used successfully by Roy Berg (among others) at the University of Alberta; the other two bulls went elsewhere in the United States, but Dr. Hill lost track of them.

Risk Takers

88. For details on these controversies and a copy of the letter from Brian Mulroney, see Henwood and Carruthers, *White Gold*, pp. 46-48

22   Island Getaways

89. Mack Braly explained that the capital city of St. Pierre et Miquelon is spelled out, "Saint Pierre," which is consistent with the postmark on a letter I received from there in 1993.

90. At the time, Beveridge was, among other things, president of the Permanent Committee of World Veterinary Associations. Willems was chairman of Permanent Committee of European Organization for Epizootic Diseases.

91. There's a difference of opinion as to the importance of performance in France before the Importation. Geneticist Ray Woodward, who selected many cattle for ABS, told me he was not impressed with French performance testing except with Simmentals. Howard Fredeen, an equally eminent geneticist, was particularly impressed by the Limousin testing he saw in France.

92. Henri Gautier passed away in 1973. His son, Pierre, is still in the import-export business at Saint Pierre and was most helpful in researching this book.

93. The infamous tariff of Senator Reed Smoot and Representative Willis Hawley is often held responsible for triggering the world trade disaster of 1930 known as the Great Depression. Readers of my earlier book, *The Range*, may remember the Smoot-Hawley tariff as the trigger that closed the U.S. border to Canadian cattle and sent Ed McKinnon and other Alberta ranchers off to England to sell their cattle. By design or not, it's interesting to find the same tariff implicated as host to a "rider" that closed our entire continent to most of the world's cattle for several decades. Hint of the tariff reappeared during the widely publicized NAFTA (North American Free Trade Agreement) debate of November 1993; on television, Vice President Al Gore presented Ross Perot with a framed photograph of Messrs. Smoot and Hawley.

23   Exotic Breeds

94. Rouse, in vol. 3 of *World Cattle*, wrote that the importation of purebred stock increased rapidly in the three decades following the Civil War. It was during this period that such dairy breeds as Dutch Black and Whites (later known as Holstein-Freisians) and Brown Swiss cattle came to America from Europe; although other continental breeds were also imported, the Holsteins and Brown Swiss remain the only ones of importance to the present day.

   Rouse also explains that small herds of Simmental, Normandie, and Danish Reds, as well as French-Canadian cattle from Quebec, were imported into the U.S. in the late 1800s; some even had their own breed societies, but little, if any, trace of them was evident by 1965.

95. Doug Blair says twenty-six breeds came to North America from Europe in the 1960s and 1970s. With literally dozens of breeds available, this should not be surprising; still, I can think of only seventeen breeds from continental Europe: Blonde d'Aquitaine, Braunvieh, Charolais, Chianina, Fleckvieh, Gelbvieh, Limousin, Marchigiana, Maine Anjous, Meuse-Rhine-Yssel, Pie Blue, Piedmontese, Pie Rouge, Pinzgauer, Romagnola, Salers, and Simmental.

I recently herd from a breed secretary that there are now 139 breeds in the United States. This includes such combinations as Charobray, Simbra, Chi-Angus, and Chi-Maine. Regardless of whether all are "true" breeds, most keep pedigree records and go in for showing.

96. Figures are the most current available from the appropriate U.S. breed associations in September 1993.

97. *Prince Pompadour*, NIM-1, came from French Charolais breeder Adrien de Moustier, through his company, BovImport, of Denver. The bull was quarantined on Grosse Ile first, then at a Catholic agricultural college in Quebec until he could be moved to Denver.

   Prince Pompadour was born in 1967 at Domaine de Pompadour, home of Marquise de Pompadour, mistress to King Louis XV. French bulls born in 1967 were given names beginning with "C"—in this case, *Castor*. Promoter Dick Goff thought *Castor* sounded odious while *Prince Pompadour* sounded classy. The Pie Rouge (French Simmental) bull *Parisien* was born in 1966, so his official French name would have started with the letter "B." Again, the name *Parisien* was considered more appealing to North Americans.

98. ELPA was probably the French performance group that impressed Dr. Howard Fredeen (see note 91).

99. *Prairie Pride*, CIM 3, was born in 1968 and imported by "Prairie Bill" and Stella Hart, of Prairie Breeders, Priddis, Alberta. The widely touted *Prairie Pride* and sidekick *Prairie Dancer* settled thousands of heifers in the 1970s.

100. "Double-muscling" is present in many breeds, often with such side effects as low fertility and difficulty walking or even standing. It is not a desirable characteristic in ranch cattle; however, where mobility and fertility in offspring are not considered a problem   as in some dairy herds   double-muscling (resulting in more heavily muscled veal calves) is in demand. The Piedmontese breed has been selected for double-muscling in Italy and is now very popular with U.S. dairymen.

101. Harry Hays (1909-1982), a former mayor of Calgary, was the Canadian minister of Agriculture while Liberals were in power from 1963 to 1965, during the early years of the Importation.

24   Exotic Imports

102. The Canadian Wheat Board came under Industry Trade & Commerce, but the Diefenbaker government, which gained power in 1960, turned over responsibility for moving grain surpluses to Agriculture.

103. The Canadian government opened an official quarantine station on St. Pierre in 1969 to deal with the overflow, but by 1974 the big demand was over. Some of the barns were used in the 1980s to quarantine South American llamas and alpacas.

104. All authorized cattle registrations in Canada are kept on a central computer in Ottawa by the National Livestock Records.

25 Exotic Buying

105. "Straws" refers to "continental straws" invented by French businessman Robert Cassou in 1964. The hollow, strawlike tubes about six inches long have mostly replaced the bulkier glass ampules originally used for storing semen. In the older-style ampules, one semen dose equalled about 1 cc; technological advances now concentrate the spermatozoa, allowing continental straws to do the same job with only about one-quarter of the volume.

26 Big Bucks

106. The second imported Simmental bull, *Bismark*, was selected by Ray Woodward for LK ranches of Bassano, Alberta, and widely distributed by ABS.

107. The Limousin *Dandin C*, born in 1968, was imported by CDA for the Brandon (Manitoba) research station.

108. Well-known geneticist Dr. Lavone Sumption, of the USDA research station at Fort Robinson, Nebraska, was Buddy Cobb's first "bid-announcer" and probably gave him the "quiet" idea. Bruce Cornell, an insurance agent and frequent live-stock sale ring man of Augusta, Montana, took up where Sumption left off. For many years he has also helped "sell" the Charlie Russell Art Auction at Great Falls.

27 Designer Genes

109. U.S. figures are from "Directions: The State of Beef Industry, 1993," (National Cattlemen's Association, Englewood, Colo.).

110. Anne Dunford, a market analyst for CANFAX of Calgary supplied the Canadian figures.

111. Bret Fox, a market analyst for the Denver-based CATTLEFAX, and Laurie Lasater, of San Angelo, Texas, supplied the Mexican figures.

112. Much credit for the development of the Hays Converter breed goes to Dr. "Red" Williams, of the University of Saskatchewan, Saskatoon, and Dr. Jack Stothard, of CDA Research, Lacombe.

28 Terminal Strain

113. Polge's company, Animal Biotechnology Cambridge, Ltd., bridges gaps between research, production, and practice in the fields of animal breeding and molecular embryology. Its formerly government-funded AFRC Laboratory, where so many notable research "firsts" occurred, has been privatized as the Animal Research Station, Cambridge.

114. Dr. Willadsen went to Calgary in 1986. As of early 1994, according to Doug Blair, the cloning of cattle embryos is still not commercially practical. Interestingly, at least 20 percent of the clones were super-sized at birth — up to 150 pounds. But yearling weights (which are expected to follow birth-weights) were not exceptional in these heavy clones, and a high percentage of the bulls had reproductive problems.

The "sexing" of semen, much talked of since the 1970s, is almost here in 1994 with the advent of DNA information.

115. Louis's company, France Embryon, actually shipped about 750 Limousin embryos to countries around the world in 1993.

   According to Dr. Jerry Callis, of Plum Island (speaking in 1988), embryos are washed ten times in waters 100 times the volume of the embryos. In the fifth and sixth washes, an enzyme is added to destroy any virus; great care must be taken to prevent the enzyme from harming the pellucid shell.

116. Doug Blair is president of Alta Genetics, Inc., which went public in July 1993 with a capitalization of C$13 million.

Bibliography

PAPERS

"Annual Review of Genetics," in *Annual Reviews*, Palo Alto, 1983.

Barlough, Jeffrey E., et al. "The Marine Calcivirus Story." *Compendium on Continuing Education for the Practicing Veterinarian* 8, Nos. 9 and 10 (September and October 1986).

Berg, R. T., V. E. Mendel, R. B. Church, et al. "Feeders' Day Report." University of Alberta, Edmonton, June 1963.

"Directions: The State of Beef Industry, 1993." National Cattlemen's Association, Englewood, Colo.

Heflin, Alan. "Campaign in Mexico Against Foot-and-Mouth Disease, 1947-1952." Unpublished. USDA Agricultural Research Service, 1954.

Keller, D. G. "The Cattalo Experiment." Canada *Agriculture* 3, No. 3 (Summer 1978).

Knapp, Bradford, et al. "Estimates of Heritability." USDA, Miles City, 1947.

Leopold, A. Starker, et al. "The Jawbone Deer Herd." *Game Bulletin No. 4*. California Department of Natural Resources. Museum of Vertebrate Zoology, Berkeley, 1951.

Smith, J. MacGregor. "Binder and Knotter Troubles," University of Alberta Bulletin No. 10, Edmonton, 1944.

BOOKS

Berg, R. T., and Rex M. Butterfield. New *Concepts of Cattle Growth*. Sydney, Australia: Sydney University Press, 1976.

Burlingame, Merril G. and K. Ross Toole. *A History of Montana*. New York: Lewis Historical Publishing Co., 1957.

de Baca, Robert C. *Courageous Cattlemen*. Huxley, Iowa: the author, 1990.

Emmett, Chris. *Shanghai Pierce*. Norman: University of Oklahoma Press, 1953.

Ewing, Sherm. *The Range*. Missoula: Mountain Press Publishing Co., 1990.

Farley, Frank W. *Hereford Husbandry*. Kansas City: Hayes Walker Publications, 1941.

Goff, Richard, and Robert H. McCaffrey. *Century in the Saddle*. Denver: the author and the Colorado Cattlemen's Association, 1967.

Henwood, Sharon, and Bonnie Carruthers. *White Gold: The Story of Charolais in Canada.* Calgary: Canadian Charolais Association, 1986.

King, T. E. *The Great White Cattle.* Chicago: Wolf & Krautter, 1967.

Lasater, Laurence M. *The Lasater Philosophy of Cattle Raising.* El Paso: Texas Western Press, 1992.

Lasater, Laurence M., and Bob Kingsbery. *Welcome to the New Cattle Industry.* Woodinville, Wash.: Kingsbery Communications, 1987.

Luyet, B. J., and P. M. Gegenio. *Life and Death at Cold Temperatures.* Normandy, Mo.: Biodynamica, 1940.

McKusick, Victor A. *Human Genetics.* Englewood Cliffs, NJ: Prentice-Hall, 1964.

Peacock, Donald. *Barefoot on the Hill.* Vancouver: Douglas & McIntyre, 1986.

Prentice, E. Parmalee. *Breeding Profitable Beef Cattle: A Source of New Wealth.* Boston and New York: Houghton Mifflin Company, 1935.

Rouse, John E. *World Cattle.* 3 vols. Norman: University of Oklahoma Press, 1970–73.

Runion, Dale F., and June A. Runion. *The History of Limousin in North America.* Fountain Hills, Ariz.: the authors, 1987.

Snyder, Roy G. *Fifty Years of Artificial Insemination in Canada, 1934-1984.* Toronto: Canadian Association of Animal Breeders, 1982.

Von Richthofen, Baron Walter. *Cattle Raising on the Plains of North America.* 1885; rpt. Norman: University of Oklahoma Press, 1964.

Index

Pinzgauer, 290
Red Angus, 66-69, 307, 315
Saler, 314
Santa Gertrudis, 72, 312
Shorthorn (Durham), 11-14, 16, 61, 74, 312, 348
Simmental, Fleckvieh, Pie Rouge, 251-53, 262, 277, 287, 297, 314, 359, 360
Tarentaise, 262-63, 314
Texas Longhorn, 16, 61-62, 171, 314, 348
Welsh Black, 314
beef cattle breed associations
AICA (American International Charolais Association), 212-13, 238
American Chianina, 39
CCA (Canadian Charolais Association), 218, 220-21, 237-38
CHBI (Charolais Herd Book International), 212, 215
Red Angus of America, 69
PACA (Pan American Charolais Association.), 213-14, 229, 238, 356
beef cattle breeding systems, crossbreeding, 21, 134-35; inbreeding, 65, 140; linebreeding, 21, 65; "negative," 61
beef cattle efficiency, 29, 39, 43-44, 66, 122
beef cattle numbers, 308, 361
beef cattle performance, 20, 28, 37
beef cattle shows and showing, 59; American Herdsman Institute, 41, 42; American Royal, 34; National Polled Hereford, 45; National Western, 42; show-ring mentality, 36-37
beef cattle strains
Beefbooster, 125, 142, 307, 309, 312-316, 317
Burke Creek, 311
Chi-Angus, 310
Hytester™, 353
Kinsella, 141
Line One, 20-8, 126, 140, 160
Miles City strains, 353
Newford, 126, 217
Whitemud, 311
beef cattle types, compact, 32; comprest (pony), 23, 34, 36, 37, 47, 208; importance of length, 23; trend to small,

30, 32, 62; fixed by selection, 65. *See also* baby beef
Beefbooster, 314. *See also* beef cattle strains
Beefmaster, 70-75. *See also* beef cattle breeds
Bennett, Fletcher and Eleanor, 261
Berg, Roy T., xi, 36, 47, 65, 110, 112, 128, 221, 270, 313; on inbred lines, 138-40; on Kinsella project, 141; on disease control, 181; on genetics of growth, 323-34
Beresford, Rex, 32, 33
Bermuda grass (Midland), 56
Berringer, Richard and Mary, 90
Big Spring, Billy, 169
blackleg, 15, 99
Blair, Douglas G., 253-54; on exotic breeds, 253, 262; on import permits, 276; on buying in France, 286; on import values, 291; on selling exotics, 297; and *Extra*, 299-300; on frozen embryos, 323, 361
blue tongue, 183, 354
Boudry, Pierre, 285
Bourbon (French breeder), 288
Brackley, Dave, 90
Braly, George, 284
Braly, Mack M., 55-60; on Eleuthera, 224; and BAI, 230-32; on FMD, 242; in France, 242-45; at St. Pierre-Miquelon, 238-41, 246, 264; importing semen, 248; PRI, 261; on Canadian embargo, 283-84. *See also* Blair; de Neuville; Goff; Lalonde
Breen, Dan, 172-73, 212
Brest, 244
Brittany peninsula, 231, 244. *See also* Brest
Bronson, Rik, 260
brucellosis, 188-89, 210-11, 356
Broussard, Alphe, 204-5
bulls, 124-25, 351
Burcher, C. Gordon, 181-84
Burns, Jim and Janice, 316
Burton, Gordon L., 15, 83, 347; and Jean, 84; on Harry Hays, 267; on import permits, 277
Burton, Rick and Jay, 83, 311

Callis, Jerry, on FMD, 193, 200, 234, 247-48; on importation, 273

Ensminger, M. E., 91, 349
Ewing, Charles M. and family, 8, 70, 87, 95
Ewing, Claire, 36, 84, 85, 120, 255, 261, 273

Falfurrias (Texas) Cream Co., 72-73
Farmer—Stock Breeder, 221
Farr, W. D. "Bill," 103; on fat, 49, 53; on hydraulics, 87; on "exotics", 308
fat (beef carcass), 47-49
Ferris, Clint, 209, 213, 219, 226, 230
FMD (foot-and-mouth disease), earliest report, 193, 355; compensation for loss, 183, 186-87, 196; cost, 184, 185, 193; symptoms and effects, 194, 355; Saskatchewan outbreak (1952), 184-88; Mexican outbreak (1946-52), 193-202; Mexican virus, 198; commissions to eradicate and prevent, 195-6, 202, 206; Mexican concern, 216; virus, 228; 230; authorities on, 242-43; vaccination, 286
Forbes, Sarah P. "Sally," 69-70, 261; on Red Angus, 66-69
foot-and-mouth. *See* FMD
Forbes, Waldo, 66, 68, 69
Fort Collins. *See* cow colleges
Fort Keogh. 18, 21-24. *See also* Miles City
Fox, Jonathan III, 39, 44, 91; on AI, 147; on Polled Hereford breed, 42-44; on importation, 283; on Chianina, 291; on buying in Italy, 295
Fredeen, Howard, on type, 32; on Dr. Lush, 111, 113; on Charolais, 220
Freeman, Orville, 272, 321
Frenkel, H. S., 242, 248

Garst, Mary, on ranch management, 114; on Chianina, 291
Garst, Roswell, 107, 115
Garst, Sarah, 251
Garst, Steve, on hybrid corn, 107-8: on management, 115; on "exotic" sales, 302
Garza Elizondo, Manuel, 266; on Charolais imports to Mexico, 171-72, 203-4; on Max Michaelis, 175; on ranching in Mexico, 171; on Rancho La Rosita, 203; on CHBI, 212, 215; on Harry Hays, 215
Garza Gomez, Gudelio, 172, 212

Gautier, Henri, 239-41, 264, 358
Gautier, Pierre, xi, 247
Gilchrist, Bill and Helen, on Charolais, 218; on breeding cattle, 311-12
Gilchrist, Joe, 9, 25, 98, 305, 329
Gilchrist, Lois S., on "exotic" era, 317-18
Gilchrist, Rube, 98, 189
Gilchrist, Tom, 313, 316; on importation, 285; on Deer Creek herd, 317-18
Gilly family, 203, 205, 212
Goff, Richard "Dick," 13, 254; on Breen and Gonzalez, 173; on Mexican imports, 207; on PACA and AI acceptance, 213, 219, 229, 244; on "exotic" sales, 305
Gonzales, Martín H., on FMD in Mexico, 195-96
Graham, William S. "Bill" and family, 92, 94
Graham School, 91-97, 349; attendance, 143
Gray, Jim, 17, 27; on Italian cattle, 170
Grosse Ile (Quebec), FMD diagnosis at, 184, 188; photos, 250; during European importation, 274-75, 281-82

Hamilton, Alvin, 212, 237, 266; on Regina FMD outbreak, 187; on European importation, 269; on Eleutheran imports, 270-71
Hargrave, Bert, 25, 169, 217, 352
Hargrave, Harry, 18, 25, 27, 128, 129, 217, 220-21, 261
Harsh, Leo "Bud," 88, 89
Hart, Orrin, 128
Harvie, Neil, building Glenbow herd, 124-25, 351; 313-14, 317
Harvie, Robin, 313
Havre (North Montana Experiment Station), 122
Hays, Harry, 215, 266, 268, 272, 309, 360
Health of Animals Canada, 230
Heemstra, L. C., 231
heritability, estimates of, 21, 61, 118
Hill, Harold J., on fertility testing, 102, 103, 349; AI pioneer, 145-46; on frozen semen, 154-56; on Eleuthera, 225-30
Hrytsak, Roman, xi, 312, 316
Hughes bulls, 126
Hughes, G. Curtis, 25, 25, 27, 261, 347

vibriosis, 25, 143, 347, 354
Vidora, Saskatchewan, 11
virology, virus, 190-92; FMD, 193, 228

WBS (Western Breeders Service, Ltd.), 292, 299. *See also* Blair
WSGA (Western Stock Growers' Association), short course, 91, 349
Wallace, Henry, 107, 111, 117, 138
Wells, Kenneth, 298; on Regina FMD break, 184-85; 222, 224; 264-65; 270, 284; on semen importation, 271; on live cattle importation, 268-69, 273; on Grosse Ile, 275
Wells, Wally, 261, 352
West, Albert, 302

Williams, S. B. "Syd," on import decision, 271; on the contessa, 293
Willits, Clair, on ABS and Rock Prentice, 149-51; on Montana Proved Sires, 160-61; on AI schools, 161
Willson, Fred, 121, 122, 127
Winters, Laurence M., 21, 112, 113, 127, 138-39, 350
Woodward, Ray R., 312, 317; on Miles City project, 18, 21, 28; on show-biz, 37; hosting PRI meet, 261; on buying in Europe, 262, 285; Saddle and Sirloin Club, 357
World War II, influence on beef grading, 51; influence on importation, 169-70

Yates, Cap, 207, 210

About the Author and Artist

Sherm Ewing is a man of rare talents. Although "rancher" describes him, the term falls short of defining him. He is a student really, who has spent a lifetime learning, remembering, and applying his knowledge. He was not born to a ranching family, but he knew from an early age that a rural western life was right for him. After earning a degree in economics from a prestigious eastern school, he headed west and began a career on the land that lasted 40 years and continues still in his research and writing.

Sherm and his wife, Claire, raised their family on ranches in Montana and Alberta. With dual citizenship in the United States and Canada, Sherm remains active in numerous ranching organizations, including the Western Stockgrowers Association, the Alberta Beef Cattle Performance Association, the (Canadian) Cattlemen's Memorial Foundation, the North American Limousin Foundation, and the Society for Range Management. Such affiliations have taught him as much about people and politics as about animals and nature.

Now retired from the seasonal obligations of ranching, Sherm has turned his attention to writing about the land, people, and lifestyle that sustained him and his family over the years. A student still, he writes to return something of value to his favorite way of life.

Sherm and Claire live in Great Falls, Montana.

Wanina Travis credits her parents, Sherm and Claire Ewing, and her teachers for encouraging her interest in art. She studied in Alberta, British Columbia, Colorado, Wyoming, and especially Montana. She painted cover art and drew inside illustrations for both of her father's books, *The Range* (1990) and now the *The Ranch*. She lives with her husband, Chuck, and two daughters in a historic ranch house/stage station/post office at the foot of the Porcupine Hills west of Claresholm, Alberta.

Sherm Ewing. —Nan Bull

Wanina Travis. —Nick Morrison